A TREASURY
of THE SATURDAY EVENING POST

A TREASURY
of THE SATURDAY EVENING POST

A selection of words and pictures, new and old, from the pages of America's favorite family magazine.

THE CURTIS PUBLISHING COMPANY,
INDIANAPOLIS, INDIANA

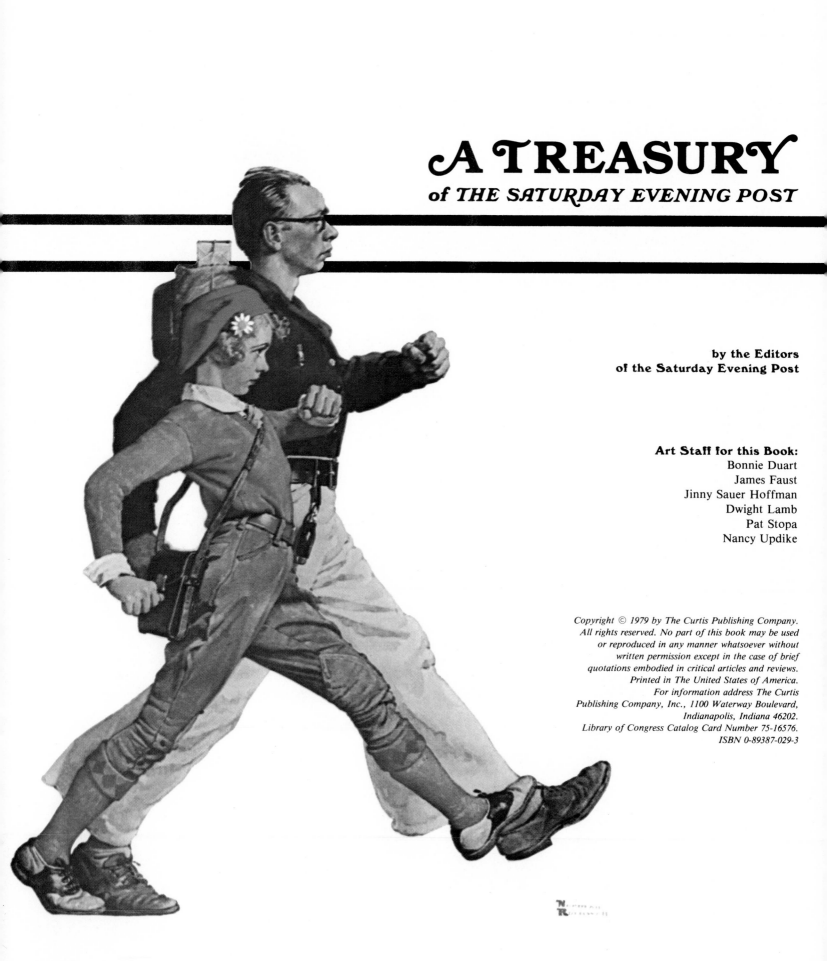

A TREASURY
of THE SATURDAY EVENING POST

by the Editors
of the Saturday Evening Post

Art Staff for this Book:
Bonnie Duart
James Faust
Jinny Sauer Hoffman
Dwight Lamb
Pat Stopa
Nancy Updike

Contents

Introduction 7

The Face of America 9

Beginnings 18

One Nation Under God 34

Heroes 52

Buying and Selling 70

The Promised Land 86

The American Woman 106

How We Looked 122

Conflict 138

Show Business 164

Innovation 190

The American Sporting Scene 212

The American Story 238

Boom and Bust 270

Spare Time 286

The American Dream 302

Acknowledgments 320

Norman
Rockwell

Introduction

Ben Franklin was twenty-two when he started the magazine. It was the day before Christmas, 1728. There were already five periodicals in the Colonies, economic conditions were unstable, times would get worse before they got better (said his friends), paper was hard to get and expensive, distribution a nightmare. They said people didn't read anymore and a great many other things older, successful people always tell young people who want to go into business for themselves.

Undaunted, Franklin sold the ads, wrote the copy, set the type, folded the paper and hawked his creation in the streets of Philadelphia, like a common laborer, which, in a colony of lace-jaboted aristocrats, was what he was.

He also had the sure instincts of a journalist: brevity (" . . . they who desire to acquaint themselves with any particular art or science would gladly have the whole before them in much less time"), entertainment (" . . . no care and pains shall be omitted that will make the *Pennsylvania Gazette* as agreeable and useful an Entertainment as the nature of the things will allow") and fearlessness ("Gentlemen of the House of Representatives . . . I take the trouble . . . to open the Eyes of the deluded People whom you represent, and whom you are at so much Pains to keep in Ignorance of the true State of their Affairs.")

The little paper thrived, taking on a distinctly American tone though it was three years before George Washington was even born, and most colonists thought of themselves as English. Franklin devoted himself to other interests after two decades, but before he left the editorship he started people thinking about a house united. One of the nation's first political cartoons showed the rattlesnake—the creature many felt should be America's emblem—cut up into colonies and the caption, an admonition against the dangers of the French and Indian war, "JOIN or DIE."

Until the magazine moved to New York in 1960 and Indianapolis in 1971, it was always printed within a few yards of Independence Hall in the heart of Philadelphia. It was published in the same printshop for a century after Franklin founded it and Franklin's type was still being used in 1821 when the editors changed the name to *The Saturday Evening Post*.

Circulation and literary quality zoomed in the nineteenth century. One editor befriended an erratic and unsuccessful young poet and his child bride. The writer, Edgar Allan Poe, under the steadying influence of regular meals gave the magazine "The Black Cat," now a classic and the prototype of the mass-magazine story. Circulation was 90,000 before the Civil War. By 1897 it was down to a thousand, which is exactly what the man from Maine, Cyrus H.K. Curtis, paid for it.

Then Curtis showed the extent of his belief. He slashed the price of the magazine from a dime to a nickel. He threw 260,000 uninflated dollars away in a promotion campaign that brought in not one single new ad for the magazine. His accountants winced. So he threw good money after bad to the tune of one million more. Ben Franklin had had guts but this, as they say, was ridiculous. It worked. The *Post* caught on. Advertising matched circulation. It became the magazine to beat, it became "an American institution."

Fifty years the magazine swelled. Then there was a switch. America turned it on, this switch, and the long front porches of rocking and reading, the firesides of one's own amusement vanished. We were faced, eye to eye, with television. Magazines made a desperate effort to match picture with picture, but casualties were many, and in 1969 the *Post* suspended publication. It had happened before—in 1765 to protest the Stamp Act—but that was small consolation. It lay—this behemoth that had been stared down by a twenty-one-inch eye—smoldering on the American memory with such intensity of heat that it had to rise again.

The *Post* is older than the Republic, into its third century. It has been to war with the country, predicted events and trends, amused and instructed the nation (many people learned to read by the *Post*). Its mistakes have shown that age is not always indicative of excellence. But its unpretentious triumphs point to hope and faith in the printed page as a continuing chronicle of America's progress.

The Editors
The Saturday Evening Post

(Left) For nearly 250 years the Post *logo has been familiar to American homes. Dissatisfaction with a good thing led to numerous changes, but the logo at the center reappeared in 1971.*

The Face of America

Alexis de Tocqueville wrote the material on this and the following pages on a visit to this country in 1831. Time has not dimmed his perception of the American spirit.

There is a close bond and a
necessary relation between these two elements—
freedom and productive industry.
Freedom is especially favorable to the
production of wealth;
Nor is it difficult to perceive that despotism
is especially averse to the
same result.

America is a land of wonders
in which everything is in constant motion
and every change seems an advancement. Thus, men
of democratic ages require
to be free in order to more readily procure
those physical enjoyments
for which they are always longing.

Perhaps there is no country
in the world where fewer idle men
are to be met with than in America, or where all
who work are more eager
to promote their own welfare.

Thus, Americans,
who arrived but yesterday
on the territory they inhabit, have already changed
the whole order of nature for
their own advantage.

(Left) Oregon pours her gold out to the harvest which helps feed the world. Purple mountains majesties tremble, as efficiency struggles with beauty in the glory of the American landscape.

Why Americans Are Friendly

Though the nation was barely formed, de Tocqueville already noted signs of national character.

Two Americans

are at once friends,

simply because they are Americans.

In America, where the privileges

of birth never existed and where riches confer no

peculiar rights on their possessors,

men unacquainted with each other

are very ready to frequent

the same places, and find neither peril nor

advantage in the free exchange of their thoughts.

If they meet by accident, they neither seek

nor avoid intercourse; their manner is

therefore natural, frank, and open;

it is easy to see that they hardly expect or

apprehend anything from each other,

and that they do not care

to display, any more than to conceal,

their position

in the world. If their demeanor is often

cold and serious, it is never haughty

or constrained; because they are not in a humor

to talk—not because they think it is

in their interest to be silent.

(Right) Amish boys inform the photographer of their true sentiments about publicity while waiting for their parents to get out of church in Lancaster, Pennsylvania. Here, de Tocqueville's comments about being natural, frank and open seem to apply.

Pioneers felt they had entered a new planet when they came to Monument Valley, so different did it seem from the old world.

The Face of America 12

Centuries of scorching wind have sculpted these rocks into the fantastic shapes which the Indians in Arizona call the Eternal Mittens.

The Right of Assembly

De Tocqueville notes the innocence of most American gatherings, though Resurrection City and national marches bespeak the seriousness of association in the 20th century.

When citizens have the faculty and habit

of associating for everything,

they will freely associate for little

purposes as well as great.

Where enjoyment is concerned, people

associate to make the festivities grander

and more orderly.

The passions that stir the Americans

most deeply are commercial and

not political ones.

In Europe we habitually regard

a restless spirit,

immoderate desire for wealth,

and an extreme love of independence

as great social dangers.

But precisely those things assure a long

and peaceful future for American republics.

Without such restless passions the population

would be concentrated around a few places

and would soon experience, as we do,

needs which are hard to satisfy.

What a happy land the New World is!

(Right) Main Street in Winchester, Virginia loves a parade as much as Fifth Avenue. American songwriters George Gershwin and Irving Berlin wrote about the feeling; and no Boy Scout, majorette, soldier or trombonist ever drooped passing a review stand.

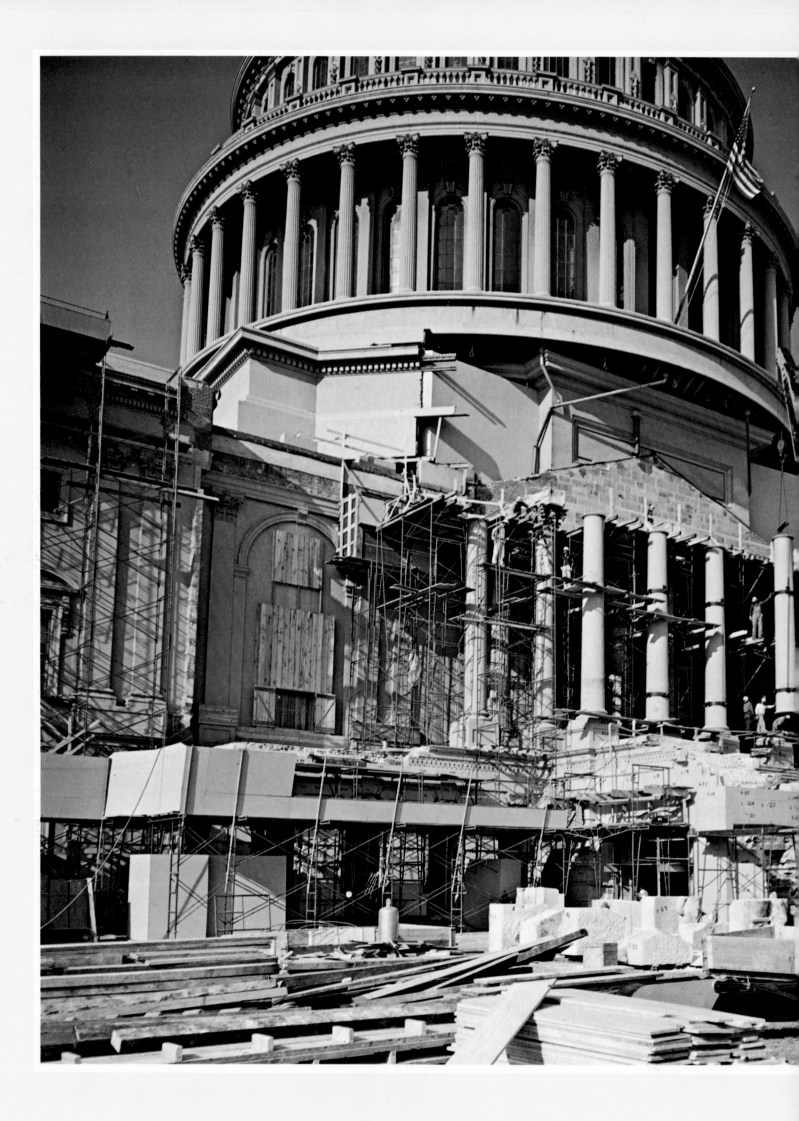

"The Capitol"

The "imaginary metropolis" de Tocqueville speaks of is now a city of sixty-seven square miles, a million inhabitants.

The several States of the Union are every day

planning and erecting for themselves

prodigious undertakings, which would astonish

the engineers of the great European nations.

For example, the Americans have traced out

the circuit of an immense city on the

site which they intended to make their

capital, but which, up to the present time

is hardly more densely peopled than Pontoise.

According to them, it will one day contain a

million inhabitants and they have already

rooted up trees for ten miles around, lest

they should interfere with the future

citizens of this imaginary metropolis. They

have also erected a magnificent palace for

Congress in the centre of this city, and

have given it the pompous name of

The Capitol.

In democratic communities the imagination

is compressed when men consider themselves;

it expands indefinitely when they think of

the State. Hence it is that the same men

who live on a small scale in narrow dwellings

frequently aspire to gigantic splendour

in the erection of their public monuments.

(Left) George Washington laid the cornerstone in 1793. Lincoln ordered the towering dome in 1861. In 1959, Congress appropriated $10 million merely to give the dome a more solid base.

BEGINNINGS

CERTAIN INALIENABLE RIGHTS

All of the great movements of civilization arrived on the American shore almost simultaneously. The renaissance—we see it in Thomas Jefferson's concept of the whole man; the Industrial Revolution—visible in Franklin's passionate concern for a better life for every man, by inventions and cheap production; the spiritualism of the medieval period—most of the states were founded as havens for religious dissenters; Rousseauistic democracy—evinced in the Declaration of Independence and the Revolution. These movements were the new Nation's natural resources. America was founded on a practical ideal—practical because capitalism enlists man's natural acquisitiveness for the good of the state. The men who made this practical ideal work were largely yeomen. Owning land had been for them in the old country an impossible dream. Having a voice in the government had been inconceivable. Yet here they had both. Tempering this brawn was the refined Greco-Roman brain of the Virginia aristocracy who gave our country twelve presidents and the theory of earned rather than indiscriminate power, the vision of a new and shining republic.

The language was ready-made, the land temperate, the soil fertile, the cornucopia overflowing. These qualities, unmatched anywhere in the world, formed the base for the renaissance in man's thinking that became America, and eventually did away with imperial authority the world over, replacing it with constitutional and parliamentary government, government by the few replaced by government by the many, the chance for man to explore his outer limits, to exchange his own interests for a grander design. The founding principles dared us to be altruistic above and beyond the self-preserving profit motive, and twice, in the Civil War of the 1860's and the civil rights movements of the 1960's, Americans went to war for the rights of the powerless and the poor, expensive clashes at the time in men and in money, but in the long run, bargains in the marketplace of liberty.

(Right) Norman Rockwell painted this portrait of Franklin on the 150th anniversary of the signing of the Declaration, a document which might have been Franklin's own credo.

SESQUI·CENTENNIAL·CELEBRATION
OF·THE·SIGNING·OF·THE
DECLARATION·OF·INDEPENDENCE

Norman
Rockwell

Dawn's Early Light

The founding principles should be the creed of our political faith, the test of civic instruction, the touchstone by which to try the services of those we trust; and should we wander from them in moments of error or of alarm, let us hasten to retrace our steps to regain the road which alone leads to peace, liberty and safety.

—Thomas Jefferson,
near the end of his presidency

I have made it a rule, whenever in my power, to avoid becoming the draftsman of papers to be reviewed by a public body. I took my lesson from an incident which I will relate to you. When I was a journeyman printer, one of my companions, an apprentice hatter, having served out his time, was about to open a shop for himself. His first concern was to have a handsome signboard with a proper inscription. He composed it in these words: "John Thompson, hatter, makes and sells hats for ready money." But he thought he would submit it to his friends for their amendments. The first he showed it to thought the world "hatter" tautologous. It was struck out. The next observed the word "makes" might as well be omitted because the customers would not care who made the hats. He struck it out. A third said he felt the words "for ready money" were useless, as it was not the custom of the place to sell on credit. The inscription now stood: "John Thompson sells hats." "*Sells* hats?" said his next friend. "Why nobody would expect you to give them away." It was stricken out; "hats" followed it, as there was one painted on the board. So his inscription was reduced to "John Thompson" with the figure of a hat subjoined.

—Benjamin Franklin to
Thomas Jefferson, when
Jefferson admitted the changes made
to his draft of the Declaration of
Independence disturbed him

Happily, the government of the United States gives to bigotry no sanction, to persecution no assistance.

—George Washington

In forty years, the Americans have quadrupled their population, and stretched their territory from the waters of the Ohio and the Mississippi to the Pacific. They have assumed, as if by instinct, a mighty system of private law, a bold precision of diplomacy; a large code of commerce and national interests. Slavery itself, the plague spot of human society, is fast verging into decay. We look forward with joy to the illustrious period, when the growing tide of population shall have fully fertilized the western wilderness; and a mighty race, one in virtue, one in interest, shall be busied in lighting up and transmitting the lamp of knowledge.

—An English Post *Correspondent in 1852*

Your life, your liberties, your property, will be at the disposal only of your Creator and yourselves. You will know no power but such as you create, no authority unless derived from your grant; no law, but such as acquires full their obligations from your consent.

—John Jay,
one year into independence

There seem to be but three ways for a nation to acquire wealth. The first is by war, as the Romans did, in plundering their conquered neighbors. This is robbery. The second is by commerce, which is generally cheating. The third by agriculture, the only honest way, wherein a man receives the real increase of the seed thrown into the ground, in a kind of continual miracle, wrought by the hand of God in his favor, as a reward for his innocent life and his virtuous industry.

—Benjamin Franklin

Nothing, in my opinion, can convey a more unjust idea of the spirit of a true American than to suppose he would even compliment, much less make an adulating address to, any person sent here to trample on the right of his country or that he would kiss the hand which is prepared to rivet his own feathers.

—Samuel Adams in 1771

Is life so dear or peace so sweet as to be purchased at the price of chains and slavery? Forbid it, Almighty God. I know not what course others may take, but as for me, give me liberty or give me death.

—Patrick Henry's address
to the Virginia Convention, 1775

Americans at the time of the Revolution strove to overcome the boundaries, both spatial and political, of European life. The small building-lots and farms, the rigid caste systems of the old world were out of scale and temper with the new country, the frontier a state of mind to which the new settler had to adjust. Like a child learning to walk and speak, he imitated the ways of those who could, first the English, then the Indians. When finally, he hit his own stride, it was a gait of many cultures. The boy above, leveling his tricorne for the country's 200th anniversary, shows the mixture of dream and determination that drove and sustained his forebears in the new world.

City of Brotherly Love

Philadelphia at the time Franklin hung out his shingle was the second largest city in the English-speaking world, exceeded only by London. Though Franklin's house does not survive, many parts of the city look as they did in Franklin's

day. On Society Hill, a panorama of eighteenth-century houses invites the mind back to the first years of this country's freedom. Most Americans at the time worked downstairs and lived above their shops; it was a time-, labor-, and space-saving device which protected cities against urban blight and suburban sprawl. Franklin's power came as much from his occupation as from the zeal with which he pursued it; the print shop was the communications center of colonial America.

The Real John Paul Jones

by Samuel Eliot Morison

(August 1959)

Almost every American and Englishman has heard of John Paul Jones, and every visitor to Annapolis is shown his tomb in the crypt of the Naval Academy chapel. He was the most famous sea fighter of the War of American Independence. Born a poor boy in Scotland, he joined the British merchant marine at the age of thirteen, rose to command by the time he was twenty-one and, having "fallen in love with America at first sight," as he later expressed it, joined the Continental Navy as a lieutenant when it was being organized at Philadelphia in 1775.

As captain of armed sloop *Providence* and later of armed ship *Alfred* in 1776, John Paul Jones made prize-taking cruises in the North Atlantic. In command of the new sloop of war *Ranger* in 1778, he made a memorable cruise off the coasts of Ireland and Scotland, raided the town of Whitehaven, England to burn enemy shipping and captured a British sloop of war, H.M.S. *Drake*, after a slugging match of over an hour. Next year, flying his commodore's broad pennant in U.S.S. *Bonhomme Richard*—an old crate of a ship but the best he could get—and with a motley task force of French and American armed vessels under him, he won the greatest naval victory of the war capturing H.M.S. *Serapis* in the Battle off Flamborough Head, when his own ship was in a sinking condition. That was one of the toughest and hardest fought of all naval battles in days of sail. Discharged at the end of the war, he accepted a rear admiral's commission in the Imperial Russian Navy and helped win two victories over a Turkish fleet in the Black Sea. He died obscurely in Paris at the age of forty-five, but had the posthumous honor of having his remains transferred to Washington by a squadron of United States cruisers in 1905, and reinterred in the gorgeous sarcophagus at Annapolis.

John Paul Jones became fabulous even in his lifetime; and the myths and fables, growing ever since his death, have almost smothered the real man. Some forty chapbooks—precursors of the dime novels of yesterday and the comics of today—were printed about him before 1840. These penny-plain and sixpence-colored pamphlets were filled with lurid tales which had no foundation, presenting Jones as adventurer, self-seeker and even pirate. In truth he always lived up to his motto, *Pro Republica*, showed exemplary humanity to prisoners and consideration to his crews, and never engaged in that licensed and respectable branch of piracy, privateering.

Perhaps the worst thing that happened to Jones's fame was to be made the subject of a misleading biography, around 1900, by one Augustus C. Buell, a professional writer of novels dressed up as true lives. Buell's two-volume biography of John Paul Jones is still popularly accepted as authentic, although frequently shown up by historians. It was Buell who placed Jones in the romantic setting of a Virginia planter who, after brawling with a British naval officer and having his plantation burned down by Tories, enlisted in the United States Navy. And there exist some thirty novels of which Jones is a leading character, each twisting his personality and career to suit the writer's purpose.

The facts are very different, and the real Jones is a far more interesting person than any of the mythical Joneses. There are two central themes in his career: first, last and always he was a sailor; and he followed the popular American pattern of the poor boy who made good. Born John Paul, son of a Scots gardener, he went to sea before the mast at the age of thirteen, rose to command at the age of twenty-one and was ready to retire with a modest competence five years later. Then a series of circumstances drew him in the Continental Navy and placed him on the road to fame.

The mythmakers have even altered Jones's appearance, making him out to be a dark, scowling, beetle-browed tough such as pirates are supposed to be. Actually, he was a sandy-haired, hazel-eyed little Scot about five feet, five inches tall. He was a complete gentleman in social intercourse and fascinating to the ladies, but a good deal of a sundowner—a martinet—on the quarterdeck. He had a hot temper, quarreling sooner or later with almost everyone close to him, yet showed such superb courage and resourcefulness as a fighting sailor that men like Benjamin Franklin, Thomas Jefferson and Robert Morris promoted his career in the Navy.

It is no wonder that authors have romanced about Jones, because he was a chivalrous figure.

The reader may well infer that Jones was an egotist. He was indeed a colossal egotist. To read his letters one would suppose that he was almost the only fighting captain in the Navy. The only executive officer to whom he ever gave any credit was Richard Dale, the attractive young officer from Virginia who served as first lieutenant in the *Bonhomme Richard*.

Besides being an egotist, John Paul Jones was a good deal of a snob. After receiving command of the *Ranger*, but before sailing for France, he adopted a coat of arms and had it painted by some local artist.

Captain Jones knew thoroughly all the rudiments of his profession, from splicing to gunnery. He was outstanding as a navigator and ship handler, and expert in all ruses of war that eighteenth-century sailors practiced. He saved *Ariel* from crashing on the Penmarch rocks by bold maneuvers that astonished even the sailors of Brittany. He fitted out his ships with great care and skill, and insisted on having plenty of spare yards, sails and other parts on board. He caused the armament, masting and rigging of every vessel that he commanded to be radically altered so that she would sail faster and fight more efficiently. For the health and welfare of his people he was always considerate, providing extra rations and grog out of his own pocket, advancing pay when in foreign waters, and fighting both French bureaucrats and American politicians to get the prize money that was due to his sailors. Although there are plenty of complaints on record by Jones's seamen of being worked too hard and of his outbursts of bad temper—such as kicking Midshipman Fanning down a hatchway—nobody ever complained of the food on board his ships. That is significant, as the first thing sailors growl about is their "chow."

Despite all he did for their welfare and glory, Jones was unpopular with his Yankee crews because he tried to maintain taut Royal Navy discipline; when he was relieved as captain of *Ranger*, her officers and men were delighted. But for *Bonhomme Richard* he recruited sailors, soldiers, beachcombers and desperadoes of six or seven different nations. They recognized him for the great leader and fighter that he was and enabled him to win a glorious victory.

Paul Jones liked to do things a little differently from other American naval officers. Navy regulations prescribed a blue uniform coat, with red waistcoat and blue breeches; Jones didn't like this outfit and fitted out his officers in *Bonhomme Richard* with blue coats, white waistcoats and breeches, as in the Royal Navy; a practical change because it enabled his ships to masquerade as British, close the enemy to short range and surprise him. Navy regulations allowed captains one gold epaulet, but Jones wore two. Even his flags were different. He revered the Stars and Stripes as the "Flag of Freedom"—his favorite phrase—but the stripes on the American ensigns flown by his ships were red, white and blue.

The meeting of John Paul Jones, the American Navy's greatest lover, with the Empress Catherine of Russia, most beloved of crowned heads, has naturally intrigued the novelists and stimulated the mythmakers. The opportunity for a grand love affair is too great to be missed. Actually there was nothing between them but the professional relationship, and not much of that; Jones was indeed impressed by the empress's charm and sagacity; but she was fat and sixty, and at the time he met her, had installed a lusty young guards officer as her official lover. Jones was promptly received by the empress at Tsarskoe Selo, and promptly sent to his command in the Black Sea. There he fought two of the most interesting sea battles of his naval career; but he could not get on with his superior in command, Field Marshal Potemkin, who put him "on the beach"; and when he returned to St. Petersburg, the empress gave him a cold reception.

When dismissed from the Russian Navy, Jones, still in excellent health and only forty-two years old, returned to Paris by easy stages. There he spent two more years very unhappily, as all his old friends had emigrated, and he detested the French Revolution. In the summer of 1792, the consequences of his long quarterdeck vigils in wet and wintry weather caught up with John Paul Jones. First jaundice, then nephritis, and finally bronchial pneumonia developed, and alone, except for his valet de chambre, he died at the age of forty-five.

Thus, John Paul Jones was not altogether an enviable or a happy person. No "founder" or "father" of the American Navy, he was a young lieutenant with neither pull nor public, who rose to the top through sheer grit, guts and merit. And he is justly considered our greatest naval hero of the American Revolution.

Benjamin Franklin

As A Diplomat

After the outbreak of the Revolutionary War, Franklin was in Europe as American Commissioner to the French Court in Paris. His wit, broad-ranging intelligence and amazing vitality soon made him the Toast of Paris and, in the eyes of the French, the embodiment of American independence and vigor. Combining this basic appeal with his keen grasp of practical affairs, he was able to gain vital military and economic assistance for the Revolutionary cause from the French Government. Franklin crowned his diplomatic career by playing a pivotal role in the three-way negotiations between America, Britain and France which followed the British surrender. Thus, his indomitable career as a diplomat spanned the entire Revolutionary period and his French mission ranks as a premier achievement in American diplomacy.

—William Rogers,
former secretary of state

As A Humanitarian

In his autobiography, Franklin says, "In 1751, Dr. Thomas Bond, a particular friend of mine, conceived the idea of establishing a hospital in Philadelphia (a very beneficent design, which has been ascribed to me, but was originally his), for the reception and cure of poor sick persons, whether inhabitants of the province or strangers." Dr. Bond tried to raise subscriptions for the hospital but was not successful. He then came to see Franklin and told him there was no such thing as carrying a public-spirited project through without Franklin being concerned in it. So Franklin "not only subscrib'd to it myself, but engaged heartily in the design of procuring subscriptions from others." Through his newspaper he also urged a public subscription.

—Morris Fishbein, M.D.,
former president of the
American Medical Association

As A Firefighter

Benjamin Franklin can rightly be called the father of many things, but it is little known that he was also the father of American fire departments. On April 4, 1732, when he was just thirty years old, he founded the first organized volunteer fire company in the world. Called the Union Fire Company, it has continued uninterrupted service to this day, and now goes by the name Engine Company Number 8 of the Philadelphia Fire Department. Fronting the firehouse stands a five-foot bust of Franklin sculptured out of 80,000 Lincoln-head pennies contributed by Philadelphia school children. Once I asked the old fire captain, "Why pennies? Why not fifty-cent pieces on which Franklin's head appears?" "Because," the captain said, "he never said, 'a half-dollar saved is a half-dollar earned.' "

—Dennis Smith,
fireman and author of
Report from Engine Co. 82

As A Scientist

Benjamin Franklin's researches in pure science were in the field of electricity. He showed there were two types of electric charge, opposite in nature, and demonstrated that the lightning bolt was an electric charge identical, except in size, to those in the laboratory. He then applied his theories to the invention of the lightning rod in 1752, a simple device which quickly proved to be an efficient guard against the lightning stroke. It was the *first* time scientific theory was used to counter natural disaster and demonstrated the fact that people could turn to science for answers to their problems.

—Isaac Asimov,
scientist and author

As An Educator

Benjamin Franklin was perhaps the first American to apply the idea of "useful knowledge" to education. His greatest achievement in education was the founding of the University of Pennsylvania, a college he wanted to respond to the needs of the time. In Franklin's "Proposals Relating to the Education of Youth in Pennsylvania," he included athletics, accounting, English, modern languages, history, geography, and the natural sciences in his proposed curriculum, a startling deviation from the usual college study of classical thought and literature. His pithy "he was so learned that he could name a horse in nine languages, so ignorant that he bought a cow to ride on" sums up his feeling.

—Martin Meyerson,
president, University of Pennsylvania

As A Labor Leader

Unlike the other founding fathers, Franklin was a working man. All his life he had to make a living. He followed the steps of the medieval guilds: first, he was an apprentice. He slept in his brother's print shop in Boston and learned the business by doing the dirty work. Then he became a journeyman—literally, for he ran off for Philadelphia—and was, according to eighteenth-century law, a fugitive from justice. He printed money for colonial America, pamphlets, and, eventually, *Poor Richard's Almanack.* His hands were dirty and his back was strong. He saw the value of organization, both for the working man and the colonies.

—Jimmy Hoffa,
former president, Teamster's Union

"Keep your shop and your shop will keep you," admonished Franklin, and he practiced, with a few dalliances, what he preached. His printing press is displayed at left, and to judge from the amount of his work which survives, it was rarely allowed to lie idle. Among other things, he invented bifocal lenses so he could do close and distant business at the same time. Unlike his compatriots Paul Revere and Tom Paine, Franklin was not an inflammatory pamphleteer. He believed reconciliation with England might be brought about by calm, businesslike procedures. Besides, he often said, he liked living in England.

July 10, 1776. NUMB. 2481.

The Pennsylvania Gazette

Containing the Frefheft Ad- *vices, Foreign and Domeftic.*

In CONGRESS, JULY 4. 1776.

A DECLARATION

By the REPRESENTATIVES of the UNITED STATES of AMERICA, in GENERAL CONGRESS affembled.

WHEN, in the Courfe of human Events, it becomes neceffary for one People to diffolve the political Bands which have connected them with another, and to affume among the Powers of the Earth, the feparate and equal Station to which the Laws of Nature and of Nature's God entitle them, a decent Refpect to the Opinions of Mankind requires that they fhould declare the caufes which impel them to the Separation.

We hold thefe Truths to be felf-evident, that all Men are created equal, that they are endowed by their Creator with certain unalienable Rights, that among thefe are Life, Liberty, and the Purfuit of Happinefs—That to fecure thefe Rights, Governments are inftituted among Men, deriving their juft Powers from the Confent of the Governed, that whenever any Form of Government becomes deftructive of thefe Ends, it is the Right of the People to alter or to abolifh it, and to inftitute new Government, laying its Foundation on fuch Principles, and organizing its Powers in fuch Form, as to them fhall feem moft likely to effect their Safety and Happinefs. Prudence, indeed, will dictate that Governments long eftablifhed fhould not be changed for light and tranfient Caufes; and accordingly all Experience hath fhewn, that Mankind are more difpofed to fuffer, while Evils are fufferable, than to right themfelves by abolifhing the Forms to which they are accuftomed. But when a long Train of Abufes and Ufurpations, purfuing invariably the fame Object, evinces a Defign to reduce them under abfolute Defpotifm, it is their Right, it is their Duty, to throw off fuch Government, and to provide new Guards for their future Security. Such has been the patient Sufferance of thefe Colonies, and fuch is now the Neceffity which conftrains them to alter their former Syftems of Government. The Hiftory of the prefent King of Great-Britain is a Hiftory of repeated Injuries and Ufurpations, all having in direct Object the Eftablifhment of an abfolute Tyranny over thefe States. To prove this, let Facts be fubmitted to a candid World.

He has refufed his Affent to Laws the moft wholefome and neceffary for the Public Good.

He has forbidden his Governors to pafs Laws of immediate and preffing Importance, unlefs fufpended in their Operation till his Affent fhould be obtained; and when fo fufpended, he has utterly neglected to attend to them.

He has refufed to pafs other Laws for the Accommodation of large Diftricts of People, unlefs thofe People would relinquifh the Right of Reprefentation in the Legiflature, a Right ineftimable to them, and formidable to Tyrants only.

He has called together Legiflative Bodies at Places unufual, uncomfortable, and diftant from the Depofitory of their public Records, for the fole Purpofe of fatiguing them into Compliance with his Meafures.

He has diffolved Reprefentative Houfes repeatedly, oppofing with manly Firmnefs his Invafions on the Rights of the People.

He has refufed for a long Time, after fuch Diffolutions, to caufe others to be elected; whereby the Legiflative Powers, incapable of Annihilation, have returned to the People at large for their exercife; the State remaining in the mean Time expofed to all the Dangers of Invafion from without, and Convulfions within.

For fufpending our own Legiflatures, and declaring themfelves invefted with Power to legiflate for us in all Cafes whatfoever.

He has abdicated Government here, by declaring us out of his Protection and waging War againft us.

He has plundered our Seas, ravaged our Coafts, burnt our Towns, and deftroyed the Lives of our People.

He is, at this Time, tranfporting large Armies of foreign Mercenaries to compleat the Works of Death, Defolation and Tyranny, already begun with Circumftances of Cruelty and Perfidy, fcarcely paralleled in the moft barbarous Ages, and totally unworthy the Head of a civilized Nation.

He has conftrained our Fellow-Citizens, taken captive on the high Seas, to bear Arms againft their Country, to become the Executioners of their Friends and Brethren, or to fall themfelves by their Hands.

He has excited domeftic Infurrections amongft us, and has endeavoured to bring on the Inhabitants of our Frontiers the mercilefs Indian Savages, whofe known Rule of Warfare is an undiftinguifhed Deftruction of all Ages, Sexes and Conditions.

In every Stage of thefe Oppreffions we have petitioned for Redrefs in the moft humble Terms: Our repeated Petitions have been anfwered only by repeated Injury. A Prince, whofe Character is thus marked by every Act which may define a Tyrant, is unfit to be the Ruler of a free People.

Nor have we been wanting in Attentions to our Britifh Brethren. We have warned them from Time to Time of Attempts by their Legiflature to extend an unwarrantable Jurifdiction over us. We have reminded them of the Circumftances of our Emigration and Settlement here. We have appealed to their native Juftice and Magnanimity, and we have conjured them by the Ties of our common Kindred to difavow thefe Ufurpations, which would inevitably interrupt our Connections and Correfpondence. They too have been deaf to the Voice of Juftice and of Confanguinity. We muft, therefore, acquiefce in the Neceffity, which denounces our Separation, and hold them, as we hold the reft of Mankind, Enemies in War, in Peace, Friends.

WE, therefore, the Reprefentatives of the UNITED STATES of AMERICA, in GENERAL CONGRESS affembled, appealing to the Supreme Judge of the World for the Rectitude of our Intentions, do, in the Name and by Authority of the good People of thefe Colonies, folemnly Publifh and Declare, That thefe United Colonies are, and of Right ought to be, FREE AND INDEPENDENT STATES; that they are abfolved from all Allegiance to the Britifh Crown, and that all political Connection between them and the State of Great-Britain is and ought to be totally diffolved; and that as FREE AND INDEPENDENT STATES, they have full Power to levy War, conclude Peace, contract Alliances, eftablifh Commerce, and to do all other Acts and Things which INDEPENDENT STATES may of right do. And for the Support of this Declaration, with a firm Reliance on the Protection of divine Providence, we mutually pledge to each other our Lives, our Fortunes, and our facred Honour.

Signed by Order and in Behalf of the Congrefs,

JOHN HANCOCK, Prefident.

Juft publifhed, and to be fold by JOHN DUNLAP, *in Market-ftreet, Philadelphia,*

OBSERVATIONS

ON THE

Nature of CIVIL LIBERTY, the Principles of GOVERNMENT, and the Juftice and Policy of the WAR with AMERICA.

To which is added,

An APPENDIX, containing a ftate of the National Debt, an eftimate of the money drawn from the Public by the taxes, and an account of the National Income and Expenditure fince the laft War.

Heu miferi cives; non Hoftem, inimicaque caftra,
------- Veftras Spes uritis. VIRG.

By RICHARD PRICE, D.D. F.R.S.

This learned, judicious and liberal author had the thanks of the Common Council, and the Freedom of the City of London prefented to him in a gold box, for this his much admired moft excellent pamphlet on Civil Liberty --- And for which he alfo deferves the united thanks of America.

July 2, 1776.

SEVEN POUNDS Reward.

RUN away, laft Sunday night, from the fubfcriber, living in Chefter county, the two following fervants, viz.— Edward Gray, about 5 feet 6 inches high, pock-marked, ftraight black hair, about 26 years of age, fays he was born in London, and ferved his time with William Hicklin, in New-Caftle county, underftands all forts of plantation work, and fays he worked at the Miller's bufinefs two years with one Reynolds, in Nottingham; had on, when he went away, white country linen fhirt and trowfers, new coat and jacket, and a leather apron; took with him a fcythe and hangings: Said Gray was bailed out of goal by the fubfcriber, and for my fecurity indented himfelf to me; it is hoped that every honeft perfon will endeavour to apprehend faid Gray, not for the reward but in order to bring him to juftice. The other, named John Dillis, about 25 years of age, born in New-England, a ftout well built fellow, about 5 feet 10 or 11 inches high, with dirty coloured hair, his fore teeth wide apart; fays he belongs to the Row-gallies, and has been feen about Port-Penn; had on, when he went away, white fhirt and trowfers, a red under jacket, without fleeves, no fhoes nor ftockings; he is fond of ftrong drink and company, and a very great liar. Whoever takes up the faid runaways, and fecures them, fo as the fubfcriber gets them again, fhall have Five Pounds for Gray, and Forty Shillings for Dillis, and reafonable charges for Dillis, paid by WILLIAM KERLIN.

N B. Dillis run away the 2d of June

Eafton, Jul. 2, 1776.

BY virtue of a writ to me directed, will be expofed to fale, on the premifes, on Tuefday, the 30th day of July inftant, at 2 o'clock in the afternoon, two certain tracts or parcels of land, fituate in Macoongie townfhip, in the county of Northampton, one of them bounded by the lands of Reuben Haines, Henry Probft and John Fogle, and containing 107 acres, whereon are a ftone tenement and log tenement, a large log barn, ftables and other out-houfes, and a confiderable quantity of good meadow; and the other of the faid tracts, bounded by the lands of Peter Hafs and the faid Haines, and containing 37 acres woodland; late the property of Henry Shade; feized and taken in execution by HENRY FULLERT, Sheriff.

STOLEN or STRAYED away, from the fubfcriber, living in Chanceford townfhip, York county, Pennfylvania, the 20th of June laft, a white Horfe and a black Mare, the horfe about 12 years old, between 13 and 14 hands high, branded on the near fhoulder I. C. his mane trimmed, a long bufh tail, and is a natural pacer; had a bell on when he went away; the mare 4 years old, both trots and paces, between 14 and 15 hands high, no brand, fhe has a fwitch tail, a fmall ftar in her forehead, and wants one of her fore teeth in the upper jaw; both newly fhod before, when they went away. Whoever takes up the thief, fhall have ... more, fo as the owner may have ... pounds reward, or for the horfe ... paid by ... Shillings ...

Founding Fathers

What do we mean by the Revolution? The war? That was no part of the Revolution: it was only an effect and consequence of it. The Revolution was in the minds of the people, and this was effected, from 1760 to 1775, in the course of fifteen years before a drop of blood was shed at Lexington.

—*John Adams*

I believe there are more instances of the abridgment of the freedom of the people by gradual and silent encroachment of those in power than by violent and sudden usurpation.

—*James Madison*

The basis of our government being the opinion of the people, the very first object should be to keep that right; and were it left to me whether we should have a government without newspapers or newspapers without government, I should not hesitate a moment to prefer the latter.

—*Thomas Jefferson*

To be prepared for war is one of the most effectual means of preserving peace.

—*George Washington*

(Bottom) John Adams and James Madison, Thomas Jefferson and George Washington admired Greek and Roman ideals and imagined the United States as a classic republic. (Top) The Declaration of Independence appeared for the first time in print in Franklin's Pennsylvania Gazette. *(Right) Inside Independence Hall today recordings tell the story of the hall and the Liberty Bell in seven languages to accommodate the 1½ million people who visit the shrine every year.*

INDEPENDENCE HALL

PHILADELPHIA

Midnight Rider

by F. X. O'Connor, Jr.

Paul Revere was a first generation American. His father, Apollos Rivoire, fled France during the Huguenot persecution, arrived in Boston at age fourteen, anglicized his name, and was apprenticed to a goldsmith. Currency was insecure in the eighteenth century, and wealth was regularly transformed into gold and silver.

Revere was often employed as a messenger for the Massachusetts Committee of Correspondence as he was on the evening of April 18, 1775. He was a good rider and not known to loiter in taverns though his hotheadedness earned him a court-martial for insubordination. Exonerated in 1782, the soldier-craftsman became rich by opening copper-rolling mills in Canton, Massachusetts. "He was well adapted to form plans, and to carry them into successful execution—both for the benefit of himself and the service of others," eulogized the *Boston Intelligencer* on Revere's death, May 16, 1818.

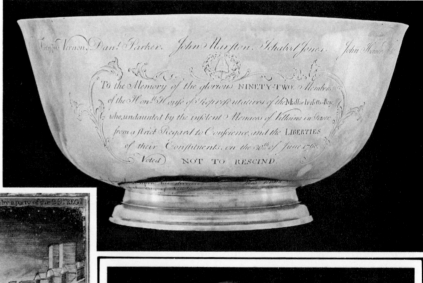

(Top and right) Sugar basin and liberty bowl worked by Revere. The bowl commemorates "the Glorious Ninety-two" Massachusetts House members who defied King George by protesting the Townshend Acts. Revere's engraving, bottom, "borrowed" from another artist, inaccurately records the first shooting of the Revolution. J.S. Copley painted the patriot-smith (bottom right) in exchange for gold and silver miniature frames in 1768. Revere is pictured with his engraving tools.

The Week That Was

by Roger Butterfield

Thomas Jefferson, who could never pass up a curious sight, paid a shilling to see a monkey. He didn't say what kind of monkey it was—probably some sailor's pet in a waterfront tavern. At any rate, he went to look at the monkey a few days before writing the Declaration of Independence.

During the time he was actually writing the Declaration, Jefferson paid one shilling sixpence for a new pencil, seven shillings for a new map and six shillings for wine.

He was very proud of his version of the Declaration and his feelings were hurt when parts were changed or omitted on July 3rd and 4th. Old Doctor Franklin tried to soothe him, but for several days afterward, Jefferson was upset. On the sixth, however, Jefferson must have felt better. His account book showed he had paid a shilling for beer.

(Bottom) Monticello, the house on the nickel. (Top) Jefferson built the clock which tells the days of the week by a series of cannonballs suspended on pulleys. His room at right shows his bed, designed to be raised during the day to give the room more space. Jefferson also submitted designs for the White House, the Capitol and the University of Virginia.

(Left) The federal city's namesake, depicted by J.C. Leyendecker, examines the plan of the capital. He commissioned the Capitol building (right) though it is unrecognizably altered from its original design.

Road to Frederick Town

Washington

by William McKinley

(June 1898)

We celebrate the birthday of a great patriot, who assured the beginning of a great nation. It would not be possible to follow Washington in his long and distinguished services at the head of the armies and as Chief Executive of the Government. Washington's public life is as familiar to the American student as the history of the United States. We love to recall his noble unselfishness, his heroic purposes, the power of his magnificent personality, his glorious achievements for mankind, and his stalwart and unflinching devotion to independence, liberty and union. A slaveholder himself, he yet hated slavery, and provided in his will for the emancipation of his slaves. Not a college graduate, he was always enthusiastically the friend of liberal education. He used every suitable occasion to impress upon Congress and the country the importance of a high standard of general education. And how reverent was this great man; how prompt and generous his recognition of the guiding hand of Providence in establishing and controlling the destinies of the colonies and of the republic!

(Right) The city of Washington was laid out by Pierre l'Enfant, a French army engineer with grandiose ideas. He envisioned miles of greensward with radial streets bursting like stars from gleaming neoclassical buildings. Citizens of Washington have recorded it is a difficult city to walk in but its beauty and perspective never fail to delight the visitor, and a few presidents have conceded they too are impressed.

ONE NATION UNDER GOD

WE THE PEOPLE...

Religion in America has two sides, spiritual and social. Churches have thrived according to their ability to congregate and maintain a family life warm with aspects of covered dishes and healthy social activities. Many of the great movements of our times, including abolition in the nineteenth century and the civil rights movement of the 1960's, have grown out of the churches, though few Americans feel churches have any real power. Paradoxically, churches, founded within the premise of separation of church and state, took on many of the responsibilities traditionally associated with temporal government. Many of America's first settlers were champions of the evangelical movement in England, and to them education was a religious duty, the natural opposite of idleness. Of the 182 colleges founded before the Civil War in the United States and still alive, 178 were established by denominational church groups. Oddly, these colleges and universities persisted in maintaining higher academic standards than their state-founded counterparts. The original purpose of many church-founded institutions was to supply their pulpits with ministers. For this, Latin and Greek were required, disciplines that spilled over to the undergraduate and secondary-school levels, thus perpetuating the classic ideals of the founding fathers. The breadth and depth of the original concept of America as a land of tolerance and faith has had a happy influence on political pursuits in this country. Deep and abiding faith in the connection of our founding principles with the Judaic concept of right and the law has been an onerous but inspiring ideal for the American people to fulfill. Certainly there has been no established church, no state religion, but a tone persists, in schools where the Pledge of Allegiance is still recited, on coins, in the White House; to be good is to be religious, it seems to say. The blessings of this nation's posterity begin with the blessings of birth in this fortunate land, but they continue only as the rights of others are protected.

(Right) With his band of farmers, Washington took on the mightiest nation on earth. The victory was a significant one for the new nation. The army subsisted mainly on prayer.

Valley Forge

Out of Many, One

We have not been told about that Great Spirit which makes everything. But your brother and the other people wish to have us know about it. I shall be very kind to the missionaries. I call your brother my son. I am his father. I have given him a house. I have given him land, and fish pond and goats. I shall be glad to see my children taught and become good.

—Tamoree, King of Atooi (Sandwich Islands, Hawaii) to Isaac A. Ruggles, brother of a missionary, June 1822

If I'd known as a young man the problems I'd become a part of, the human anguish I'd be invited to see, I don't think I'd have had the courage to become a pastor.

—Pastor Noah Imbody, of Immanuel Lutheran Church, Evanston, Illinois

We had all the material things. Fame and all that. But there was still something needed, you see. It can't be one hundred percent without the inner life, can it?

—Former Beatle George Harrison, meditating with Maharishi

Prayer is the hardest kind of work, but it is the most important work we can do.

—Dr. Wernher von Braun

Let us picture for a moment what a reborn church would be. A life, not a creed, would be its test; what a man does, not what he professes; what he is, not what he has. What the world craves today is a more spiritual and less formal religion. I plead not for a modification of form, but for its subordination to the spirit, not for the abolishing of ordinances, but for their voluntary rather than obligatory observations.

—John D. Rockefeller, Jr.

Believing with you that religion is a matter which lies solely between man and his God, that he owes account to none other for his faith or his worship, that the legislative powers of government reach actions only, and not opinions, I contemplate with sovereign reverence the act of the whole American people which declared that their legislature should "make no law respecting an establishment of religion, or prohibiting the free exercise thereof," thus building a wall of separation between church and state.

—Thomas Jefferson, in a letter to the Baptist Association of Danbury, Connecticut in 1802

Educators, business leaders and statesmen admit that the problems of our day are staggering. Obviously we need more than human wisdom. Sir Winston Churchill before his death said, "Our problems are beyond us. We are a generation staggering around the rim of hell" . . . Plainly the answer lies only with the Lord.

—Pat Boone

I was converted (to Judaism) because of one fact. Inside every man there is a need to try to reach God in his own way. My dad is a Baptist, my mother was a Catholic. Her maiden name is Sanchez. She came from Puerto Rico. I tried Catholicism, but while it's the answer for millions of people, it was no answer for me. Nor did I change to Judaism because any of my friends influenced me, although some people say, "He's around Jews so much he wanted to be a Jew." The thing I found in Judaism which appealed to me is that it teaches justice for everyone.

—Sammy Davis, Jr.

I want to say that despite our troubles and the implacable enemies in many parts of the world who threaten our way of life, we will come through. We will come through because we have the best form of government man ever devised, because we have great creative and productive genius, because we have freedom and courage to protect it and, above all, because we believe in God. That last is a priceless advantage that our atheistic enemies don't have.

—President Herbert Hoover, in the dark days of the Depression

My faith in Christ and God has been helpful in keeping me peaceful, accepting defeats and disappointments not only in tennis but in other areas and in appreciating the things I've been given by my God.

—Tennis star Stan Smith

Changing attitudes about religion in America are shown in Rockwell's most popular and best remembered Post cover, "Saying Grace," which appeared Thanksgiving, 1951. Crowded travel conditions persisted from the war; tables were often shared. Travelers brought with them the articles of faith by which they lived. The country had not yet moved to the city, and families still bowed their heads to ask a blessing. The two men at the left regard the old woman and her grandson almost with longing, with nostalgia for a more stable time, a time of agrarian bedrock values, primitive dependence on the earth to provide man with his daily bread. The clouds of smoke from trains seen in the restaurant window indicate America has moved on, but the sentiment of the painting suggests it has lost something important. Rockwell's idea for the painting came from an Amish family he saw praying in a Pennsylvania restaurant.

Many Mansions

by Reinhold Niebuhr

(July 1960)

While both our foreign and domestic problems demand technical competence for their solution, they obviously confront us with moral issues which transcend the mere adaptation of means to ends. They raise the question of the meaning of human existence and of the meaning of the strange drama in which all nations are now so fatefully involved.

Three great religious traditions prevail among us—all three with the same Biblical roots: Judaism, Catholicism and Protestantism, the latter divided into a multitude of sects. Fortunately, they have much in common, despite their diversities. They worship a God who is the Creator, Redeemer and Judge of all men and nations. They are all ethical religions in that they try through various structures to implement the commandment, "Love thy neighbor."

All these common aspects of the three great religious traditions are potentially relevant to our moral concerns and historical perplexities. Yet it is not so much this relevance that has revitalized religions, but rather their concern with the incongruities of the individual, with his hopes and fears, with the grandeur and misery characteristic of the human condition.

All the Biblical faiths deal with this problem by defining the mystery of the divine as the mystery of the relation of ultimate justice to ultimate mercy. They assign the historically relevant meaning to the divine mystery, either in the covenant of God with Moses in the Old Testament, or in the New Testament conception of a "second covenant" established in the drama of Christ's life, death and resurrection.

Religious faith has always drawn its vitality from the knowledge man is an incongruous creature, immersed in the flux of time, yet transcending it.

Rehearsing for his Bar Mitzvah, a thirteen-year-old Jewish boy reads aloud, in Hebrew, from the ancient Scriptures that comprise the Torah. This ritual marks his first active part in the worship of the synagogue, an occasion for rejoicing that generally takes the form of a family party. The cap he wears is called a yarmulke; the prayer-shawl, a talis. Most other faiths have similar ceremonies of initiation, or rites of passage, for their young people. They may be called Confirmation, First Communion, or, more simply, joining the church.

The ritual sharing of bread and wine called the Mass or the Eucharist is the heart of a formal Christian tradition preserved in America by the Roman Catholic and Episcopal churches (top left). At the other end of the spectrum (right), simplicity and sincerity characterize the kind of religion brought to these shores by the Puritans, and preserved today in country churches where neighbors still gather for midweek evening "prayer meeting" and gospel hymn-sings.

Why I Didn't Quit the Ministry

by Norman Vincent Peale

(March 1963)

Three times since my ordination almost forty years ago I have seriously considered leaving the ministry. Twice I have reached the point of actually writing out my resignation. Some of my friends may be startled to learn this, but I doubt that many ministers will be surprised. They know the moments of deep discouragement that come to us all.

It's not just that most ministers are underpaid and overworked; I think that every man who is ordained is ready and willing to face that. It's the less obvious things that try the soul. The frustration that comes from being strangled by detail, never having enough time to pray, to study, to meditate, to be alone. The constraint that comes over some people when a minister is among them. The resentment that anyone but a saint would feel when people who want all the privileges of church membership contribute little or nothing in terms of time or money to meet the church's needs. The jealousy of some colleagues, the unreasonableness of some superiors.

Tough? Of course it's tough! It's hard on ministers' wives too. The other day a young pastor's wife came up to my wife. "Mrs. Peale," she said, "I'd like to ask you just one question. Can a minister's wife have a best friend?" And Ruth said to her gently, "No, I'm sorry, but in my opinion she can't. Her loyalty belongs to the whole congregation. If she singles out one woman for special confidences, special intimacies, others may be offended."

These and many other difficulties are very real, but I am still in the ministry. Like thousands of others, I haven't quit. I know now that I never will.

Before trying to explain what keeps this particular minister going, perhaps I should sketch the circumstances under which on three separate occasions I almost stopped. The first time was during the Depression, in New York. I had accepted a call to a big Fifth Avenue church with eagerness and enthusiasm. But church attendance was low, and the people who did come were harassed and fearful. Nothing I could do or say seemed to get through to them, and finally a great dark wave of self-doubt swept over me. I became convinced that I was totally inadequate, a failure who was trying to fill a pulpit too big for him. I told my wife that I thought I ought to quit and go back to the newspaper business, which I had left to become a minister.

I'll never forget what Ruth said to me. "Norman," she said, "right now you *are* a failure, but not in the way you think. You're a failure because you're thinking primarily of yourself, of your own success or lack of it. You're not thinking about what God may have in mind for you. Maybe He thinks it would be good for you to fail. Anyway, why don't you do what you're always telling other people to do: Trust God, put your life in His hands and ask for His guidance?"

I took her advice and weathered that first crisis. But twice, in later years, I became even more discouraged. In 1955 some members of the clergy criticized my books and sermons so bitterly that I wrote out my resignation. Only my father's faith in me as a man and a minister kept me from handing it in.

Five years later, I became involved in a controversy even more stormy. In the late summer of 1960 I attended a conference of ministers who had gathered in Washington, D.C., to discuss religious freedom in general and separation of church and state in particular. We felt that the latter issue was not being fully discussed in the presidential campaign then underway, and said so. This ended the uneasy silence on the subject with a bang. So great, indeed, was the ensuing furor that I feared it might bring discredit on my church. This time I did submit my resignation. It was rejected.

But even if the elders and deacons had accepted my resignation, I would have gone on being a minister somewhere. I would have *had* to go on, because this business of helping other people become better people by bringing them closer to God is the most exciting, the most stimulating, the most challenging, the most rewarding work in the world, and quitting it would be like dying—only worse.

When you think of the opportunities a minister has, the problems and difficulties and irritations of his job shrivel down to nothing—absolutely nothing. Consider what he is! He's a front-line fighter in the war against evil, where often the battleground is a human soul. In this endless struggle he has all the confidence and pride and sense of rightness that comes from being openly and unashamedly on God's side. His job is one of literally infinite importance because he is concerned, not just with the here-and-now problems of human beings, but with their destiny for all eternity. Day after day he is invited to look deep into the mysteries of the human heart.

Every minister, regardless of creed or denomination, has seen great things happen to people, things that in the last analysis can be explained only by the workings of the Holy Spirit. I remember one man, an apparently hopeless alcoholic, who put himself in the hands of a New York physician, seeking a cure. The doctor put him in a hospital, sobered him up, gave him some psychotherapy. But then, when he released him, he said, "I've done what I can for you, and I think you're better. But there's about 5 percent of your personality that I can't get at. And judging from my experience, that 5 percent will trip you sooner or later."

The man said, "Isn't there anyone who can help me, anyone at all?"

The physician smiled. "There is a doctor," he said, "but he's very expensive. He'll take all you have. I think you know the one I mean."

Well, the man left the hospital and walked through the city streets until darkness fell. It was a cold, rainy, miserable winter's night, and he told me afterward that a part of him wanted a drink desperately. Not just 5 percent—95 percent. Finally he came by chance to our church and stood outside the door. Again, a part of him wanted to go in, but a stronger part held him back. He stood there in the rain, unable to touch the door, until finally with a kind of desperation he took out one of his business cards. On it he wrote: "Dear Dr. Jesus, please help me." And he dropped it through the letter-slot and burst into tears. With the tears came an indescribable feeling of warmth, of relief, of release. The desire for drink was gone, completely gone. It has never come back.

To be sure, dramatic episodes do not occur every day in the life of a minister, but every day does offer him the chance and the challenge to push on toward his ultimate goal, which is to build the ideas and the ideals of his religion into the fabric of society.

Of course, at times progress will seem painfully slow. You've got to be a realist as well as an idealist. There will always be some problems you can't solve, some people you can't change. Sometimes a minister gets the feeling that his best efforts are useless, that the gap between the true Christian ethic and the performance of the average churchgoer is so wide that it's unbridgeable. This sort of discouragement, I think, is often the result of what might be called too-great-expectations. A good many ministers leave divinity school with radiant visions of themselves as benign and saintly shepherds eager to guard and guide a flock of snow-white sheep. Actually, there are few saints among us, and certainly no flocks of snow-white sheep.

Often you see the most unexpected people display miracles of quiet fortitude. I remember once we had as a new member at our church an artist employed by a magazine whose editorial approach was based entirely on that old, familiar commodity: sex—pornography, really, controlled to the point where it could just squeak through the mails. Our artist member kept coming to church, and the more he grew spiritually the more disgusted he became with his part in producing such degrading trash. Finally he told his boss he could do it no longer.

His boss told him not to be a fool. It was in the late years of the Depression. Jobs were very scarce. If the artist refused to do the work, the boss said, he would simply find someone else to do it. So what good would quitting do?

The artist said that he was sorry, but that he was trying to live the way he thought Jesus Christ wanted him to live, and that this did not include drawing dirty pictures. So he resigned.

Well, for five mortal months that man was out of work. He suffered. His family suffered. We all suffered, really; our young adult group prayed for him daily. But there was also great power in the drama of this man who found new principles and stuck to them regardless of cost. At last he did get another job. And he got it because his former boss recommended him to another editor. The artist, he said admiringly, was the only truly honest man he had met in New York. Today he's art director of a great advertising agency.

How can anyone turn his back on people like that? How, if you're a minister, can you give up the greatest calling in the world—a life of service to God and man? You can't; you simply can't.

An Answer

by Billy Graham

(March 1972)

The vast majority of American young people are still alienated, uncommitted and uninvolved. There is a deep vacuum within them. They are searching for an individual identity. They are searching for a challenge and a faith. Whoever captures the imagination of the youth of our generation will change the world. Youth movements of the past have been perverted and led by dictators and demagogues. Perhaps the American young people will be captured by Jesus Christ.

I say to them: If you are fifteen to twenty-two years old—the U.S. Census reports that you now number over thirty million—you are probably still wrapped in educational swaddling clothes and taking subjects under the general heading of "preparation for life." The trouble is, you believe you are ready for life.

Ideals? You have bales of them. You see men dying in wars around the world. You see crime, disease and violence in cities, suburbia and country. You see diseases unhealed and hunger unsatisfied. Why? you ask. And no one answers! Already, many of you have moved from what Professor Reich of Yale calls Consciousness I and Consciousness II into the state of consciousness he calls Consciousness III. Consciousness III people are determined to make a better world.

But you are powerless, as you soon discover. You are shackled by financial, social and familial check-reins. I see that you are impatient. I see that you are angry, and I see that you have your chance to change the world. I say that you can succeed in your dreams. I pray that you will succeed as no other generation in history has succeeded, for several reasons: because you have a better education, because you are brighter than earlier generations, because you are healthier and will live longer, and because you and your friends, by the thousands, are discovering Jesus Christ.

When I was your age, I felt almost exactly as you do. I loved. I hated. My world at times seemed to be falling apart. The Great Depression of the Thirties was on. A few "ridiculous" people were predicting a second world war. I understood little and resented my parents, my teachers and my humdrum life. There has always been a gap between the generations—I rather expect it was meant to be. What nettles many young people is the refusal of their elders to bend to the winds of change.

The church, too, is at fault in turning from Biblical proclamation to social and political activism. Too many clergymen are just plain phonies in the eyes of youth. How long will it take to learn that astronomical congressional appropriations are no substitute for spiritual awakening?

(Right) For two hundred years the church steeple was the skyscraping landmark in most towns, a tower of strength and use since it not only reassured citizens but was used to sound fire alarms and to call people to town meetings. Bank towers have long since become the dominant feature in cityscapes, symbolic perhaps of the struggle between God and Mammon.

One Nation Under God

Freedom of Speech

by Booth Tarkington

(February 1943)

In a chalet on the mountain road from Verona to Innsbruck, two tourists sat. The great hills rose in peace that summer evening in 1912. The two patrons, both young, both dusty from the road, sat across the room from each other.

One was of robustly active figure, dark, with a bull head; the other was thin and mousehaired. It was somewhat surprising to see him take from his knapsack several sketches in water color. Upon this, the dark young traveler, who'd been scribbling notes in a memorandum book, decided to speak.

"You're a painter, I see."

"Yes. You, sir, I take to be a writer?"

The dark young man brought his glass of red wine and his plate of cheese and hard sausage to the painter's table. "You permit?" he asked as he sat down. "By profession I am a journalist."

"An editor, I think," the water-color painter responded. "I might guess that you've written editorials not relished by the authorities."

"Why do you guess that?"

"Because," the painter said, "when other guests were here, a shabby man slipped in and whispered to you. A small thing, but I observed it, though I am not a detective."

"Not a detective," the dark young man repeated. "And yet perhaps dangerously observant. This suggests that possibly you do a little in a conspiratorial way yourself."

"Why do you say that?"

"Because of your appearance. You're precisely a person nobody would notice, but you have an uneasy yet coldly purposeful eye. And because behind us it's only a step over the mountain path to Switzerland, where political refugees are safe."

"Yes, no doubt fortunately for you!" The painter smiled. "As for me, I am in no trouble with the authorities, but I admit that I have certain ideas."

"I was sure you have." The journalist drank half his wine. "Ideas? With such men as you and me that means ambitions. Socialism, of course. That would be a first step only toward what we really want. Am I right?"

"Here in this lonely place"—the painter smiled faintly—"it is safe to admit that one has dazzling thoughts. You and I, strangers and met by chance, perceive that each in his own country seeks an extreme amount of success. That means power. That is what we really want. We are two queer men. Should we both perhaps be rightly thought insane?"

"Greatness is easily mistaken for insanity," the swarthy young man said. "Greatness is the ability to reduce the most intricate facts to simple terms. For instance, take fighting. Success is obtained by putting your enemy off his guard, then striking him where he is weakest—in the back, if possible. War is as simple as that."

"Yes, and so is politics. Our mutual understanding of greatness helps to show that we are not lunatics, but only a simple matter of geography is needed to prove our sanity."

"Geography?" The journalist didn't follow this thought. "How so?"

"Imagine a map. Put yourself in England, for instance, and put me and my dazzling ideas into that polyglot zoo, the United States. You in England can bellow attacks on the government till you wear out your larynx. In America I could do the same. Do you not agree?"

"Certainly," the journalist said. "In those countries the people create their own governments. Those countries are poor fields for such as you and me, because why conspire in a wine cellar to change laws that permit themselves to be changed openly?"

"Exactly." The water-color painter smiled his faint strange smile. "Speech is the expression of thought and will. Therefore, freedom of speech means freedom of the people. If you prevent them from expressing their will in speech, you have them enchained, an absolute monarchy. Of course, nowadays he who chains the people is called a dictator."

"My friend!" the dark young man exclaimed. "We understand each other. But where men cannot speak out, they will whisper. You and I will have to talk out of the sides of our mouths until we have established the revolutions we contemplate. For a moment, suppose us successful. We are dictators, let us say. Then in our turn do we permit no freedom of speech? If we don't, men will talk out of the sides of their mouths against us. So they may overthrow us in turn. You see the problem?"

"Yes, my friend. Like everything else, it is simple. We shall not be able to last a day unless we destroy freedom of speech."

"But how?"

"By means of a purge."

"Purge?" The word seemed new to the journalist. "What is that?"

Once more was seen the water-color painter's peculiarly icy smile. "My friend, if I had a brother who talked against me, either out of the side of his mouth or the front of it, and lived to run away, he might have to leave his wife and child behind him. A purge is a form of carbolic acid that would include the wife and child."

"I see." The dark youth looked admiring, but shivered slightly. "On the one hand, then, there is freedom of speech and on the other this fatal acid you call a purge. The two cannot exist together in the same country. The people of the earth can take their choice, but you and I can succeed only where we persuade them to choose the purge. They would be brainless to make such a choice—utterly brainless!"

"On the other hand," said the painter, "many people can be talked into anything, even if it is terrible for themselves. I shall flatter all the millions of my own people into accepting me and the purge instead of freedom."

He spoke with a confidence so monstrous in one of his commonplace and ungifted appearance that the other stared aghast. At this moment, however, a shrill whistle was heard outside. Without another word the dark young man rose, woke the landlord, paid his score and departed hurriedly.

The painter spoke to the landlord: "That fellow seems to be some sort of shady character, rather a weak one. Do you know him?"

"Yes and no," the landlord replied. "He's in and out, mainly after dark. One meets all sorts of people in the Brenner Pass. You might run across him here again, yourself, someday. I don't know his whole name, but I have heard him called 'Benito,' Herr Hitler."

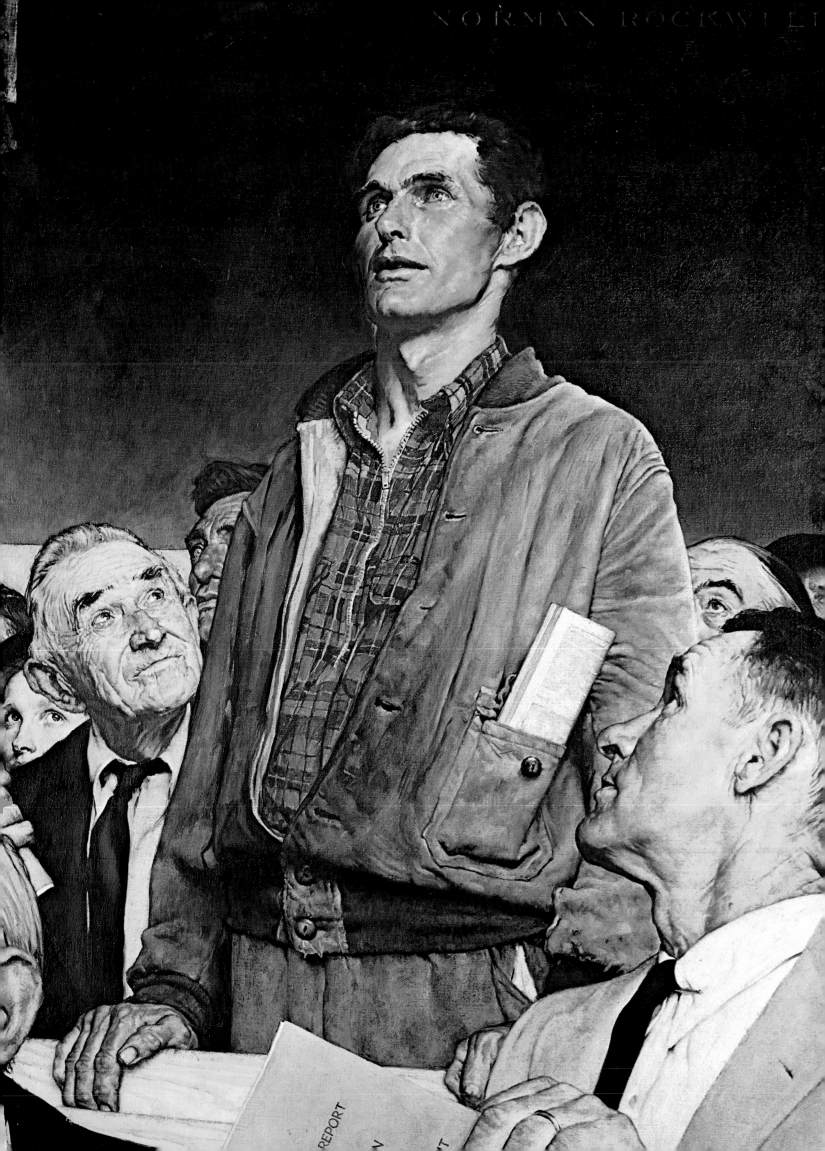

Freedom of Worship

by Will Durant

(February 1943)

Down in the valley below the hill where I spend my summers is a little white church whose steeple has been my guiding goal in many a pleasant walk.

Often, as I passed the door on weekdays when all was silent there, I wished that I might enter, sit quietly in one of the empty pews, and feel more deeply the wonder and the longing that had built such chapels—temples and mosques and great cathedrals—everywhere on the earth.

Man differs from the animal in two things: he laughs, and he prays. Perhaps the animal laughs when he plays, and prays when he begs or mourns; we shall never know any soul but our own, and never that. But the mark of man is that he beats his head against the riddle of life, knows his infinite weakness of body and mind, lifts up his heart to a hidden presence and power, and finds in his faith a beacon of heartening hope, a pillar of strength for his fragile decency.

These men of the fields, coming from afar in the uncomfortable finery of a Sabbath morn, greeting one another with bluff cordiality, entering to worship their God in their own fashion—I think, sometimes, that they know more than I shall ever find in all my books. They have no words to tell me what they know, but that is because religion, like music, lives in a world beyond words, or thoughts, or things. They have felt the mystery of consciousness within themselves, and will not say that they are machines. They have seen the growth of the soil and the child, they have stood in awe amid the swelling fields, in the humming and teeming woods, and they have sensed in every cell and atom the same creative power that wells up in their own striving and fulfillment. Their unmoved faces conceal a silent thankfulness for the rich increase of summer, the mortal loveliness of autumn and the gay resurrection of the spring. They have watched patiently the movement of the stars, and found in them a majestic order so harmoniously regular that our ears would hear its music were it not eternal. Their tired eyes have known the ineffable splendor of earth and sky, even in tempest, terror and destruction; and they have never doubted that in this beauty some sense and meaning dwell. They have seen death, and reached beyond it with their hope.

And so they worship. The poetry of their ritual redeems the prose of their daily toil; the prayers they pray are secret summonses to their better selves; the songs they sing are shouts of joy in their refreshened strength. The commandments they receive, through which they can live with one another in order and peace, come to them as the imperatives of an inescapable deity, not as the edicts of questionable men. Through these commands they are made part of a divine drama, and their harassed lives take on a scope and dignity that cannot be canceled out by death.

This little church is the first and final symbol of America. For men came across the sea not merely to find new soil for their plows but to win freedom for their souls, to think and speak and worship as they would. This is the freedom men value most of all; for this they have borne countless persecutions and fought more bravely than for food or gold. These men coming out of their chapel—what is the finest thing about them, next to their undiscourageable life? It is that they do not demand that others should worship as they do, or even that others should worship at all. In that waving valley are some who have not come to this service. It is not held against them; mutely these worshipers understand that faith takes many forms, and that men name with diverse words the hope that in their hearts is one.

It is astonishing and inspiring that after all the bloodshed of history this land should house in fellowship a hundred religions and a hundred doubts. This is with us an already ancient heritage; and because we knew such freedom of worship from our birth, we took it for granted and expected it of all mature men. Until yesterday the whole civilized world seemed secure in that liberty.

But now suddenly, through some paranoiac mania of racial superiority, or some obscene sadism of political strategy, persecution is renewed, and men are commanded to render unto Caesar the things that are Caesar's, and unto Caesar the things that are God's. The Japanese, who once made all things beautiful, begin to exclude from their realm every faith but the childish belief in the divinity of their emperor. The Italians, who twice littered their peninsula with genius, are compelled to oppress a handful of hunted men. The French, once honored in every land for civilization and courtesy, hand over desolate refugees to the coldest murderers that history has ever known. The Germans, who once made the world their debtors in science, scholarship, philosophy and music, are prodded into one of the bitterest persecutions in all the annals of savagery by men who seem to delight in human misery, who openly pledge themselves to destroy Christianity, who seem resolved to leave their people no religion but war, and no God but the state.

It is incredible that such reactionary madness can express the mind and heart of an adult nation. A man's dealings with his God should be a sacred thing, inviolable by any potentate. No ruler has yet existed who was wise enough to instruct a saint; and a good man who is not great is a hundred times more precious than a great man who is not good. Therefore, when we denounce the imprisonment of the heroic Niemoller, the silencing of the brave Faulhaber, we are defending the freedom of the German people as well as of the human spirit everywhere. When we yield our sons to war, it is in the trust that their sacrifice will bring to us and our allies no inch of alien soil, no selfish monopoly of the world's resources or trade, but only the privilege of winning for all peoples the most precious gifts in the orbit of life—freedom of body and soul, of movement and enterprise, of thought and utterance, of faith and worship, of hope and charity, of a humane fellowship with all men.

If our sons and brothers accomplish this, if by their toil and suffering they can carry to all mankind the boon and stimulus of an ordered liberty, it will be an achievement beside which all the triumphs of Alexander, Caesar and Napoleon will be a little thing. To that purpose they are offering their youth and their blood. To that purpose and to them we others, regretting that we cannot stand beside them, dedicate the remainder of our lives.

ACH ACCORDING TO THE DICTATES OF HIS OWN CONSCIENCE

RMAN ROCKWELL

Freedom From Want

by Carlos Bulosan

(March 1943)

If you want to know what we are, look upon the farms or upon the hard pavements of the city. You usually see us working or waiting for work, and you think you know us, but our outward guise is more deceptive than our history.

Our history has many strands of fear and hope, that snarl and converge at several points in time and space.

It is the dignity of the individual to live in a society of free men, where the spirit of understanding and belief exists; of understanding that all men are equal; that all men, whatever their color, race, religion or estate, should be given equal opportunity to serve themselves and each other according to their needs and abilities.

But we are not really free unless we use what we produce. So long as the fruit of our labor is denied us, so long will want manifest itself in a world of slaves. It is only when we have plenty to eat—plenty of everything—that we begin to understand what freedom means. To us, freedom is not an intangible thing. When we have enough to eat, then we are healthy enough to enjoy what we eat. Then we have the time and ability to read and think and discuss things. Then we are not merely living but also becoming a creative part of life. It is only then that we become a growing part of democracy.

We do not take democracy for granted. We feel it grow in our working together—many millions of us working toward a common purpose. If it took us several decades of sacrifices to arrive at this faith, it is because it took us that long to know what part of America is ours.

Our faith has been shaken many times, and now it is put to question. Our faith is a living thing, and it can be crippled or chained. It can be killed by denying us enough food or clothing, by blasting away our personalities and keeping us in constant fear. Unless we are properly prepared, the powers of darkness will have good reason to catch us unaware and trample our lives.

The totalitarian nations hate democracy. They hate us, because we ask for a definite guaranty of freedom of religion, freedom of expression and freedom from fear and want. Our challenge to tyranny is the depth of our faith in a democracy worth defending. Although they spread lies about us, the way of life we cherish is not dead. The American dream is only hidden away, and it will push its way up and grow again.

We have moved down the years steadily toward the practice of democracy. We become animate in the growth of Kansas wheat or in the ring of Mississippi rain. We tremble in the strong winds of the Great Lakes. We cut timbers in Oregon just as the wild flowers blossom in Maine. We are multitudes in Pennsylvania mines, in Alaskan canneries. We are millions from Puget Sound to Florida.

But sometimes we wonder if we are really a part of America. We recognize the main springs of American democracy in our right to form unions and bargain through them collectively, our opportunity to sell our products at reasonable prices, and the privilege of our children to attend schools where they learn the truth about the world in which they live. We also recognize the forces which have been trying to falsify American history—the forces which drive many Americans to a corner of compromise with those who would distort the ideals of men that died for freedom.

Sometimes we walk across the land looking for something to hold on to. We cannot believe that the resources of this country are exhausted. Even when we see our children suffer humiliations, we cannot believe that America has no more place for us. We realize that what is wrong is not in our system of government, but in the ideals which were blasted away by a materialistic age. We know that we can truly find and identify ourselves with a living tradition if we walk proudly in familiar streets. It is a great honor to walk on the American earth.

If you want to know what we are, look at the men reading books, searching in the dark pages of history for the lost word, the key to the mystery of living peace. We are factory hands, field hands, mill hands, searching, building and molding structures. We are doctors, scientists, chemists, discovering and eliminating disease, hunger and antagonism. We are soldiers, Navy men, citizens, guarding the imperishable dream of our fathers to live in freedom. We are the living dream of dead men. We are the living spirit of free men.

Everywhere we are on the march, passing through darkness into a sphere of economic peace. When we have the freedom to think and discuss things without fear, when peace and security are assured, when the futures of our children are ensured—then we have resurrected and cultivated the early beginnings of democracy.

We have been marching for the last one hundred and fifty years. We sacrifice our individual liberties, and sometimes we fail and suffer. Sometimes we divide into separate groups and our methods conflict, though we all aim at one common goal. The significant thing is that we march on without turning back. What we want is peace, not violence. We know that we thrive and prosper only in peace.

We are bleeding where clubs are smashing heads, where bayonets are gleaming. We are fighting where the bullet is crashing upon armorless citizens, where the tear gas is choking unprotected children. Under the lynch trees, amidst hysterical mobs. Where the prisoner is beaten to confess a crime he did not commit. Where the honest man is hanged because he told the truth.

We are the sufferers who suffer for natural love of man for another man, who commemorate the humanities of every man. We are the creators of abundance.

We are the desires of anonymous men. We are the subways of suffering, the well of dignities. We are the living testament of a flowering race.

But our march to freedom is not complete unless want is annihilated. The America we hope to see is not merely a physical but also a spiritual and an intellectual world. We are the mirror of what America *is*. If America wants us to be living and free, then we must be living and free. If we fail, then America fails.

What do we want? We want complete security and peace. We want to share the promises and fruits of American life. We want to be free from fear and hunger.

Freedom From Fear

by Stephen Vincent Benét

(March 1943)

What do we mean when we say "freedom from fear"? It isn't just a formula or a set of words. It's a look in the eyes and a feeling in the heart and a thing to be won against odds. It goes to the roots of life—to a man and a woman and their children and the home they can make and keep.

Fear has walked at man's heels through many ages—fear of wild beasts and wilder nature, fear of the inexplicable gods of thunder and lightning, fear of his neighbor man.

He saw his roof tree burned with fire from heaven—and did not know why. He saw his children die of plague—and did not know why. He saw them starve, he saw them made slaves. It happened—he did not know why. Those things had always happened.

Then he set himself to find out—first one thing, then another. Slowly, through centuries, he fought his battle with fear. And wise men and teachers arose to help him in the battle.

His children and he did not have to die of plague. His children and he did not have to make human sacrifices to appease the wrath of inexplicable gods. His children and he did not have to kill the stranger just because he was a stranger. His children and he did not have to be slaves. And the shape of Fear grew less.

No one man did this by himself. It took many men and women, over many years. It took saints and martyrs and prophets—and the common people. It started with the first fire in the first cave—the fire that scared away the beasts of the night. It will not end with the conquest of far planets.

Since our nation began, men and women have come here for just that freedom—freedom from the fear that lies at the heart of every unjust law, of every tyrannical exercise of power by one man over another man. They came from every stock—the men who had seen the face of tyranny, the men who wanted room to breathe and a chance to be men. And the cranks and the starry-eyed came, too, to build Zion and New Harmony and Americanopolis and the states and cities that perished before they lived—the valuable cranks who push the world ahead an inch. And a lot of it never happened, but we did make a free nation.

"How are you ever going to live out there, stranger?"

"We'll live on weevily wheat and the free air." If they had the free air, they'd put up with the weevily wheat.

So, in our corner of the world, and for most of our people, we got rid of certain fears. We got rid of them, we got used to being rid of them. It took struggle and fighting and a lot of working things out. But a hundred and thirty million people lived at peace with one another and ran their own government. And because they were free from fear, they were able to live better, by and large and on the whole, than any hundred and thirty million people had lived before. Because fear may drive a burdened man for a mile, but it is only freedom that makes his load light for the long carry.

And meanwhile around us the world grew smaller and smaller. If you looked at it on the school maps, yes, it looked like the same big world with a big, safe corner for us. But all the time invention and mechanical skill were making it smaller and smaller. When the Wright brothers made their first flights at Kitty Hawk, the world shrank. With those first flights the world began

to come together and distant nations to jostle their neighbor nations.

Now, again in our time, we know Fear—armed Fear, droning through the sky. It's a different sound from the war whoop and the shot in the lonesome clearing, and yet it is much the same for all of us. It is quiet in the house tonight and the children are asleep. But innocence, good will, distance, peaceable intent will not keep those children safe from the fear in the sky. No one man can keep his house safe in a shrunken world. No one man can make his own clearing and say, "This is mine. Keep out." And yet, if the world is to go on, if man is to survive and prosper, the house of man must be kept safe.

So, what do we mean by "freedom from fear"?

We do not mean freedom from responsibility. It is not enough to say, "Here, in our country, we are strong. Let the rest of the world sink or swim. We can take care of ourselves." That may have been true at one time, but it is no longer true. We are not an island in space, but a continent in the world. While the air is the air, a bomb can kill your children and mine. Fear and ignorance a thousand miles away may spread pestilence in our own town. A war between nations on the other side of the globe may endanger all we love and cherish.

War, famine, disease are no longer local problems or even national problems. They are problems that concern the whole world and every man. That is a hard lesson to learn, and yet, for our own survival, we must learn it.

A hundred and sixty odd years ago, we, as a nation, asserted that all men were created equal, that all men were entitled to life, liberty and the pursuit of happiness. Those were large assertions, but we have tried to live up to them. We have not always succeeded, we have often failed. But our will and desire as a nation have been to live up to them.

Now, in concert with other free nations, we say that those children you see and other children like them all over the world shall grow to manhood and womanhood free from fear. We say that neither their minds nor their bodies shall be cramped or distorted or broken by tyranny and oppression. We say they shall have a chance, and an equal chance, to grow and develop and lead the lives they choose to lead, not lives mapped out for them by a master. And we say that freedom for ourselves involves freedom for others—that it is a universal right, neither lightly given by providence nor to be maintained by words alone, but by acts and deeds and living.

We who are alive today did not make our free institutions. We got them from the men of the past and we hold them in trust for the future. Should we put ease and selfishness above them, that trust will fail and we shall lose all, not a portion or a degree of liberty, but all that has been built for us and all that we hope to build. Real peace will not be won with one victory. It can be won only by long determination, firm resolve and a wish to share and work with other men, no matter what their race or creed or condition. And yet, we do have the choice. We can have freedom from fear.

Here is a house, a woman, a man, their children. They are not free from life and the obligations of life. But they can be free from fear. All over the world, they can be free from fear. And we know they are not yet free.

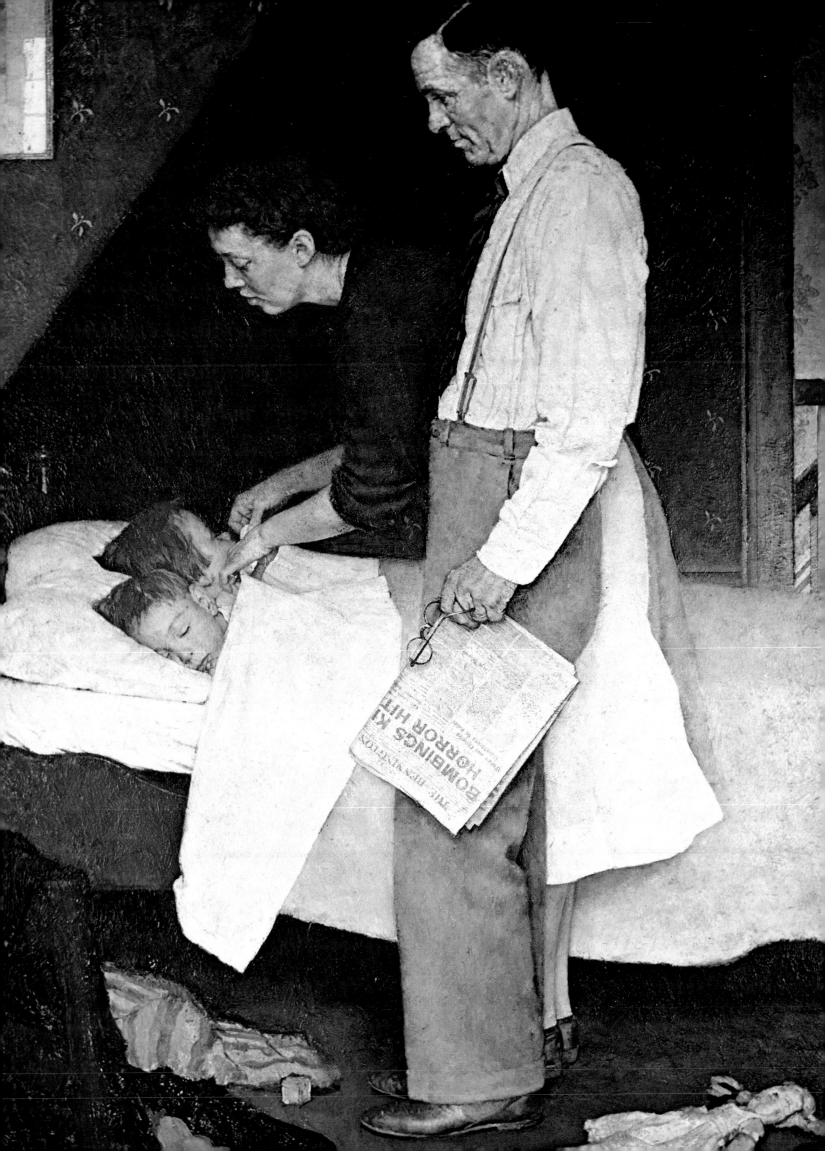

HEROES

CREATED BY DEMAND

Pragmatism is anathema to heroes. They do or die to the tune of abstract convictions or souped-up adrenalin glands the rest of us never hear or feel. We remember our worthies in marble and granite because monumentally they forgot themselves. Franklin once noted that the golden age is never the present age. So it is with heroes. Time and public relations have a way of working on a man or a woman until the face only a mother could love becomes the coin of the realm, instantly recognizable to millions of strangers but unfamiliar to the hero's next-door neighbor. The demigods of yesterday might simply be the survivors of today. Lincoln, alive today, would be a tough precinct politician, a thorn in the side of special interest groups. Audubon would be considered a hippie, Paul Revere a hustler, Lindbergh a naive, dreaming boy, Eleanor Roosevelt a busybody.

In heroism, the end justifies the means; what is left behind is what matters. Lincoln left a country, Robert E. Lee a code of honor, Audubon a book whose concept was that America belongs to nature, not the reverse. These national treasures built a culture which endures according to the number and excellence of those who heed the call of idealism, of those who give back more than they take.

Heroes can be modest only in their person, not in their accomplishment. They must break unbreakable records, tread the ground of the impossible dream and appear surprised by their own achievement. It is a difficult role to perform, perhaps they succeed only because they are not acting. A flagrant disregard for the sensible marks these legendary figures, and a delight in bold resolution.

America admits a large dose of mythology in the truth of these men, but a nation has to hang its laurel leaves as well as its hat. And despite the revelations of overly assiduous historians, these Americans manifest themselves as substantial pegs, reliable, workers of verifiable magic on the diamond-hard surfaces of time.

(Right) Lincoln belongs to the ages, but the ages take their toll on limestone. Here a worker repairs damage done to the great emancipator's nose by ice and snow at Mount Rushmore.

Sterner Stuff

It was involuntary. They sank my boat.
—*John F. Kennedy*
on how he became a war hero

If a man has a talent and he cannot use it, he has failed. If he has a talent and he uses only half of it, he has partly failed. If he has talent and learns somehow to use the whole of it, he has gloriously succeeded, and won a satisfaction and a triumph few men ever know.
—*Thomas Wolfe*

Woodrow Wilson is a human being. He is just folks like the rest of us. He is a plain and rather unassuming American citizen. He is smarter than most of us, but not half so smarty as the bulk of us.
—*Samuel G. Blythe in 1914*

The difference between a moral man and a man of honor is that the latter regrets a discreditable act, even when it has worked and he has not been caught.
—*H.L. Mencken*

I do the very best I know how—the very best I can; and I mean to keep doing so until the end. If the end brings me out all right, what is said against me won't amount to anything. If the end brings me out wrong, ten angels swearing I was right would make no difference.
—*Abraham Lincoln*

I leave this rule for others when I'm dead—be always sure you're right—then go ahead.
—*Davy Crockett's*
advice to young men

I used to think I was the only one who loved him. In the years to come I was to learn more and more that I wasn't. A nation loved him—not because he hit 714 home runs and did all sorts of wonderful things on a baseball field, but also because the people knew he was one of them. He had their faith and their weaknesses. They loved him because they sensed that he was, above all else, a great human being. And they were—and are—so right.
—*Mrs. Babe Ruth*
on her husband

Mr. Carlyle has told us of the hero as divinity; the hero as prophet; the hero as poet; the hero as priest; the hero as a man of letters; and the hero as king. Did he not recognize the hero as a man of science? Did he not know that during the time that he was writing there traveled alone, somewhere in the vast forests of America, a natural of native original insight, of manhood, and heroic nobleness?
—*An 1842* Post
editorial about
John James Audubon

It's good just to see him on the field. He's our leader. He can give us the big hit when we need it, but so can some of the rest of us. It's more than that. When you see how he has had to play, what he's done to play, those legs, now the arm—you've got to be proud of him, proud to play with him. You play harder with him around.
—*Elston Howard*
on Mickey Mantle after surgery

When they told me yesterday what had happened, I felt like the moon, the stars and all the planets had fallen on me.
—*Harry Truman after his*
first full day in office

It is well, I die hard, but I am not afraid to go.
—*George Washington's*
last words

Had I so interfered on behalf of the rich, the powerful, the intelligent, the so-called great, or in the behalf of any of their friends, every man in this court would have deemed it an act of reward rather than punishment.
—*John Brown*
at his trial

The refrain of one of the popular ballads proclaimed that old soldiers never die; they just fade away. I now close my military career and just fade away.
—*Douglas MacArthur's*
farewell address

Motion is a large part in heroism. We move from old country to new, east to west, and back to the old country. The time, however, improves.

The Nature of Things

by John James Audubon

(May 1842)

What a terrible destruction of life. The buffalo tongues only were brought in, and the flesh of these fine animals was left to beasts and birds of prey. The prairies are literally *covered* with the skulls of the victims. Provost tells me that the buffaloes become so very poor during hard winters. They lose their hair, become covered with scabs, on which the magpies feed, and the poor beasts die by hundreds. Daily we see so many that we hardly notice them more than the cattle in our pastures about our homes. But this cannot last; even now there is a perceptible difference in the size of the herds, and before many years, the buffalo, like the Great Auk, will have disappeared. I cannot eat beef after being fed on buffaloes. I am getting to be an old man, for this evening, I missed my footing on getting into the boat, but at seventy and over I cannot have the spring of seventeen.

(Top left) The passenger pigeon once darkened American skies. Audubon feared for its slaughter as he did for the bison. (Bottom) French, Audubon was influenced by the romantic concept of the noble savage. As an American, he learned the realities of poverty and discomfort.

Franklin wanted to make the wild turkey the national bird. He felt it was wily, clever, a survivor by intelligence rather than aggression, while the eagle, imperious and aloof, preyed on weaker beings and had to kill to exist. The eagle won, however, when in 1782 Congress voted the bald eagle our national symbol. Both birds have been on the verge of extinction, proving that survival in animals as in human beings is a matter of interdependence; that the destruction of nature means the destruction of man. Wildlife protection laws have saved this native fowl, present at the Pilgrim feasts, while the heath hen and other sustainers of the early settlers in New England have vanished.

I Saw Lee Surrender

by a Yankee Bugler

(January 1940)

When Robert E. Lee surrendered to Ulysses S. Grant at Appomattox Court House seventy-five years ago, I was there; luck and the ability to toot a bugle explained my presence.

As far as I know, I am the last survivor. Running away from home, I had enlisted in Company H, Fifth Cavalry, in June 1862. I gave my name as Charles M. Seaver, and my age as eighteen, knowing that the army shared my family's opinion that a fifteen-year-old was too young for war. Sixteen months of stiff campaigning incapacitated me as a fighting private, so I transferred to Company F as a bugler, a change that eventually brought me to Appomattox.

In the spring of '65, my new company was assigned to escort General Grant. The Confederate leader had agreed to meet General Grant. The staff officers construed this to be an assurance of surrender, for every last man of them burst into cheers. The only one who took no part in the celebration was General Grant.

Appomattox Court House slumbered in the spring sunshine, was soon to awaken and discover itself famous. A few hundred yards ahead we saw a little party of gray-clad figures, and several horses by the roadside. One of the men was sitting under a small tree. As we neared the spot, the man beneath the tree rose and exchanged salutes.

It was not difficult to recognize the famous commander of the Army of Northern Virginia. He measured up fully to my expectations, and those expectations were rather elaborate. Though I was only a lad of eighteen, I had been in fifteen or sixteen battles during three years, and had come to have a wholesome esteem for the Johnny Rebs and their leader. He had become a sort of legendary figure.

Grant looked like an old and battered campaigner as he rode into the yard. His blouse of blue was unbuttoned and underneath could be seen his undershirt. He was unlike Lee.

What a brave pair of thoroughbreds Lee and Traveler were! That horse would have attracted attention anywhere. General Lee's uniform was immaculate and he presented a superb martial figure. But it was the face beneath the gray felt hat that made the deepest impression on me. I have been trying to find a single word that describes it, and I have concluded that "benign" is the adjective I am after; because that means kindly and gracious. There was something else about him that aroused my deep pity that so great a warrior should be acknowledging defeat.

There we were, a group of eager troopers in blue, and a lone orderly in gray. General Lee came from the house, his soldierly figure erect, even in defeat. We stiffened up and gave him a salute and the man in gray courteously returned it. At the moment his soul must have been heavy with sorrow, but he could return the salute of Yankee troopers. Soldiers do not carry hatred; they leave that to the stay-at-homes.

(Right) The smoke of defeat curls about Lee and his famous mount, Traveler. A superb strategist, Lee graduated at the head of his class at West Point. He was asked by President Lincoln to assume field command of the Union forces before the war began. Lee was never sure he had made the right decision, but he could make no other. The major victories were his during the first two years of the conflict, but manpower and equipment began to overcome daring and brilliance by 1864, and the tide turned. (Above) Lee poses on the porch of his modest Virginia home before his final trip to Washington to visit his old adversary, President Grant. Lee devoted his last years to Washington College.

ROBERT E. LEE

JAN. 19, 1807

OCT. 12, 1870

"Photo by Brady"

by Wesley Winans Stout

(January 1939)

The world was blind one hundred years ago. Men had been groping toward photography, but Daguerre and Niepce were the first to make a permanent image. When news of the French breakthrough reached America, Mathew Brady was a sixteen-year-old boy in New York.

Brady photographed every American president from John Quincy Adams to William McKinley, excepting only William Henry Harrison, who died a month after taking office, and before the Brady studio began business. Brady sought out every celebrity. Later they sought him out; to sit for him was a social distinction.

When the Civil War began, Brady foresaw the opportunity to record a war photographically for the first time. The reproduction of photographs in print was still a

slow and expensive process. Harper's and Leslie's weeklies recorded the war in line drawings made by staff illustrators in the field.

Brady plagued Lincoln and Allan Pinkerton, head of the Secret Service, until they gave him permission to go where he pleased, photographing battle and camp. At his own expense, of course.

He was in the thick of first Bull Run and the panic flight of the Union forces, the tails of his white linen duster streaming behind. He was with the armies through 1861 and 1862, each of his units carrying several hundred eight-by-ten glass plates in dustproof boxes and all the chemicals needed to prepare them in a converted delivery wagon which the soldiers called a "What-is-it?" Confederates searched out these wagons, fearing them to be some new Yankee gun.

(Top left) a self-portrait of Brady. In his studio on Pennsylvania Avenue in Washington, he used a clamp to make sure the sitter's head did not move, accounting for many a pained expression in the finished plates. His candids show Grant and his staff (above right) and Lincoln (bottom) in the field. Brady's photographs constitute the most comprehensive record and singular view of any war in history.

Sergeant York

by George Pattulo

(April 1919)

Alvin C. York comes from Pall Mall, Fentress County, Tennessee, and is second elder in the Church of Christ and Christian Union. The sect is opposed to any form of fighting; they are conscientious objectors. But York refused to ask exemption, went to war, and as Corporal York of Company G, 328th Infantry, killed twenty Germans on October Eighth, captured one hundred and thirty-two prisoners, including a major and three lieutenants, and put thirty-five machine guns out of business.

This Tennessee mountaineer seems to do everything correctly by intuition. York is entirely the working of instinct, for until November 14, 1917, he was living on a small farm on Wolf River, five miles from the Kentucky border. On that day, he joined the Army at Camp Gordon, Georgia.

"I used to drink and gamble some. When I got to drinking I was kind of liable to fight, and it was like to get me into a real smart of trouble. A feller does a heap of things he's ashamed of later, don't he?"

"What do you suppose Pastor Pile will say when he hears of your exploit?"

"What can he say? What can any of them say? 'Blessed is the peacemaker,' isn't he? Well, there was sure some stir-up in this country!"

After the War was over, Sergeant York returned to the mountains of Tennessee, leaving the movie version of his life to Gary Cooper. It was as though York wished to disappear. Here, still dressed in his old khakis, he gets a helping of well water at a revival meeting while the young girl's expression indicates she has not forgotten what he seemed so anxious the world would forget.

33 Hours to Paris

by Charles A. Lindbergh

(June 1953)

May 20, 1927, 7:52 a.m.,
Roosevelt Field, Long Island.

I buckle my safety belt, pull goggles over my eyes, turn to the men at the wheel blocks and nod. A yank on the ropes—the wheels are free. Pace quickens—turf becomes a blur—the tail skid lifts off. I pull the stick back firmly, and—the wheels leave the ground. The wheels touch again. I ease the stick forward—almost flying speed, and nearly 2,000 feet of field ahead. The Spirit of St. Louis takes herself off the next time full flying speed; the controls taut, alive, straining. Five feet off the ground—twenty—forty—wires flash by underneath—twenty feet to spare. A curtain of mist moves along with me. What lies beyond the curtain?

12:52 p.m. Over Nova Scotia.

Wind is rising, and I'm crabbing fifteen degrees to offset drift. I drop my hand to the bag of sandwiches, but I'm not hungry. Why eat simply because it's lunchtime? A drink of water will be enough. In hanging up the canteen, I let my map slide toward the open window. One corner flutters in a puff of air. I jerk it away with a start. If I lost this sheet of paper, this key to Paris, I'd have to turn back. "On course, plenty of fuel, all readings normal, but the chart blew out the window." What an explanation that would make!

During early spring test flights, designer Donald Hall, Ryan Airlines salesman Adolf Edwards, Lindbergh and Lt. Col. Harry Graham, Rockwell Field Commander, are snapped in a non-pose.

1:52 p.m., Six Hundred Miles Out, Over Canada.

A wilderness lies beneath my wings. Valleys are filled with the deep green of virgin timber. Flocks of duck rise out of lakes and marshes. The edge of a storm is receding toward the north. The compass is fastened to the top of the fuselage where I can't read it directly. On the day it was installed, in a hangar on Long Island, we had no mirror. A girl of college age, watching us through the hangar door, offered the small mirror from her compact. How much chance did she think her mirror had of reaching Paris? How many hours to Paris? There's a chasm of eternity to cross. In The Spirit of St. Louis I live in a frame of time and space not to be measured in hours.

4 p.m., Off the Newfoundland Coast.

The men in San Diego who built my plane in two record-breaking months, my partners in St. Louis who helped pay for it—they have a right to know that all is well when I leave the North American continent. My mother, teaching chemistry in Detroit—she's probably been at her desk all day, worrying, trying to fix her attention on laboratory experiments in an unsuccessful effort to curtain off thoughts of a pilot and his plane.
I must keep my mind from wandering.
I'm in an airplane. How satisfying it is to have 800 miles behind—No! Sleep has crept up a notch. Thoughts of anything are relaxing. I can't afford to relax.
I come upon it suddenly—the little city of St. John's. Twilight deepens as I plunge down into the valley. This northern city is the last point on the last land of America—the end of land, the end of day. At daybreak the wind may be blowing from a new direction. The problem now is to fight sleep and hold the compass steady. Day has almost vanished; I glance back—just a trace of it left, a wash on the western sky.

(Right) "Lucky Lindy" with The Spirit of St. Louis. *The plane is now hanging in the Smithsonian Institution, Washington, D.C.*

Lindbergh stands second from left with employees of Ryan Airlines, San Diego. Douglas Corrigan, third from right, later won notoriety with his "wrong way" flight to Ireland.

8:35 p.m., Over the Atlantic.

There was a key sentence in the last weather forecast before my takeoff: "A large high-pressure area is forming over the North Atlantic." I'm flying with my head thrown back, looking up through the skylight at faint stars, glancing down at intervals to read my compass. The stars blink on and off. This fog, this cloud, is rising too fast. At any moment those stars may blink their last, leaving me stranded thousands of feet below the surface. If I start flying blind, I might have to go on that way all night, always watching the instrument board. And then there's the question of staying awake. Yesterday morning, I awoke bright and rested. But I had a busy day, and last night I went without sleep. I've kept awake now—let's see, it's after eight p.m.—about thirty-six hours. The stars blink off again.

1:52 a.m., Daybreak Over the Atlantic,
May 21, 1927.

The night is ending. The uncontrollable desire to sleep falls over me in quilted layers. This is the hour I've been dreading, the early hour of the second morning of flight—the third morning since I've slept. I've lost command of my eyelids. They start to close, I can't restrain them. I've got to keep alert. There's no alternative but death and failure. I keep repeating the thought—*no alternative but death and failure*—using it as a whip on my mind.

3 a.m. New York Time, Over the North Atlantic.

There are deep chasms on the cloud floor. In the bottom of them I see a darker shade—the ocean. I nose down steeply. As minutes pass I fall into the state of eye-open sleep again. There's a part of me—a third element ruling body and mind—which is directing my flight, knowing when the alarm must be given to my ordinary senses. I'm twenty degrees off course. The clock says I'm twenty-one hours from New York. Will the fog never end? Over and over again, I fall asleep with my eyes open, knowing I'm falling asleep, unable to prevent it, and then, seconds or minutes later, waking up. When I fall asleep this way, my eyes are cut off from my ordinary mind which grows increasingly competent. *Right rudder, twelve degrees.*

7:52 a.m. New York Time—24 Hours Since Takeoff.

The greater part of the ocean is behind me. My immediate problem is to correct my heading for Ireland, the first landfall. I'm wide awake. It's almost noon of the day I'll land in Europe—at Paris—on Le Bourget aerodrome. The hours of afternoon stretch out, empty, warm and safe, like the limitless sky ahead. I reach into my flying suit pocket for a handkerchief. My fingers touch a small hard object. It's a St. Christopher's Medal. From whom did this gift come? It was slipped into my pocket by a person who was not asking for any thanks.

Dusk, Approaching Ireland.

I'm flying along dreamily when it catches my eye, a speck on the water two or three miles away. A boat! I squeeze my eyelids together and look again. Several small boats, scattered on the ocean! I fly over the boat bobbing up and down on the swells. A man's head appears, thrust out of a cabin porthole, motionless,

(Top) The next day. The French who had mobbed Lindbergh the night before have regained their usual shruggable composure. (Right) There was no wind sock to gauge the affection of the crowds. Here tin-hatted gendarmes link rifles to protect the shy young man who captured the imagination of the world.

(Left) Top-hatted, bemedaled welcomer Grover Whalen manages a profile while Lindbergh and Mayor Jimmy Walker balance an uneasy perch for New York's news photographers.

staring up at me. I glide down within fifty feet of the cabin and shout as loudly as I can: "Which way is Ireland?"

10:52 a.m. New York Time, Over Dingle Bay, Ireland.

It looks like land but I don't intend to be tricked by a mirage. I stare at it intently. Ireland! The fields are too green for Scotland, the mountains too high for Brittany or Cornwall. I'm almost exactly on my route. Only 600 miles to Paris. There are golden hours of the afternoon still left, and the long evening twilight. I'll see France before dark.

1:52 p.m. New York Time;
Just After 6 p.m., French Time.

There's the English Channel up ahead. The coast of France comes like an outstretched hand to meet me glowing in the light of sunset. Cherbourg—the sun almost touches the horizon as I look down on my first French city. I'm so far ahead of schedule that I may not find anybody waiting for me at Le Bourget. All the east foreshadows night. I nose the Spirit of St. Louis lower while I study farms and villages. People come running out as I skim over their houses.

4:20 p.m. New York Time, Approaching Paris

All details on the ground are masked out in night. A light flashes from the darkness up ahead. Paris is rising over the edge of the earth. There are thousands of lights along one side. There's a black patch to my left, large enough to be an airport. And there are lights all around it. If that isn't Le Bourget, where else can it be? I circle. Yes, it's definitely an airport.

The wheels touch gently. Not a bad landing. The Spirit of St. Louis swings around and stops rolling in the center of Le Bourget. I start to taxi back toward the floodlights and hangars—but the entire field is covered with running figures. When my wheels touched earth, I had no way of knowing that tens of thousands of men and women were breaking down fences and flooding past guards. My cockpit windows were blocked with faces. The Spirit of St. Louis trembled with the pressure of the crowd.

"Does anyone here speak English?" I shouted.

(Top) The tons of ticker tape strewn for Lindbergh's return set the standard for future heroes, and for the New York Sanitation Department who had to clean up following the big parade.

Willie Gillis

Norman Rockwell

Willie Gillis, Norman Rockwell's world war hero, protects a Care package from enemies more domestic than foreign. Like thousands of other boys, Willie went to war, enjoyed adventures that would change his life and his country's way of thinking, then returned home to tell about it.

Heroes

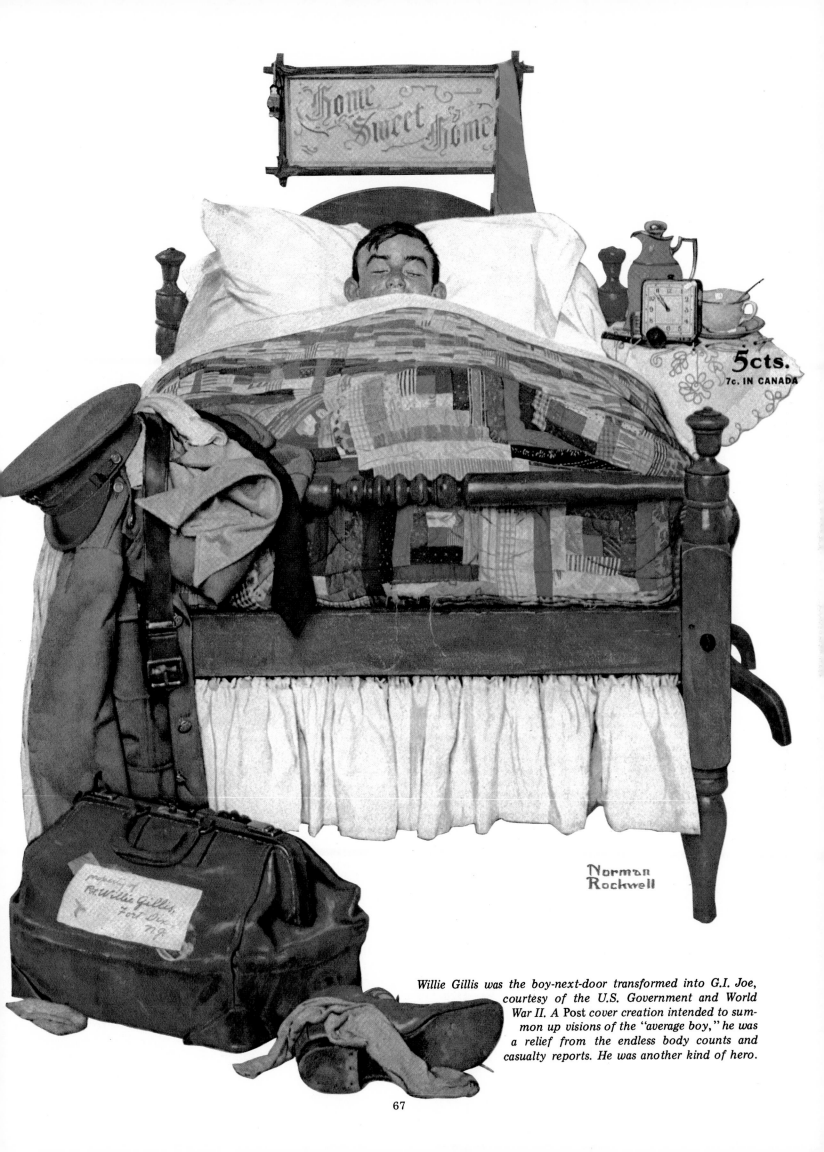

Home Sweet Home

5cts.
7c. IN CANADA

property of
Pvt. Willie Gillis,
Fort Dix
N.J.

Norman
Rockwell

Willie Gillis was the boy-next-door transformed into G.I. Joe, courtesy of the U.S. Government and World War II. A Post cover creation intended to summon up visions of the "average boy," he was a relief from the endless body counts and casualty reports. He was another kind of hero.

In Praise of Heroes

by Arthur M. Schlesinger, Jr.

(November 1958)

Ours is an age without heroes—and, when we say this, we suddenly realize how spectacularly the world has changed in a generation. Most of us grew up in a time of towering personalities. For better or for worse, great men seem to dominate our lives and shape our destiny.

Today no one bestrides our narrow world like a colossus; we have no giants who play roles which one can imagine no one else playing in their stead. Whatever one thought, whether one admired or detested Roosevelt or Churchill, Stalin or Hitler, one nevertheless felt the sheer weight of such personalities on one's own existence. We feel no comparable pressures today.

Why have the giants vanished from our midst? One must never neglect the role of accident in our history; and accident no doubt plays a part here. But too many accidents of the same sort cease to be wholly accidental. One must inquire further. Why must our age not only be without great men, but even seem actively hostile to them?

Surely one reason we have so few heroes now is precisely that we had so many a generation ago. Greatness is hard for common humanity to bear. As Emerson said, "Heroism means difficulty, postponement of praise, postponement of ease, introduction of the world into the private apartment, introduction of eternity into the hours measured by the sitting room clock." A world of heroes keeps people from living their own private lives.

No man is infallible, and every man needs to be reminded of this on occasion. Still, our age has gone further than this—it objects not only to hero worship but to heroes. The century of the common man has come into its own.

This term, "common man," suggests the deeper problem. There is more involved than simply a dismissal of those colossi whom the world identified with a season of blood and agony. The common man has always had a tendency to regard the great man with mixed feelings—resentment as well as admiration, hatred as well as love.

"I attribute the small number of distinguished men in political life," wrote Alexis de Tocqueville after visiting the United States in the 1830's, "to the ever-increasing despotism of the majority. . . . The power of the majority is so absolute and irresistible that one must give up one's rights as a citizen and almost abjure one's qualities as a human being, if one intends to stray away from the track which it prescribes." James Bryce even titled a chapter in his *American Commonwealth*, "Why Great Men Are Not Chosen President."

History has shown these prophets unduly pessimistic. Distinguished men do enter American politics; great men have been chosen President. Democracy demonstrates a capability for heroic leadership quite as much as it does a tendency toward mediocrity. Yet Tocqueville and the others were correct enough in detecting the dislike of great men as a permanent potentiality in a democracy.

Though we continue to speak of ourselves as rugged individualists, our actual life has grown more and more collective and anonymous. As a Monsanto Chemical film put it, showing a group of technicians at work in a laboratory: "No geniuses here; just a bunch of average Americans working together." Our ideal is increasingly smooth absorption into the group rather than self-realization in the old-fashioned, strong-minded, don't-give-a-damn sense. Where does the great man fit into our homogenized society?

"The greatness of England is now all collective," John Stuart Mill wrote a century ago. "Individually small, we only appear capable of anything great by our habit of combining." He might have been writing about contemporary America; but where we Americans are inclined to rejoice over the superiority of the "team," Mill added somberly, "It was men of another stamp than this that made England what it has been in the past; and men of another stamp will be needed to prevent its decline."

But was Mill right? Do individuals really have impact on history? A powerful group of philosophers has denied any importance at all to great men. Such thinkers reject heroes as a childish hangover from the days when men ascribed everything to the action of gods.

Individuals, of course, must operate within limits. They cannot do everything. They cannot, for example, propel history into directions for which the environment and the human material are not prepared.

To say there is a case for heroism is not to say there is a case for hero worship. The surrender of decision, the unquestioning submission to leadership, the prostration of the average man before the Great Man—these are diseases of heroism, and they are fatal to human dignity. But, if carried too far, hero worship generates its own antidote. "Every hero," said Emerson, "becomes a bore at last." And we need not go too far. History amply shows that it is possible to have heroes without turning them into gods.

And history shows, too, that when a society, in flight from hero worship, decides to do without great men at all, it gets into troubles of its own.

Our contemporary American society, for example, has little use for the individualist. Individualism implies dissent from the group; dissent implies conflict; and conflict suddenly seems divisive, un-American and generally unbearable. Our greatest new industry is evidently the production of techniques to eliminate conflict, from positive thoughts through public relations to psychoanalysis, applied everywhere from the couch to the pulpit. Our national aspiration has become peace of mind, peace of soul. The symptomatic drug of our age is the tranquilizer. "Togetherness" is the banner under which we march into the brave new world.

Obviously society has had to evolve collective institutions to cope with problems that have grown increasingly complex and concentrated. If Khrushchev worried because his collectivist society developed a cult of the individual, maybe we Americans should start worrying as our so-called individualist society develops a cult of the group. We instinctively suppose that the tough questions will be solved by an interfaith conference or an interdisciplinary research team or an interdepartmental committee or an assembly of wise men meeting at Arden House. But are not these group tactics essentially means by which individuals hedge their bets and distribute their responsibilities? And do they not nearly always result in the dilution of insight and the triumph of mishmash? If we are able to survive, we must have ideas, vision, courage. These things are rarely produced by committees. Everything that matters in our intellectual and moral life begins with an individual confronting his own mind and conscience in a room by himself.

A bland society will never be creative. "The amount of eccentricity in a society," said John Stuart Mill, "has generally been proportional to the amount of genius, mental vigor and moral courage it contained. That so few now dare to be eccentric marks the chief danger of the time."

If this condition frightened Mill in Victorian England, it should frighten us much more. For our national apotheosis of the group means that we systematically lop off the eccentrics, the originals, the proud, imaginative, lonely people from whom new ideas come. What began as a recoil from hero worship ends as a conspiracy against creativity. If worship of great men brings us into perdition by one path, flight from great men brings us there just as surely by another.

Great men enable us to rise to our highest potentialities. They nerve lesser men to disregard the world and trust to their own deepest instinct. Which one of us has not gained fortitude and faith from the incarnation of ideals in men, from the wisdom of Socrates, from the wondrous creativity of Shakespeare, from the strength of Washington, from the compassion of Lincoln, and above all, perhaps, from the life and death of Jesus? "We feed on genius," said Emerson. "Great men exist that there may be greater men."

Yet this may be only the smaller part of their service. Great men have another and larger role—to affirm human freedom against the supposed inevitabilities of history. It takes a man of exceptional vision and strength and will—it takes, in short, a hero—to try and wrench history from what lesser men consider its preconceived path. And often history tortures the hero in the process. Yet, man is still able to hold his own against the gods. Brave men earn the right to shape their own destiny.

An age without great men is one which acquiesces in the drift of history. Such acquiescence is easy and seductive; the great appeal of fatalism, indeed, is as a refuge from the terror of responsibility. When a belief in great men reminds us that individuals make a difference, fatalism reassures us they can't. It thereby blesses our weakness and extenuates our failure. Let us not be complacent about our supposed capacity to get along without great men. If our present society has lost its wish for heroes and its ability to produce them, it may well turn out to have lost everything else in addition.

BUYING AND SELLING

THE AD GAME

Americans are not such sharp traders as they are sharp producers and publicists. Advertising and the assembly line, like jazz and the movies, are essentially Yankee art forms. Advertising, never known as a bastion of taste, has nonetheless taken the euphemism out of cleanliness and health. We can face the fact of our bodies now. The lure of purchase and possession, the association of perfection with ownership, have made buying an entertainment and an ideal which work at both ends of the production line, eliminating class structure, and creating purchase as the only true power. In the supermarket, every woman is a queen; the whole world is at her feet. Americans live better than any people on earth and in many ways it is because advertising has made a virtue of necessity, and necessity through the mass media has become a boundless country. Daily bread no longer suffices. It has been iced and raisined, and the production line, driven by our desires, has become such a mighty conga line that America has helped to feed and clothe the entire world. America's interests overseas have in the main been efforts to create markets for American products. This is nothing new in terms of world history, but what is new is the availability to the world of the imperial concept, the idea that royalty is a democratic concern, that every man may drive a shining coach, own his own palace, send his children to college, and aspire to any office in the.land including that of the kingpin himself, the president. Happily, no one knows his place here.

Everyman is essentially a salesman, hawking his goods and his soul to the highest bidder, hoping for retirement or heaven, whichever comes first, going from door to door or standing before the world market, his sample case in hand, his spiel on the ready. The death of a salesman is a diminishment of the gross national product for America lives by trade. Copy and banter only succeed according to the quality of the product, and when times are hard, mere longing is kept well under control.

(Right) The merchandise exchanges hands but the bidding never stops. Supply and demand are the eternal haggle of the American marketplace, buying and selling the liquidator of all class distinction.

Super Market

This is no Humbug! By sending 30 cents, and stamp with age, height, color of eyes and hair, you will receive by return mail, a correct picture of your future husband or wife, with name and date of marriage. Address W. Fox, P.O. no. 40, Fultonville, New York.

—1869 Classified ad

A heavy beard in five weeks is warranted to those who use Russell's Italian Compound. It will not injure the skin and never fails. Sent, closely sealed and post-paid for 50 cents. W.C. Russell & Co., Watertown, New York.

—An appeal to smooth-skinned men, 1867

We gave to millions a new concept of baked beans.

—Van Camp's 1920 ad slogan

Constant vigilance on the part of parents is the price of bodily vigor and health in children. How closely are you guarding the food for the little ones? Sturdy girls and boys cannot be built out of soggy pastries. Nearly all children have wheat-hunger—a craving for the body-building elements found in whole wheat, the most perfect food given to man—his "staff of life" for four thousand years. It is through the cooking and shredding process used in making SHREDDED WHEAT that the whole wheat is prepared in its most digestible form. The Shredded Wheat Company, Niagara Falls.

—A 1911 ad pitch

R.R.R.—Radway's Ready Relief. A Cure for All Summer Complaints. A halfteaspoonful in half a tumbler of water will in a few moments cure Cramps, Spasms, Sour Stomach, Nausea, Vomiting, Heartburn, Nervousness, Sleeplessness, Sick Headache, Diarrhea, Dysentery, Cholera Morbus, Colic, Flatulency, and all Internal Pains. For Cholera and severe cases of the foregoing Complaints see our printed directions.

—Typical Cure-All ad of the 1880's

Guarding the Gateway to 500,000 Minds. The eye is the *main gate* to the mind of your boy. Are you leaving it unguarded, for evil reading to enter and cause havoc? Your most important duty is to put a trained, loyal sentry on guard—to give your boy reading that will develop his active, inquiring mind and urge him to "make good." Why not choose the guard already on duty for 250,000 careful parents—THE AMERICAN BOY? The Sprague Publishing Company, 293 American Building, Detroit, Michigan.

—Magazine ad in 1915

All the Comforts of Home includes the great temperance drink—HIRE'S ROOT BEER. It gives New Life to the Old Folks, Pleasure to the Parents, Health to the Children. Good for All—Good All the Time.

—1893 Root Beer ad

OLD EYES MADE NEW. A Pamphlet directing how to speedily restore sight and give up spectacles, without aid of Doctor or medicine. Sent by mail on receipt of 10 cents. E.B. Foote, M.D., 1130 Broadway, New York.

—An ad of the Civil War era

Let's End the Great Scalp Drought. It's almost universal, this masculine complaint about excessively dry scalp. And all so unnecessary. Let's end this great drought here and now by spending a few minutes a week on "corrective exercises." Oh yes, your scalp needs exercise just like any other muscles and it needs a lubricant, too, to help overcome that tight, dry feeling. Try this system: Every week a liberal application of "Vaseline" Hair Tonic and a thorough massage, working the scalp until it feels loose and tingly. Then a regular shampoo. Simple, isn't it? The trick is to do this regularly, once a week. And the result—a return to scalp normalcy, and a new lease on life for your hair.

—1932 Saturday Evening Post

People thought shave lotions were odd when they first appeared in the 1930's; guys were reluctant to smell like that until they discovered girls liked the smell. That's the big question you ask about any new idea in this business. Will the girls like it.

—George Mennen, president of
the Mennen Company

(Right) A world away from all the jokes about traveling sales-men and farmers' daughters, a lonely drummer bores him-self to sleep with a game of solitaire in a strange hotel room.

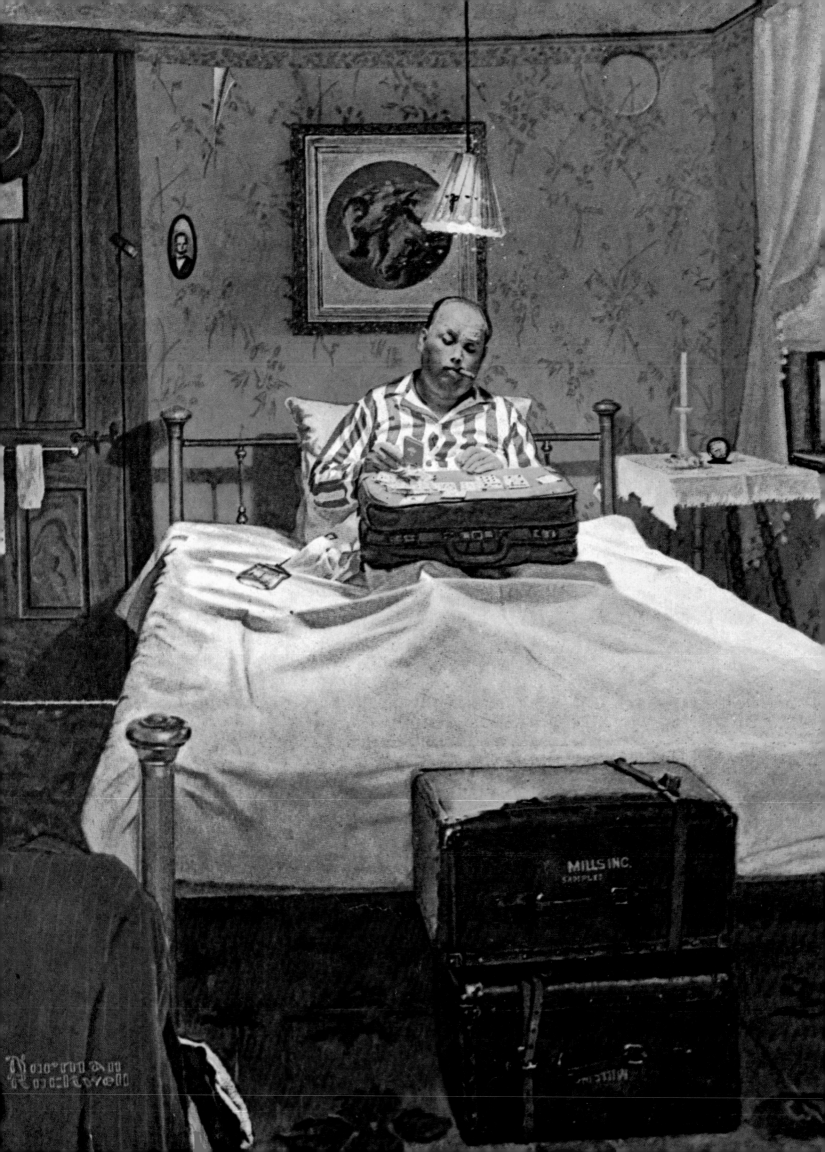

The boss hated to have him in his office

THE boss liked his work and personality but avoided being near him. One fault blocked his progress.

Millions are overcoming this humiliating hot weather handicap of body odor simply by using the *right soap*.

The first time you bathe with Lifebuoy your wholly new sense of fresh, supercleanness explains better than words why Lifebuoy actually prevents body odor by removing the cause.

The rich, gentle lather is so soothing and leaves the skin so smooth and glowing that most people use Lifebuoy simply because they like it. But its deeper value as a guardian of health is proved by this searching, complete removal from pores of body waste and acids of perspiration which cause body odor. Only antiseptically clean skin is odorless—only an antiseptic soap can give antiseptic cleanness.

The clean health odor of Lifebuoy rinses away completely—never clings. Lifebuoy is orange red—the color of its pure palm fruit oil. Lever Bros. Co., Cambridge, Mass.

LIFEBUOY
HEALTH SOAP
—stops body odor

THE DAINTIEST MEMBER OF THE JUNIOR SET..

Yet she has "Athlete's Foot!"

ONLY this morning she had noticed it again—and her pretty brows had puckered with vexation. Charming—sought after—exquisitely groomed—it seemed to her almost a reproach upon her delicacy— yet there it was, that affection, unnaturally white, unpleasantly moist,* between her smallest toes!

Not that it hurt her so much—it seldom *does* in the beginning—but the *thought* of it distressed her more and more. In the midst of a perfectly divine dance— during the "big" scene at the play—in wakeful moments at night—it obtruded itself upon her mind— it was *maddening!*

She is just one of millions who suffer from "Athlete's Foot" and *don't know what it is!*

Tinea Trichophyton—a National *Affliction*

Her escort, the big Princeton end, had he known of her worry, could have told her that she was suffering from a form of ringworm infection caused by tinea trichophyton and nicknamed "Athlete's Foot"! Also he could have told her *what to do* for her trouble, for college coaches everywhere now know that Absorbine Jr., the familiar antiseptic, *kills and helps prevent its spread.*

This is fortunate, for "Athlete's Foot" is such a *stealthy* infection . . . so easily overlooked at first . . . that it has stolen up on the Nation until it is found

---

* WATCH FOR THESE DISTRESS SIGNALS THAT WARN OF "ATHLETE'S FOOT"

Though "Athlete's Foot" is caused by the germ *tinea trichophyton* —its early stages manifest themselves in several different ways, usually between the two smallest toes: redness, skin-cracks, tiny itching blisters, a white, thick, moist condition or dryness with little scales. *Any one of these calls for immediate treatment!* If the case appears aggravated and does not readily yield to Absorbine Jr., consult your physician without delay.

simply *everywhere!* The United States Public Health Service even asserts in one of its Bulletins that *"it is probable that at least one-half of all adults suffer from it at some time"* . . . suffer from it without knowing what it is.

Again, tests conducted in such widely separated Universities as those of California and Pennsylvania reveal that probably 50% of the students involved are infected.

There can be no doubt that tiny *tinea trichophyton* has made itself at home in America!

It lurks where you would least expect it

One of the worst features of "Athlete's Foot" is that it is most apt to be contracted in the *very* places where people go for health and cleanliness and recreation! In spite of the most rigid sanitary precautions, the germ abounds on the locker and dressing-room floors—on the edges of swimming pools and showers—in gymnasiums, even on hotel bath-mats.

And from such places it is carried into millions of homes to infect whole families!

It has been found that Absorbine Jr. kills Tinea Trichophyton

A series of laboratory tests with the antiseptic Absorbine Jr. has proved, through bacteria counts and microphotographs, that Absorbine Jr. penetrates deeply into flesh-like tissues and that wherever it penetrates it *kills* the "Athlete's Foot" infection.

This will be good news indeed to many thousands of people who have worried over a threatening foot condition without knowing what it was that was troubling them, nor how to rid themselves of it.

It might not be a bad idea to examine your feet tonight for the distress signals* that announce the beginning of "Athlete's Foot."

At the first sign of infection begin the free use of Absorbine Jr. on the affected areas—douse it on morning and night and after every exposure. Not injurious to the tenderest tissues.

Absorbine Jr. is so widely known and used that you can get it at all drug stores. Price $1.25. For free sample, write

W. F. YOUNG, INC. SPRINGFIELD, MASS.

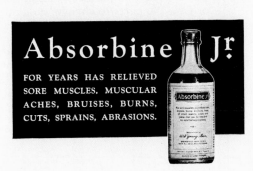

Absorbine Jr.

FOR YEARS HAS RELIEVED SORE MUSCLES, MUSCULAR ACHES, BRUISES, BURNS, CUTS, SPRAINS, ABRASIONS.

"year 'round ... it serves willingly and worthily ..."

In season and out, the whole year 'round, this Universal Combination Range seems actually to delight in pleasing you. It serves most willingly and worthily. Tempting dishes fairly flow from it. As for looks—just see for yourself its immaculate, trim appearance.

The turn of a simple lever automatically adjusts oven for use with coal, wood or gas. No parts to change; no dampers to operate. Beautifully finished in unbreakable, durable UNIVIT Porcelain—Peacock Blue or Pearl Gray. Will not chip, craze or discolor. Clean as a china dish. Can be washed like a porcelain bath. Also made in plain and nickel finish. Fits in small space and keeps kitchen cool in summer and warm in winter. At all good dealers'— cash or terms. Dealer's name and illustrated booklet on request.

CRIBBEN & SEXTON COMPANY   716 N. Sacramento Blvd., Chicago, Ill.
DENVER   PORTLAND   'SAN FRANCISCO   PITTSBURGH   NEW YORK   ALLENTOWN, PA.   BAYONNE, N. J.
Made in Canada under the name "SIMPLEX" by McClary's—London   Patented in United States and Canada   (38)

UNIVERSAL COMBINATION RANGE
Burns Natural or Artificial Gas *and* Coal or Wood

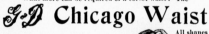
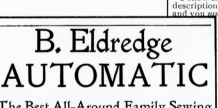

Pinching was the fashion, both at waist and ankle. Cooking stoves were efficient but retained the appearance of a Louis XV landau. Promises were dished out with the abandon of the main speaker at a political rally. Women knew they still had a lot to do.

Three dollars and fifty cents bought a pair of shoes and put you in the parade. A threatening-looking device known as a button hook got butterfingers there on time. Street car engineers were in league with girl watchers. Tram steps were just high enough.

Letter From A Self-Made Merchant to His Son

by George Horace Lorimer

(November 1902)

Dear Pierrepont: When I saw you start off yesterday I was just a little uneasy; for you looked so blamed important and chesty that I am inclined to think you will tell the first customer who says he doesn't like our sausage that he knows what he can do about it. Repartee makes reading lively, but business dull. And what the house needs is more orders.

Sausage is the one subject of all others that a fellow in the packing business ought to treat solemnly. Half the people in the world take a joke seriously from the start, and the other half if you repeat it often enough. Only last week the head of our sausage department started to put out a tin-tag brand of frankfurts, but I made him take it off the market quicker than lightning, because I knew that the first fool who saw the tin-tag would ask if that was the license. And, though people would grin a little at first, they'd begin to look serious after a while; and whenever the butcher tried to sell them our brand they'd imagine they heard the bark, and ask for "that real country sausage" at twice as much a pound.

He laughs best who doesn't laugh at all when he's dealing with the public. It has been my experience that, even when a man has a sense of humor, it only really carries him to the point where he will join in a laugh at the expense of the other fellow. There's nothing in the world sicker looking than the grin of the man who's trying to join in heartily when the laugh's on him, and to pretend that he likes it.

Speaking of sausage with a registered pedigree, last year a fellow came into the office with a shriveled-up spaniel he wanted to sell. I asked him what he wanted. The fellow wiped away a tear. He said I had a rather pleasant face and he could trust me to treat Dandy kindly; so he would let me have him for five hundred. "Cents?" says I. "Dollars," says he. I just said, "The sausage business is too poor to warrant our paying any such price for light-weights. Bring around a bigger dog and we'll talk." The fellow shook his head sadly, whistled to Dandy and walked off. There's such a thing as carrying a joke too far and the fellow who pretends to believe that he is paying for pork and getting dog is pretty apt to get the dog in the end.

A real salesman is one part talk and nine parts judgment; and he uses the nine parts of judgment to tell when to use the one part of talk. Goods ain't sold under Marquess of Queensberry rules anymore, and you'll find that knowing how many rounds the Old 'Un can last against the Boiler-Maker won't really help you to load up the junior partner with our corn-fed brand hams.

A good many salesmen have an idea that buyers are only interested in baseball, and funny stories, and Tom Lipton, and that business is a sideline with them; but as a matter of fact mighty few men work up to the position of buyer through giving up their office hours to listening to anecdotes. I never saw one that liked a drummer's jokes more than an eighth of a cent a pound on a tierce of lard. What the house really sends you out for is orders.

Of course, you want to be nice and mellow with the trade, but always remember that mellowness carried too far becomes rottenness. You can buy some fellows with a cheap cigar and some with a cheap compliment, and there's no objection to giving a man what he likes, though I never knew smoking to do anything good except a ham, or flattery to help anyone except to make a fool of himself.

Real buyers ain't interested in much besides your goods and your prices. Never run down your competitor's brand to them, and never let them run down yours. Don't get on your knees for business, but don't hold your nose so high in the air that an order can travel under it without your seeing it. You'll meet a good many people on the road that you won't like, but the house needs their business.

Some fellows will tell you that we play the hose on our dry salt meat before we ship it, and that it shrinks in transit like a Baxter Street shyster's all-wool suits in a rainstorm; that they wonder how we manage to pack solid gristle in two-pound cans without leaving a little meat hanging to it; and that the last car of lard was so strong that it came back of its own accord from every retailer they shipped it to. The first fellow will be lying, and the second will be exaggerating, and the third may be telling the truth. With him you must settle on the spot; but always remember that a man who's making a claim never underestimates his case, and that you can generally compromise for something less than the first figure. With the second you must sympathize, and say that the matter will be reported to headquarters and the boss of the canning room called up on the carpet and made to promise that it will never happen again. With the first you needn't bother. There's no use feeding expensive "hen food" to an old Dominick that sucks eggs. The chances are that the car actually weighed out more than it was billed, and that the fellow played the hose on it himself and added a thousand pounds of cheap salt before he jobbed it out to his trade.

Where you're going to slip up at first is in knowing which is which, but if you don't learn pretty quick you'll not travel very far for the house. For your own satisfaction I will say right here that you may know you are in a fair way of becoming a good drummer by three particular indications:

First—When you send us Orders.

Second—More Orders.

Third—Big Orders.

If you do this you won't have a great deal of time to write long letters, and we won't have a great deal of time to read them, for we will be very, very busy here making and shipping the goods. We aren't specially interested in orders that the other fellow gets, or in knowing how it happened after it has happened. If you like life on the road you simply won't let it happen. So just send us your address every day and your orders. They will tell us all that we're interested in knowing about "the situation."

I was cured of sending information to the house when I was very, very young—in fact, on the first trip which I made on the road. I was traveling out of Chicago for Hammer & Hawkins, wholesale dry goods, gents' furnishings and notions. They started me out to round up trade in the river towns down Egypt ways, near the city of Cairo.

I hadn't more than made my first town and sized up the population before I began to feel happy, because I saw that business ought to be very good there. It appeared as if everybody in that town needed something in my line. The clerk of the hotel where I registered wore a dicky and his cuffs were tied to his neck by pieces of string run up his sleeves, and most of the merchants on Main Street were in their shirt-sleeves—at least those that had shirts were—and so far as I could

judge there wasn't a whole pair of galluses among them. Some were using wire, some a little rope, and others just faith—buckled extra tight. Pride of the Prairie XXX flour sacks seemed to be the nobby thing in boys' suitings there. Take it by and large, if ever there was a town which looked as if it had a big, short line of dry goods, gents' furnishings and notions to cover, it was that one.

But when I caught the proprietor of the general store during a lull in the demand for navy plug, he wouldn't even look at my samples, and when I began to hint that the people were pretty ornery dressers he reckoned that he "would paste me one if I warn't so young." Wanted to know what I meant by coming swelling around in song-and-dance clothes and getting funny at the expense of people who made their living honestly. Allowed that when it came to a humorous getup my clothes were the original end man's gag.

I noticed on the way back to the hotel that every fellow holding up a hitching post was laughing, and I began to look up and down the street for the joke, not understanding at first that the reason why I couldn't see it was because I was it. Right there I began to learn that, while the Prince of Wales may wear the correct thing in hats, it's safer when you're out of his sphere of influence to follow the styles that the hotel clerk sets; that the place to sell clothes is in the city, where everyone seems to have plenty of them; and that the place to sell mess pork is in the country, where everyone keeps and raises hogs.

I wrote in to the house pretty often on that trip, explaining how it was, going over the whole situation very carefully, and telling what our competitors were doing, wherever I was able to find that they were doing anything at all.

I gave old Hammer credit for more curiosity than he possessed, because when I reached Cairo I found a telegram from him reading: *"Know what our competitors are doing: they are getting all the trade. But what are you doing?"* I saw then that the time for explaining was gone and that the moment for resigning had arrived; so I just naturally sent in my resignation. That is what we will expect from you—or orders.

Your affectionate father,
John Graham

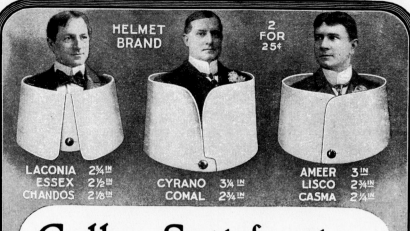
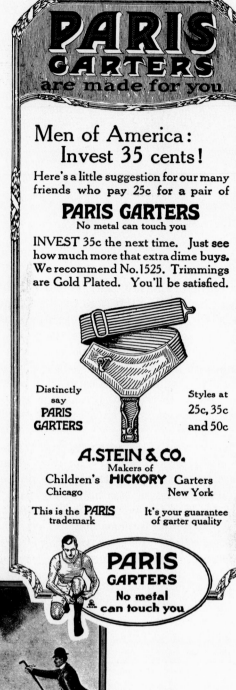

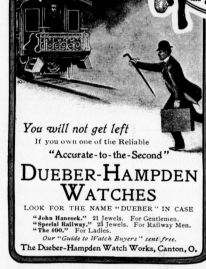
Perhaps as a holdover from the Civil War, Union suits were very much in vogue. The scarcity of central heating probably added to their popularity; most men were glad to see spring. Collars were boiled before being applied as tourniquets, and the clean face, reddened by the tightness of the collar, was making a comeback as these ads for razor strops and shaving cream suggest. Men could still miss trains but they looked better running.

FAR IN THE LEAD

MUNSING UNION SUITS STAND EVERY TEST

*"The supreme com-
bination of all that
is fine in motor cars"*

BALANCE

What Packard means by "balance" in a motor car goes far beyond the mechanical balance of parts which assures silent, vibrationless operation. Packard's clientele takes that for granted.

The balance in which Packard takes pride is that perfect balance of desirable qualities which led one enthusiastic owner to write that his Packard was *"the supreme combination of all that is fine in motor cars."*

Packard's deliberate aim for twenty-seven years has been to develop a car of all-around excellence—not a car famous merely for one out-

standing trait but of acknowledged superiority in all. Those who own Packard cars know how well Packard has succeeded.

Whatever you may expect from a motor car the Packard will provide to an unusual degree. Beauty, smartness and distinction recognized and imitated the world around. Speed unsurpassed by any but racing cars. Roominess and comfort which are proverbial. Low operating cost and long life which make Packard ownership a real economy. It is the *balanced excellence* of the Packard which makes it so universally admired and desired.

PACKARD

ASK THE MAN WHO OWNS ONE

MARMON

For more than twenty-seven years Marmon has meant the truly distinc-tive, the luxurious, the fine thing well done + + + **Today Marmon means all that and more with an** entirely new line of cars—each a straight-eight, **each abundant in ad**vanced engineering thought — each with that charm and un-usualness which is so inseparably Marmon + + + New easy riding qualities and super comfort dimensions + + + With these cars Marmon covers the entire range of fine cars—the Big Eight—the "Eight-79"—the "Eight-69" and the Marmon-Roosevelt — a car for every possible motor car need.

Marmon Motor Car Company, Indianapolis

R.F.D.—Silent Salesman

by Frederic A. Birmingham

Advertising started in American cities before the original cobblestones were laid. The first printing press ran the claims of hatters and gunmakers alongside the news.

Nineteenth-century America was predominantly rural. The country was growing up by growing west. Post offices were sprouting in every hamlet and town. Railroads were bridging the continent. And in between the Atlantic and Pacific coasts were millions of farm families who created a self-sustaining economy. Besides raising crops, they made just about everything they needed—clothes, implements, household furnishings. But that economy was bound to change. In the second half of the century, farmers were selling their crops for cash and buying what they needed from the little rural general stores which sprang up everywhere. Prices were preposterous and the middleman was the villain. In 1894, flour was $3.37 wholesale, and about $7.00 retail. The excuse was the cost of getting it "out there."

The answer to the farmer's prayer was the mail order company. Thanks to volume buying, to the railroads and post offices, and, later, to rural free delivery and parcel post, here was a happy alternative to the high-priced general stores of the area.

In the tiny hamlet of North Redwood, Minnesota, by one of those fascinating quirks of fate, was a man who was at the right place, at the right time, with the right abilities and ambitions. His name was Richard Warren Sears, a station agent for the Minneapolis and St. Louis Railroad, who was mighty facile with the telegrapher's key. But no one suspected that there by the gleaming tracks was a man also of merchandising and advertising genius who would someday outshine them all, with a name destined to become better known to history than those of most of our generals and even our presidents.

It was in 1886 that Richard embarked on the business which was to become the greatest retail establishment of all time.

A budding entrepreneur from the age of seven— when he had earned twenty-five cents a day carrying water to harvest field hands—young Richard started this fabulous business empire by opting to earn a little extra money on the side. As the trains moseyed by on the lazy little railroad, the enterprising agent took to supplying coal and lumber to local residents. When he

Some of the most marvelous tales in our history record the peacetime triumphs of humble men who created the foundation of great corporate enterprises. In this charming railroad station at North Redwood, Minnesota, a young station agent named Richard Warren Sears had the gumption to try selling a few things on the side. Thus began the greatest retail establishment in the world: Sears, Roebuck and Co.

also attempted to sell a shipment of watches unwanted by a local Redwood Falls jewelry, Sears took the epochal plunge. But he who sells watches must also repair the bad ones. So now Richard advertised in the Chicago *Daily News:*

WANTED: Watchmaker with reference who can furnish tools. State age, experience, and salary required.

And who answered? The same antic fate which decrees that salt and pepper and ham and eggs are inseparables, now and forever, reached down and produced (who else?) an Indiana-born lad of English parentage, watchmaker by trade, one Alvah C. Roebuck. Sears and Roebuck were joined, as the hidden thunders of simple domestic history rolled on.

Richard's next inspiration was to advertise by mail. At first, Sears sold only watches. But by 1895 the new firm was producing a 507-page catalogue with many other items—shoes, millinery, wagons, fishing tackle, baby carriages, everything a farmer and his family might think of, and other things besides. All were minutely illustrated in detail to whet the appetite, and seductively described in Sears's words, which, as later students of advertising came to recognize, were a veritable dictionary of sales appeal.

Cultural historians may flinch at the fact, but the most widely read book in nineteenth-century America, except for the Bible, was the Sears, Roebuck and Co. catalogue, a calling card and wish book for both parlor and privy in millions of rural American homes—rightfully dubbed "the stuff of dreams, with reading matter."

Dreams, arriving by rural free delivery, were to become the very stuff—as one surveys the endless years of catalogues and the fantastic array of merchandise—of daily life in America in 1896.

True, in 1925, in time with the times, Sears opened its own retail stores. The country had become urbanized, everyone drove his own car, and "the store" was literally or figuratively just around the corner. But the catalogue still rolls grandly off the presses. The words are more factual today; the flamboyance of the founder's prose is gone. But the dream lingers on, and millions of purchasers-to-be still linger over the bulky "wish books," since one thing never changes, as Richard Warren Sears well knew, and that is human nature.

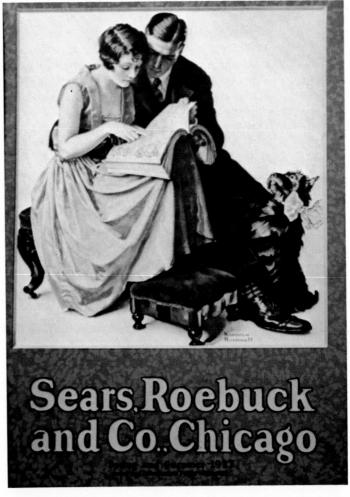

The Sears, Roebuck Catalogue, a reading favorite in both parlor and privy of millions of America's rural families, on several occasions had a cover by Norman Rockwell, the great Post *artist.*

THE PROMISED LAND

AMERICA MOVES WEST

It seems the Creator may have made a mistake. The sun should rise in the west, or at least that was where the hope and eventual destiny of many early Americans rested. So firmly is the West imprinted on the gray matter of the nation as a place of beginnings, that we still see cowboys and Indians roaming the plains, lonely and heroic, or we sit in the drugstore at Hollywood and Vine waiting to be discovered, waiting to be made perfect and eternal by plastic surgery, proper lighting and universal adulation. Even our cities expand in a westward direction.

In the 1800's, hope and the migratory urge drove many Americans in the direction where the world begins all over again. It was an incredible journey. The pioneers not only had to pack up everything they owned, they had to take enough to sustain themselves for months on the road (if it could be called that) and until the first crop (usually a disaster) came in. Television misrepresents the struggle.

When Europeans visit America it is not the cities where houses and history have been made that intrigue them, it is the West where nature allowed herself to be ravaged by her own elements, the land of myth and monument, the mix of ancient civilization and eye-aching vastness. The West was made for nomads and even today there is a quality of transience about the cities of the plain that live on imported water. To be native-born in Southern California is to qualify almost as landed aristocracy. The frontier quality persists in its being the home of the aerospace industry, the mind-rock for America's expanding new frontier.

The natural wonders of the land became the national wonders of the people. They thrived, these people, and unlike most voyageurs, they looked back, and came back, again and again, and the East was better for it, as was the West. And perhaps more than the Civil War, or the old country immigrants, the sod busters and wagon trains tied the country together in a yeoman's knot which two centuries have failed to unravel.

(Right) The West's stomach traveled with it, and the cook was a stock character in cowboy comedy, the chuck wagon as efficient and quick as a Pullman galley.

Home on the Range

Our cabin had been raised, covered, part of the floor laid, when we moved in on Christmas Day. At both the doors we had high, unsteady, and sometimes icy steps, made by piling logs cut out for the doors and the window, if it could be called a window, when perhaps it was the largest spot in the top, bottom, or sides of the cabin where the wind could not enter.

It was made by sawing out a log; and then placing sticks across, and by pasting an old newspaper over the hole and applying hog's lard, we had a kind of glazing which shed a most beautiful and mellow light across the cabin when the sun shone on it.

—William Dean Howells,
"Pioneer Days," 1898

The Civil Service Commission has wanted for some time past a woman doctor to go out among the Indians, with an assured income of $1,000 at the start, but the applicants are few. They would be reasonably sure of retaining their scalps.

—1893

New discoveries of gold are said to have been made in California. It is estimated that about a hundred thousand dollars' worth is gathered daily: The diggers, notwithstanding the immense amount of gold gathered, are in a suffering condition for the necessaries of life, and much sickness prevails. Provisions demand almost any price, and two barrels of brandy have been retailed at the mines for fourteen thousand dollars in gold dust.

—1849

Unlucky for Eastern Girls—It is stated in *Letters from the South West,* just published by Harper & Brothers, in describing the state of society near Natchez, that "unluckily for six out of every seven of the fair daughters of the East, the pioneers of the West feel disposed to pass their lives in all the solitary dignity of the bachelor state. Wrapped up in their speculations, their cigars, and their clubs, not even a second Sabine device could move them to bend their reluctant necks to the noose."

—1836

The meanest man yet has lately moved out West. A person who witnessed one of his small acts said that "ten thousand such souls might live in a mustard seed and keep furnished rooms to let at that."

—1840

The buffaloes found in the telegraph poles of the overland line a new source of delight on the treeless prairie—the novelty of having something to scratch against. But it was expensive scratching for the telegraph company . . . for the bisons shook down miles of wire daily. A bright idea struck somebody to send to St. Louis and Chicago for all the brad-awls that could be purchased, and these were driven into the poles with a view to wound the animals and check their rubbing propensity. Never was a greater mistake. The buffaloes were delighted. For the first time they came to the scratch sure of a sensation in their thick hides that would thrill them from horn to tail.

—1869

In grading near the crossing of Broad and Main Streets, the workmen have been obliged to trespass upon the old burying ground of the Indians. Day before yesterday, an Indian with his squaw and little boy happened to pass along just as the workmen struck an Indian mound. He stopped and for a short time watched the men as they rudely cast its contents out of the way, but soon, overcome by his emotions, he commenced sobbing. The kindhearted laborers gathered the bones, covered them in the mound again, and retired to another part of the work until he went away.

—1858 news item from Minnesota

We learn from the *Arkansas Gazette* that the Cherokees are much dissatisfied with the treaty made with the United States, and that present appearances justify the belief that their delegation will lose their heads as soon as they return. Poles have been erected in front of the houses of the delegation, on which their heads are to be exhibited as soon as they return.

—1828

Go West, young man!

—1850 advice to unemployed
popularized by Horace Greeley

"Everything is funny
as long as it is happening to somebody else,"
said Will Rogers as he made the West seem like
us and our politicians like somebody else.

The hazards of their occupation surround these cowboys as they huddle against the vast and lonely space of an unknown land.

Beyond the Missouri

by A Pioneer

(July 1849)

Since leaving the Kansas, we have passed at least one thousand teams, and are still behind at least two thousand others. We are scarcely ever out of sight of emigrants. A long white line, before and behind, points out the road, relieving very much of the monotony of these, to me, very dreary plains. Horsemen are constantly passing and re-passing, galloping over hill and dale; and it is very difficult to drive from the mind the idea that we are still within the precincts of civilization. Every now and then as we ford a creek or pass through a small slip of wood, I look inadvertently for the fences and habitation of the husbandman, but all that can be seen that indicates that man has been here, are the stumps of trees felled by the emigrants and a well beaten road.

Day before yesterday we broke the sandboard of our wagon, and while lying by, we were passed by several trains, among which was Captain

Indian braves watch as settlers invade the wild territory of the hunters.

W. H. D
Koerner

James White's, of St. Louis. In this company are Dr. White and family and two other females. The army of General Twiggs also passed the same day. One thousand mounted riflemen and a train of two hundred wagons presented a most grand spectacle, stretching along the road as far as the eye could see—officers and wagon masters galloping at full speed up and down the line.

As this train will proceed on the California road, as far as the South Pass, ample protection will be afforded to the emigrants in its immediate vicinity from the Indians. No open attacks are to be feared; but the strictest vigilance will be required to keep the animals from being stolen.

As near as I have been able to ascertain from the emigrants, from fifty to seventy-five deaths have occurred on the St. Joseph and Independence roads. I have been unable to learn the names of any except three or four, who have been buried. Most of the deaths have been from cholera and dysentery.

(Top, Bottom) While thousands of pioneers were taking the flying clouds west by way of the Cape—a journey by sea of 17,000 miles—more were migrating across the plains in land-clippers or Conestoga wagons. Families staked their lives on the supplies and team which bore them toward the promised land. (Right) Buffalo Bill Cody slew 4,280 buffalo in 8 months. Later, he brought attention to their dwindling numbers in his wild west shows.

Hunting the Herds

by Buffalo Bill

(April 1899)

One of the most exciting scenes in connection with hunting the buffalo is a "buffalo stampede." I recall an exciting incident of this kind. Vast herds of these monarchs of the plains were roaming around us, and we lay over one day for a grand hunt. The next day we pulled out of camp, and the train was strung out a considerable length along the road which ran near the foot of the sandhills, two miles from the river. Between the road and the river we saw a large herd of buffaloes grazing quietly; they had been down to the stream for a drink. At the same time we observed a party of returning Californians coming from the West. They, too, noticed the buffalo herd, and in another moment they were dashing upon them with terrific speed.

The buffalo herd stampeded at once, and broke down the hills. So hotly were they pursued by the hunters that several hundred of them rushed through our train pell-mell, frightening both men and oxen. The teams got entangled in their gearing and became wild and unruly. Many of the cattle broke their yokes and stampeded. One big buffalo bull became entangled in one of the heavy wagon chains. In his desperate efforts to free himself, he not only snapped the strong chain in two, but broke the ox-yoke to which it was attached, and the last seen of him he was running toward the hills with a yoke hanging in his horns.

The Post Office

by Bella Z. Spencer

(February 1860)

WANTED: Young skinny wiry fellows, not over eighteen. Must be expert riders willing to risk death daily. Orphans preferred. Wages $25 per week. Apply Central Overland Express, Alta Building, Montgomery St.

*   *   *

(May 1913)

We never open a day's mail without being informed that there is a tremendous popular demand for something or other that we have been regarding as quite negligible. If we believed all the letters and circulars we should have to imagine the entire population of the United States assembled in perpetual mass meeting, formulating demands; but we do not believe them.

For instance, we do not believe there is any popular demand for one-cent postage. Why should there be? About one-third of all the letters in the country are sent from the six largest cities. Some big-city businesses—especially mail-order houses, publishers, department stores, subscription-book concerns—might reap a benefit from reduced letter postage; but the Post Office Department even now is barely self-sustaining. If letter postage were cut in half it would be necessary to increase rates on other classes of mail, which increase would be borne by the public, or there would be a big deficit in postal revenues, which deficit would be paid by the public. Postal rates in the United States now are the cheapest in the world when distances are considered.

The rural per-capita expenditure for letter postage is about fifty cents a year. Reading and writing go together. The rural household into which little second-class mail goes is one out of which little first-class mail comes. A saving of twenty-five cents in letter postage would be more than offset by an increase on second-class mail and merchandise. Some booksellers have long had a mistaken notion that if magazines could be made more expensive through increased postage, more books would be sold; but any increased cost of magazines through higher postage would fall upon the consumer, without affecting the book trade.

The first postal receipt for U.S. Overseas Mail is dated 1639, Fairbanks' Tavern, Boston. Franklin was appointed postmaster general in 1775. By 1970, 84.8 billion pieces of mail were being delivered, 400 items for every man, woman and child in the U.S.

Lexington & Concord 1775 by Sandham

US Bicentennial 10cents

Bunker Hill 1775 by Trumbull

US Bicentennial 10c

Contributors To The Cause...

U.S. 8c

Sybil Ludington *Youthful Heroine*

The short-lived but glamorous Pony Express carried mail between Missouri and California in ten days, from April 1860 to October 1861. Frederic Remington painted this fast start from one of the 190 way-stations along the route. Usually one man carried the mail 75 miles.

She was unmarried, easy to caricature, demanding, but above all, scrupulously fair. Her curiosity was genuine and all inclusive. She did not mind handling spiders or snakes though she recoiled at human cruelty. Her knowledge of multiplication tables and grammar was frightening as was her capability of meting out deserved punishment. You had heard the man she loved had died in some remote war. Years later, you remembered her for having taught you most of what you knew, and when you returned to thank her, she was gone.

Dearest John

by Abigail Adams

(Letters 1776, 1789)

I long to hear that you have declared an independency. And, by the way, in the new code of laws which I suppose it will be necessary for you to make, I desire you would remember the ladies and be more generous and favorable to them than your ancestors. Do not put such unlimited power into the hands of husbands. Remember, all men would be tyrants if they could. If particular care and attention is not paid to the ladies, we are determined to foment a rebellion, and will not hold ourselves bound by any laws in which we have no voice or representation.

That your sex are naturally tyrannical is a truth so thoroughly established as to admit of no dispute; but such of you as wish to be happy willingly give up the harsh title of master for the more tender and endearing one of friend. Why, then, not put it out of the power of the vicious and the lawless to use us with cruelty and indignity with impunity? Men of sense in all ages abhor those customs which treat us only as the vassals of your sex; regard us then as being placed by Providence under your protection, and in imitation of the Supreme Being make use of that power only for our happiness. (1776)

It has been my lot in life to spend a large portion of it in public life, but I can truly say the pleasantest part of it was spent at the foot of Pens Hills in that humble cottage when my good gentleman was a practitioner at the bar, earned his money, during the week, and at the end of it poured it all into my lap to use or what could be spared to lay by. Nobody then grudged us our living, and twenty-five years of such practice would have given us a very different property from what we now possess. It might not have given us the second rank in the United States, nor the satisfaction of reflecting by what means and whose exertions these states have arrived at that degree of liberty, safety and independence which they now enjoy. If the United States had chosen to the vice-president's chair a man wavering in his opinions, or one who sought the popular applause of the multitude, this very constitution would have had its death wound during this first six months of its existence. (1789)

The first American to look down on Europe, Abigail Adams, largely self-taught, was only slightly surprised to find herself and her countrywomen as intelligent as the so-called well-educated ladies of the English and French courts.

Dolley Madison

by Meade Minnigerode

(November 1924)

Dolley was "a fine, portly, buxom dame, who has a smile and a pleasant word for everybody," and her sisters were "like the two Merry Wives of Windsor." She was in her forties now, but young-looking, and in the best of spirits. Dolley painted and powdered a little, although the question was hotly argued among contemporaries; she took snuff constantly, from lava and platina boxes, and used large bandanna handkerchiefs.

"This is for rough work," she is once supposed to have explained, whereas her little lace handkerchief was merely her "polisher."

She towered above the crowded levees in her rose-colored satin robes trimmed with ermine and her ostrich-feathered turbans and her amethyst eardrops; her honest laughter was always ringing out; perhaps not always so sure of herself, she strived painstakingly to put everyone at ease, even the young gentleman who in his excitement at meeting her tried to cram a teacup into his pocket.

She always appeared in her parlor with a book in her hand. Not that she ever had leisure to read, but—"in order to have something not ungraceful to say, and if need be, to supply a word of talk."

A cheerful, sweet-tempered, gracious, jolly lady, who found time to cut out hundreds of garments for the city orphan asylum, a wise, clever lady in her own appointed ways, who invited Mrs. Gallatin to represent her at drawing rooms

Dolley Payne Todd married Madison when he was 43. She was 16 years his junior, a Quaker who loved parties. The White House became a setting for successful diplomatic negotiations with European powers under her graceful hand.

after the President had quarreled with Mr. Gallatin, and who had Mrs. William Seaton to dinner when her husband became editer of the important *National Intelligencer*, and who did many little kindnesses to many people—so that finally Madison was allowed to have a second term.

And in the meantime, there was war. "The world"—Dolley was moved to so deep a thought—"the world seemed to be running mad, what with one thing and another." An embargo to begin with, in April 1812. And, in June, a war with England. An unpopular war throughout the Eastern and Middle states—Madison's War. But still Madison was reelected, thanks, primarily, to Dolley, who never lost her head.

For the second time in American history, the British were coming! At Dolley's suggestion, the gardener broke the frame containing Gilbert Stuart's portrait of Washington and gave the picture to some gentleman for safekeeping. The Castle was abandoned, to be burned by the British. But Government did return to Washington in a few days.

Carry Nation

by William Allen White

(April 1901)

On a winter's morning in Chicago, a tall, overpowering woman with determined face and rotund figure, clad in black alpaca, and not too warmly wrapped, came from a cheap Dearborn Street tavern and set out walking to see the town. The woman was Mrs. Caroline Nation, Crusader, of Medicine Lodge, Kansas.

She wandered with rather unstable purpose, and a hooting, indolent rabble followed her with curiosity. She had been well advertised. For several weeks before she came to Chicago Mrs. Nation's name had been occupying a "preferred position" in the American newspapers, and so when she began her morning's journey over the big city to purify it, the mob at her heels was ready for miracles or a fight, or both.

She went into saloons and pleaded with the barkeepers. She prayed on the streets; she exhorted; she laughed and cried and wrought herself up to a pitch of excitement wherein nothing matters much. Then she went to find the Mayor. He heard that she was coming and fled his office.

When Mrs. Nation entered the Chicago City Hall, in the mob that came after her were a dozen disciples—perhaps half a dozen—and a few half-hearted sympathizers; then there came loafers, pickpockets, criminals, a few young gentlemen with nothing better to do, a few emotional people swept away from sedentary pursuits by the hypnosis of mob spirit, and a cloud of witnesses for the newspapers. Mrs. Nation was clearly conscious of the presence of her escort—and quite proud of it.

At the head of this hooting throng, Carry Nation entered the Chicago City Hall. When she found that she could not scold the Mayor, the crusader mounted a wide, black-walnut railing in the great anteroom to the Mayor's office. There she stood, with hair disheveled, with wild, glowing eyes, with radiant face reflecting the hysteria, and began to harangue the crowd. She waved her arms; her voice creaked with excitement, her hands beat the air. At first the throng was silent, then it began to titter, then to jeer and howl.

Carry Nation was six feet tall, weighed 175 pounds and felt, since saloons were flourishing in direct violation of certain prohibition laws, it was her duty to smash them. With axes, which she later sold as souvenirs, she made kindling of bars, bottles, fraternal orders, tobacco, corsets, foreign foods, too-short skirts and paintings of nudes. Her activities helped bring about the ratification of the Prohibition Amendment in 1919 which introduced the nation to the power of big-time crime, and the fun of being thirsty in the 1920's.

The Suffragette

by Mary Roberts Rinehart

(May 1914)

The men voted to pave the street and I had to pay for it. But that is not all. The minute the street was paved, some more men came along and raised my taxes because the street was improved! So I paid three hundred dollars to have my taxes raised! Is that reasonable? Is that government? Well, that made me strong for suffrage. But I am not militant. You know as well as I do that it is coming. The American men are just doing what a father does at Christmastime. For about a month beforehand he talks about hard times and not seeing his way clear and all of that. And on Christmas morning he comes downstairs awfully glum, with one hand behind him. We always play up and tell him never mind—maybe he can do it next year. And we are always awfully surprised when he brings his hand round with checks for everybody, bigger than they had expected.

And so, just as soon as the men realize that we are really in earnest about the vote, they will give it to us with bells on it.

A suffragette marches down Constitution Avenue in Washington to draw attention to women's rights. After the parade, some of the women were arrested and hauled off to jail. When they emerged, their captors were amazed to find them adamant in their demands. The movement had begun in England in the 1800's, but it was 1920 before the Nineteenth Amendment was passed granting universal suffrage. Women now constitute 53 percent of the vote in the United States, besides holding governorships, senate seats and cabinet posts.

Woman: A Technological Castaway

by Clare Boothe Luce

(January 1974)

After a lifetime of casting about in the depths of female psychology, Sigmund Freud made this anguished entry in his diary: "What do women want, my God, what *do* they want?"

The feminist answer is "By God, they want Freedom!" They want to be free, as men are free, to fulfill their own potentials and to seek their own identities. They want political, economic, and social equality with men. And this equality, the feminists contend, is being denied them by overt and covert masculine coercion.

The feminists would seem to have their work cut out. Male supremacy is the most obvious and massive fact of our society.

All our social institutions that exercise power, generate wealth, create the law, form the minds, and guide the actions and opinions of society are male dominated.

The government, military, judiciary, labor unions, churches, universities, communications and advertising media, the banking, production, insurance, and transport systems, and all the significant professions (law, science, medicine, engineering, architecture) are male oriented. Men make all the crucial decisions for society.

In all our great institutions, whether public or private, there are not a hundred women who occupy high policy-making positions. The sporadic appearance of women in so-called top-level appointive political jobs is still largely female tokenism.

Of America's 80 million adult women, only 30 million are gainfully employed. Although women twenty and over now account for one-third of the labor force, the vast majority are working in menial, sex-typed, or dead-end jobs. Women are the "domestics" of the Male Establishment.

The only institution in which women appear in equal numbers with men is our institution of monogamous marriage (80 percent of all adult women are or have been married). Legally, marriage is the most male-dominated institution of all. It is the only institution in which women are expected to work without receiving any stipulated wages and with no fixed working hours. A woman who enters marriage penniless (as most women do) becomes totally dependent on her husband for bed, board, clothing, and whatever monies she may need for running his house and caring for their children. He can give her as much or as little as he chooses. She has no legal claim to any part of his property or income. He is legally responsible for her current debts, but he can also legally disavow future responsibility whenever he finds it too onerous.

If the marriage ends in divorce, the wife must go to work to support herself, or she must depend either on her ex-husband's charity or on the charity of the courts. This charitable handout is called alimony. Permanent alimony is awarded in only 2 percent of all divorces, and the average alimony award is less than 30 percent of the ex-husband's wages. In awarding child support, the majority of judges generally expect able-bodied women to go to work and to assume half the cost of supporting their children.

A recent government study of marriage, made on a nationwide basis, shows that only three out of twenty women profess to be happily married. Seven out of twenty "get along" but fight a lot. Ten out of twenty confess to being unhappy, but stick to their mates for "practical reasons."

Men come unstuck more easily than women. More than half the divorces granted are instigated by husbands. Husbands instigate the overwhelming number of divorces involving wives over forty. Many marriages end in the husband's desertion of the wife. Desertion, the "poor man's divorce," does not show up in the statistics.

The average woman who leaves marriage leaves it as poor as she entered it, a good deal older, and far less able to find employment with wages above the poverty level. About 40 percent of all families with a female head are below the poverty level. In every marriage there are two marriages, his and hers. His is better.

It's a man's world, no two ways about it.

The second obvious fact about our society is that, married or unmarried, this is the way most women seem to like it. The married, however, like it better. Given a (pollster's) choice between the unpaid and increasingly insecure job of "married woman" and any of the other jobs that the Male Establishment offers, women opt overwhelmingly for the job of homemaker. Hands down they prefer the gratifications of motherhood, the privileges of wifehood, and the status conferred by society on the title Mrs. to the condition of the unmarried woman working in a man's world.

But married or unmarried, happy or miserable, the vast majority of women accept their unequal social status. And when they are not indifferent to the efforts of the organized and activist feminists to achieve sex equality, they are openly hostile to them. A recent survey showed that more women than men accept the stereotype view of Women's Liberationists as sexually frustrated, hysterical, and unfeminine creatures who, if not "old bags," are probably lesbians.

The fight of any group, class, or minority for equality in a democratic society must be waged in many ways and at many levels. But if it is to be made "within the system," it has to be energetically fought at the ballot box and in the courts.

Women have had the vote for half a century. Unlike the blacks or Chicanos, women *are not* a political minority. They represent 51 percent of the electorate. They are a political majority that is treated as a minority. If women, as a class, were to demand legal equality, vote-hungry politicians could not afford to deny it. Women, as a class, have made no such demand.

All surveys show that the majority of married women prefer to leave political questions—even those already affecting their own personal rights—in the hands of their husbands. It would seem that most women are intellectually, as well as economically, dependent on men.

The temptation is to leave the feminist question right there. It's a free society, and its female citizens have the right to pursue life, liberty, and happiness in any way they choose.

If they prefer the feminine gratifications and privileges of marriage to the rights enjoyed by men, and if they don't feel themselves to be an oppressed class, well, whose business is it but theirs?

Nevertheless, the widespread indifference of women to their own unequal status in a so-called free society calls for some rational explanation.

The antifeminist holds that the physiological and psychological differences between the sexes determine the roles they play—and prefer to play—as well as their condition in society. These differences are genetically and biologically ordained. Each sex possesses a "true nature." Woman's true nature is submissive, passive, dependent, and emotional. She is born with a "feminine mentality." The true nature of man is dominant, active, independent. He is born with a "masculine mentality." To boil this proposition down to simple language, woman thinks with her womb, man thinks with his penis. Their different "mentalities," so to speak, actually *exude* from their genital organs.

The standard position of the Women's Liberationists is that, while woman's reproductive systems differs from man's, there are no other natural differences between them. (Pause, for male chauvinists to say *vive la différence*.)

Each sex is inescapably stuck with its own biological functions, and cannot transfer them to the other. But roles (the parts people choose or are given to play in life) are both assignable and transferable. Generally, they are assigned—or reassigned—according to the preferences or prejudices of those who dominate the society. Sometimes a social emergency, great or small, causes a sudden reassignment of roles. War comes, and Rosie the housemaid becomes Rosie the riveter. Mother falls ill and father takes care of the baby and does the housework. Both riveting and child care are assignable and reassignable roles. The assignment of roles to the sexes is often wholly arbitrary. Once a role is assigned, however, the tendency is to give the assignment the force of natural law, either directly or *à deuxième main*. Riveting is "naturally" man's work. But Rosie is doing the "unnatural" work only because it is "natural" for woman to back up her fighting man.

What man now calls woman's natural feminine mentality is the unnatural slave mentality he forced on her, just as he forced it on the blacks. He made her the "house nigger." (Many women's liberationists see women as "nigger.") In the end, men dropped the shackles from woman's body only because he had succeeded in fastening them on her mind. This, according to the women's liberationists, he finally did only very recently.

Man did not grant women the vote until he was reasonably certain that her slave mentality had become second nature and that she would not act to bring about her own emancipation.

Inner Vision

by Helen Keller

(March 1951)

People often express surprise that I find life great and wonderful, when I have only three senses. From others' testimony, I know that at the age of nineteen months, I was exploring the world with five senses, playing, laughing and learning a few words. Then came the illness which deprived me of sight and hearing, and as a result of deafness I lost the ability to speak.

Untaught, unstimulated, I acted and thought like a mere animal. I cannot convey verbally the state I was in—wrapped in a double silence—my own and that of others to me. I was a wild creature.

The change which occurred after Anne Sullivan began my education still causes me to thrill and glow. It was not a child that confronted her, but an animal utterly ignorant of itself, its feelings and its place among human beings. She treated me exactly as a seeing, hearing child, substituting hand-spelling for the voice and the eye from which other children learn language.

I am not a teacher or an educator, but I have always believed that infants should be taught as soon as possible—before they speak—to notice objects pretty or delightful or unusual. If the mother puts as much gentle art into this delicate fostering of all his physical powers as she does into the task of preserving his health, her reward will be past calculating. The child's five senses are faithful fairies who, if cherished and heeded, will surrender to him their priceless tokens of royalty—the splendor at the rainbow's end, the seven-league boots of imagination, lovely dreams fulfilled.

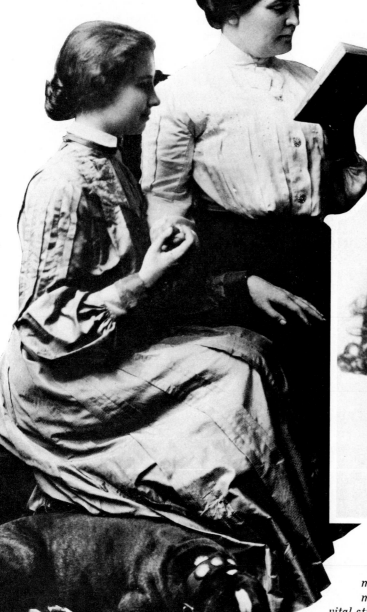

Helen Keller with Anne Mansfield Sullivan, the miracle worker who gave the deaf blind girl her speech. Miss Keller wrote, "The problems of deafness are deeper and more complex . . . than those of blindness. Deafness is a much worse misfortune, for it means the loss of the most vital stimulus—the sound of the voice—that brings language, sets thoughts astir and keeps us in the intellectual company of man." Inspired by her Bell helped to develop the hearing aid.

Evolution

by Margaret Mead

(December 1962)

We are the inheritors of a tradition of service that was established by women who left their homes, many of them never to return. In these days of great freedom, when education is as open to women as to men, when the great professions of medicine and law, teaching and scientific research are open to women, we may well ask: How do we women stand?

The answer is simple. We stand badly needed. We may well ask, why have we returned to the Stone Age? Women's main ambition today is to acquire and hold a mate, to produce or adopt children who are to be the exclusive delight and concern of a married pair. Work outside the home, whether it be such traditional occupations as teaching or nursing, office or technical work, holds no attraction in itself, unless it is subservient to the demands of an individual household. The woman who does not marry is frowned upon, given neither status nor honor. Girls are admonished to study typing rather than mathematics, and if, after the children are grown, women look for some greater meaning in life, their eyes usually are turned toward a hobby or community busy-work.

Margaret Mead discovered America in New Guinea, Samoa and Bali, found that labor divisions in most cultures were arbitrary, that women built the home, cultivated the land, traded, and practiced medicine in one society while those same occupations might be engaged in by males in other societies. Her studies of pre-industrial societies, which showed that women often divested themselves of their young after they were weaned, have persuaded American women to find new lives in new careers—34 million now work outside the home.

117

First Fall

by Pearl Buck

(April 1972)

I think we Americans, being so young and unsophisticated, have a completely wrong idea of what true sophistication is. According to Asian definition, which I myself believe to be correct, a sophisticated person is one who has experienced everything, knows everything, and has reduced everything to its essence. Sophistication is the final simplicity.

It is only an American, born and reared in an alien country, who can appreciate fully the amazing beauty of the American woods in autumn. Inexplicably, no one had prepared me for it. I had lived all my days in a calm Chinese landscape, lovely in its way with delicate, swaying bamboos, curved temple roofs mirrored in lotus pools. It was gently colorful too, in blues and greens. But when summer was gone, and chrysanthemums had glowed and faded, the colors were put away for the most part until next spring.

Thus, when, after a loitering journey eastward, I found myself walking through a wood in Virginia, how can I put the excitement into words! No one had told me how paganly gorgeous it would be. Oh, of course they had said, "The leaves turn in the fall you know," but how does that prepare one? I had thought of pale yellows and tans and faint rose reds. Instead, I found myself in a living blaze of color—robust, violent, vivid beyond belief. I shall never forget one tall tree trunk wrapped about a vine of flaming scarlet, standing outlined, a fiery sentinel, against a dark, rocky cliff.

There was a maple walk which might have been the pathway to the golden streets of New Jerusalem. Wandering anywhere, above crimson and seal brown, and yellow of purest quality. There can be nothing like it on this earth. Do the Americans realize it every year?

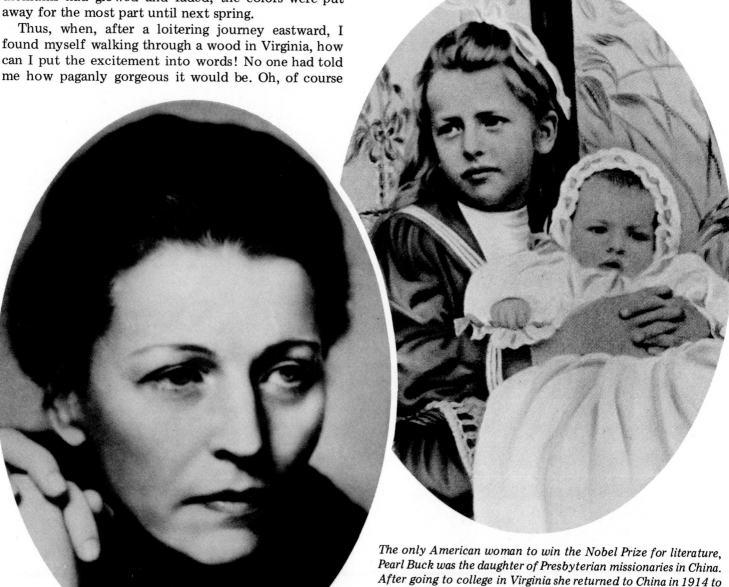

The only American woman to win the Nobel Prize for literature, Pearl Buck was the daughter of Presbyterian missionaries in China. After going to college in Virginia she returned to China in 1914 to become a university teacher in Nanking. Out of her experiences she wrote The Good Earth, *which eventually earned her the Pulitzer Prize as well as the Swedish award. Miss Buck wrote more than eighty books. Her humanitarian efforts raised $7 million for the illegitimate children of U.S. servicemen in Asia.*

On My Own

by Eleanor Roosevelt

(February 1958)

I remember the time when a young man made a study of American columnists for his college thesis and concluded that a reader should have at least two years of college to understand the columns of Walter Lippmann and Arthur Krock. But, he added, you need only a fifth-grade education to understand Mrs. Roosevelt's columns! So I am not an Egghead, but I am in favor of Eggheads in government if that means the application of our best intellects to the problems of government. I believe most voters feel the same way, and I do not think that the description of Governor Stevenson's advisers—or some of them—as Eggheads was detrimental to his campaign. I don't believe the voters want their candidates to be dumb.

A couple of "Egghead Ideas" were bitterly attacked. First, the question of abolishing the draft. We need a small career army, but the draft takes too much time out of a young man's life.

Another issue was the continued test explosion of atomic bombs. This was derided, but as everybody knows, it has become a problem of great concern to people everywhere.

FDR knits as he and Eleanor await the birth of their first child. Eleanor was the niece of Theodore Roosevelt and a cousin of her husband. When the handsome young Franklin was paralyzed by poliomyelitis, she urged him, against his domineering mother's wishes, to run for office again. To some Americans, FDR's four terms as president bordered on demaguery; to others, he pulled the country out of the Depression and ended the threat of Hitler. As controversial as the president was his wife, columnist, U.N. delegate and party power.

Women at War

by Harold W. Ickes

(February 1943)

In light of what women throughout the world are doing to help their menfolk win this war in the shortest
possible time, I am no longer in any serious
doubt that it would have been a mistake
not to make women. There may have
been occasion before Pearl Harbor
when I might not have felt that way,
and, even now, certain women snark
me into believing that they
shouldn't be here—but, for women
in general, that is my opinion.
Woman's sacrifice runs the gamut of
human experience, from the cradle to
the grave, the surrender to the slaughter of the sons she bore.

*Rosie the Riveter, modeled by Rockwell after
Michelangelo's figure of Isaiah in the Sistine
Chapel, sits with her foot nonchalantly resting on
a tattered copy of Adolf Hitler's* Mein Kampf.

Strength

by Barry Goldwater

(November 1973)

I would judge this Navajo woman to be well over eighty, and I know her to be a woman of strength. One day, while in the trading post on the south side of Navajo Mountain, I sold her a bale of hay. I told her I'd put the hay on her horse for her, but while I went back to get something else she wanted, she picked up the hay herself and had it halfway up on the horse when I got back. This was a determination born of a lifetime of having to do things for herself and she was really a bit upset when I tried to help her.

HOW
WE LOOKED

AMERICA DRESSES THE PART

At the beginning, Americans dressed like what they did. Frontiersman, blacksmith, banker, planter. But a greater need lurked in the national libido—a yearning for a king as model. Having blown George III off the continent, the nation which fought for independence then supinely accepted as royal decrees the dictates of King Fashion on what to wear and how to behave. One of the inner ironies of fashion is self-destruction: the minute you wear something, it is out of date. The evolution of obsolescence is the story of America's national drive to perpetually create and eternally destroy a source of never-ending income for designers, manufacturers, and retailers, and a font of refreshment for a public which plunges into new threads and discards the old with shrieks of delight and flourishes of greenbacks. But like any aging monarch, King Fashion is a sentimentalist. The Good Old Days return again and again as a golden theme. Witness our current infatuation with the mad, glad Twenties and the snazzy jazzy days. That was the time when fashion models were the idols of the nation, the Arrow Collar man the Burt Reynolds of the day, when the man in the Hart Schaffner & Marx or the Kuppenheimer suit had broader shoulders than any Pittsburgh Steeler, when the Jack Nicklaus of the moment wore a halo of butterflies and had a living cherub as his caddy. How exciting to dress like a bank robber with his moll, like Gatsby in search of his Daisy, or an Indian on a Kawasaki—especially if you are a divinity student! So now the great wheel has turned all the way: Americans dress the part once more, not like what they do, but like what they'd like to do. We have dethroned another King: the Fashion is to be yourself, and independence rules once more across the land.

(Right) Plus fours, wooden golf sticks, and an incongruously vested observer distinguish this Leyendecker threesome of the 1920's.

The Glass of Fashion

In putting on diamonds, the time to stop is when you don't have any more.

—Greer Garson

Navy blue remains the popular color for bathing dresses, and if flannel is selected it should be flannel of light quality, as the heavier flannels become too heavy for comfort when filled with water. There are dark gray flannel suits, but those of red flannel are not as much used as they formerly were.

—1879 fashion report

I don't pay much attention to my hair. A girl shouldn't waste time dressing her hair, if she thinks that's not the place where they're going to look.

—Marilyn Monroe

Now that telephones have grown to be common, and automobiles have begun and waxed, and country clubs have become a necessity, that delicate and tenacious vampire called style has fastened upon Mrs. Average Woman. Anything with last year's label is a badge of shame, a kind of scarlet letter. And because style is like ice and melts, quality and durability have been relegated to the background, like croquet sets and side-saddles and carriages and real buffalo robes.

—Maude Radford Warren, 1918

New fashions in dress produce new diseases. Diphtheria, that infectious form of sore throat, is said to have originated in the modern custom of wearing low, turndown collars, instead of the old still white walls, which now mark so conspicuously the middle-aged man. The national throat, guarded for so many centuries by ropes of muslin, black velvet solitaires, lace collars, and other knickknacks, was suddenly stripped of all its defenses, and thrown open to the rude winds. The result blossoms out in the disagreeable form of diphtheria, nature's terrible warning of the danger, and simultaneous correction of the folly. . . .

—1864

I don't have much time or taste, but when I'm well dressed I can look good, so I just go to Bergdorf's and tell them what I plan to do and ask them what I ought to wear. If Bergdorf's suggested a well-pressed fig leaf, I'd say OK.

—Wife of a TV executive

A hat can do more for a woman's ego than anything except a husband. A hat can say something the wearer can't—it can say "Look at me!"

—Sally Victor, haute couture milliner

Make the rocks bigger. Without diamonds, honey, I feel undressed.

—Mae West to Edith Head

Dr. T. Felix Gourand's Oriental Cream, or Magical Beautifier. Removes Tan, Pimples, Freckles, Moth Patches, Rash, and Skin diseases, and every blemish on beauty, and defies detection. It has stood the test of 40 years and is so harmless we taste it to be sure it is properly made.

—1893 cosmetic advertisement

Aren't people crazy to come in here and spend that much on a dress? Just think, mon cher, what they could do with those francs.

—Christian Dior

The careful dress of men in America is another point that strikes the visitor. Everybody, except those engaged at the moment in physical occupations, is well dressed. The fact implies a self-respect that is not lost on the English visitor. He misses the class distinctions; he misses them sometimes with a sense of loss, because they carry with them a prideful courtesy and consideration. On the other hand he is struck with the independence of all classes toward each other.

—A 1918 English visitor
on American dress

The journal Le Mode announces that furs have this season been taken into highest favor, and will be more universally worn than a great many years past. Not only will muffs, boas and pelerines be seen everywhere, but the warmth-infusing material begins already to pervade every article of the toilet.

—1840 fashion report

The 17th-century puritan maid bared nothing but her soul and that only on Sunday. The correlation between skin and sin persists in American fashion, causing skirt lengths and necklines to determine the morality of an age: flapper, short, bad. Victorian, long, good.

Colonial Couple

by Samuel G. Atkinson

(November 1822)

During the siege at Boston, General Washington consulted Congress upon the propriety of bombarding the town of Boston. John Hancock was then president of Congress, and he had all his estate at Boston. After he left the chair, he addressed the chairman of the committee of the whole in the following words:

John Hancock in 1765 wore a melton cloth suit with gold braid. Five years later he would affect the simpler clothes of the patriot. Bad management and inattention to his business caused him to lose a large part of the huge fortune he had inherited from his uncle.

"It is true, Sir, nearly all the property I have in the world is in houses and other real estate in the town of Boston; but if the expulsion of the British army from it, and the liberties of our country require their being burnt to ashes—*issue the order for that purpose immediately.*"

Dorothy Quincy was painted by Copley four years before her marriage to John Hancock. The lace on her party dress was imported from France though the mahogany table is probably American. The marriage united the richest merchant families in Massachusetts.

Fashion

by Marshall McLuhan

(July 1968)

Many people have commented on clothing as weaponry, as Carlyle did on institutions as clothing, but there are a good many unexplored facets of the topic of clothing and fashion.

For a century, to take one example, the French had made strenuous efforts to induce their Arab colonials to strip off the purdah. In the Algerian "troubles" of 1954 to 1958, things were reversed. The Arabs themselves actually had their women take off the purdah so that they might infiltrate the enemy ranks in European guise. Without the purdah these hapless females were not only unable to infiltrate European precincts, they were unable to cross the street. The stark, staring confrontation with motorcars and buses induced hysteria. Even worse, when they resumed the purdah and returned to their old surroundings, they discovered that they had become alienated from them and had undergone a radical sensory change.

At a quite different level, Africans attempting to acquire literacy have found it expedient to wear European costume for the simple reason that it retains a great deal more bodily heat and energy than their native costume. The act of reading printed matter drains off a huge proportion of human energy, as any convalescent knows. Anthropologists are well acquainted with the fact that the scantily clad native cannot go without food and water for more than twenty-four hours because of the rapid dissipation of his energies over the entire surface of his exposed body. On the other hand, the heavily clad Eskimo in a most inhuman environment can last for six or seven days without food or water. In contrast to the Western function of clothing, desert dwellers wear heavy clothing to exclude the heat.

These are all simple cases of clothing as weaponry designed to combat hostile conditions, and an inventory of such weaponry could easily be extended. Clothing as an extension of the human skin is as much a technology as the wheel or the compass. Strangely, the world of fashion has never been approached from this point of view. Is it merely a "bore war"? Is it merely an attempt to add a bit of spice and variety to the monotony of life? Possibly the fact that there is no such thing as fashion in native societies may provide an approach to this question. In these societies clothing indicates age and status and serves complex ritual functions that relate the energies of the tribe to cosmic forces, as much as we relate our energies to tanks and airplanes. Clothing is power and the organization of human energy, both private and corporate. In tribal societies they prize the integral power of the corporate far above the variations of the individual costume. In fact, when all members of the tribe wear the same costumes, they find the same psychic security that we do in living in uniform, mechanized environments. Since our environments are so drastically uniform, we feel we can afford a wide play of private expression in behavior and costume. However, when we seek to rally the corporate energies for sharply defined objectives, we do not hesitate to impose uniforms. Both the military costume of the citizen as robot and the ceremonial costume of the elite at dignified functions are exact parallels to the tribal use of costume. It is somewhere in between the military uniform and the fixity of formal attire that the world of fashion falls.

Is then fashion the poor man's art? Is it an attempt to adjust the sensory life to a changing technological environment? It would seem very likely that this is the case. The teenagers have begun to experiment with clothing as an artist does with his pigments. Many of the hippies make their own clothes, and many of the clothes worn by teenagers look as though they've never been made by anybody. There is, nevertheless, an unmistakable rapport between the shaggy and disheveled garments of the teenaged male and the sounds of the music and the look of the art to which he also gives his loyalty. After 2,500 years of visual culture the violent switch to the audile-tactile stress, and resulting indifference to visual appearance, is a fact that concerns all our institutions and experiences. The world of fashion, whether at the level of the slob or the snob, now has the same textural qualities that express rebellion against the departing visual values. Colors play a very large part in this rebellion. Color is apprehended not by the periphery of the eye but by the central macula, and the shift from the outer to the inner area of the eye is as much a part of the information implosion as television has become in our time.

Considering clothing, then, as an anti-environmental gesture, whether physical or psychical, it becomes fascinating to study this language. The study of armor as a clothing related to the stirrup makes a nice correlation with the clothing of the cowboy or of the motorcar as clothing. The rapid change of car styles reveals it as a form of human clothing.

The miniskirt, of course, is not a fashion. It is a return to the tribal costume worn by men and women alike in all oral societies. As our world moves from hardware to software, the miniskirt is a major effort to reprogram our sensory lives in a tribal pattern of tactility and involvement. Nudity itself is not a visual so much as a sculptural and tactile experience.

Whereas clothing is the enclosed space of Western literate man, the attire of the medieval or Renaissance page boy and gentleman strongly stressed a world of contours. Again, if the enclosed attire of literate man strove for individualist and specialist effects, dichotomizing the attire of male and female, the exact opposite now seems to be true. A recent Associated Press story provides some examples:

"As women begin to look like and in a sense become men, the men, freed of the responsibility of running things . . . become more flamboyant," James Laver, British fashion historian, recently told an interviewer.

"Man is trying to get women to notice him," Mr. Laver said, "and I don't think his interest in clothing and colognes and so on is necessarily going to make him effeminate."

So what has he been doing lately to make women notice him, now that his wife is bringing home half the rent money?

He's wearing:

—Turtlenecks. Men have probably struck their hardest blow for fashion independence by snubbing the necktie, bowtie and a variety of other starched harness. Though the necktie industry swears it is not choked up over the trend, the turtleneck boom is still booming.

—Fur coats. Men are wearing rugged Persian lambs cut military fashion and moleskins in hardy trench styles. When the fur is mink, it is hidden unostentatiously as lining.

—Colored shirts. Television started it. Prominent people appearing on camera were asked to wear blue shirts because white bounces light. And since others wanted to look as though they were prominent enough

to be asked to be guests on television panels, they wore blue, too. After blue, could yellow, green or even pink be far behind?

Tom Hyman wrote a feature article for *The Saturday Evening Post* on the electronic clothes created by a twenty-year-old blonde:

A tall, battered wooden door, painted Day-Glo pink and blue, opens into a small loft. Inside, the first thing that greets the eye is a set of drums, set up against the far wall, flanked on one side by an amplifier and on the other by two electric guitars. Two windows are draped with American flags. Against another wall, beneath a four-foot-long sign that says Zoooooooom! in big red letters, a workbench is cluttered with screwdrivers, pliers, soldering equipment, sketch pads, pieces of plastic, scraps of metal, strips of Plexiglas, a deck of tarot cards, paintbrushes and cans of paint. A sofa nearby sags under the weight of bolts of exotic cloth, and scattered everywhere—in boxes, on tables, chairs, stools, on the floor—lie tangles of wire, battery packs, plugs, fuses, potentiometers, switches and electroluminescent lamps. Hanging on a lamp pole is a silver-colored jump suit with wires dangling from its unzipped insides.

The room could belong to some mad engineer working on his own private space program. Or it could be a garage for repairing Hispano-Suizas. Actually, it's a dress shop.

The owner of this mechanical jungle, located in a warehouse on East 18th Street in Manhattan, is twenty-four-year-old Diana Dew, the inventor of the electronic dress, and by any standard the most far-out fashion designer in the world.

"My clothes are designed to turn people on," she said. "Get rid of their inhibitions. Like taking LSD—with none of the hangups." . . . Equally intriguing was a line of night clothes and underwear treated with phosphorescent patterns that glowed in the dark. She turned out the light in the studio so I could get the full effect. "Great for making love in," she said.

Perhaps fashion is a kind of macro-gesticulation of an entire culture having a dialogue or an interfacing encounter with its new techniques.

Girlwatching

August 1888

*The brims are often puckered
with the same fabric. White, red or
green have it well nigh all their
own way, and I have just seen a
sweet fresh face peep from behind
a hat of this kind, with a full
bind of Liberty silk.*

May 1893

*Sailor styles are rampant.
The collars have fouled anchors,
the north star and regular bo'sun's
cords and whistles are around the
necks. Tailors are working night
and day to fill the demand.*

July 1929

*Pearls are much used for evening dress. Nothing can be more
becoming, as the pearl is the woman's ornament par excellence.*

May 1929
Jonquils are mixed with violets,
both Parmese and the ordinary
blue violet. Roses are either China
roses, or yellow tea roses; the
white lilac is another favorite
flower; in fact all spring
flowers are in good taste.

June 1893
All the old-time dainty needlework, the shirring, tacking, brier work, hemstitching,
tiny plaiting of satin ribbon, quillings of ribbon or lace and a profusion of embroidery
enter into the construction of summer dresses in every young woman's wardrobe.

The Great Turnout

by George Ade

(September 1930)

Certainly Riley was the most captivating and unusual man I ever knew. If you caught him from one angle, he was as innocent and unsophisticated as a callow young farmhand. If you gained his confidence and received his observations at first hand, he seemed to be, at times, four times as wise as Solomon or any professor in Harvard.

He was a great stickler for the courtesies of life, and hated the familiarities to which the loud talkers are addicted, and had a perfect horror of being shoulder-slapped or even touched. As he put it, he didn't like to have anybody come up and handle him. He was always immaculate in his attire and perfectly groomed. He was always ready to act, on a moment's notice, as best

(Left) Tweeds, such as the one worn by poet James Whitcomb Riley, replaced the somber black suits of the late Victorian period.

Dressed for sight-seeing in shirtwaists and straw hats, these women drop their handkerchiefs in a geyser at Yellowstone National Park.

man at a noon-day wedding. He was for dignity and believed in the dignity which should accompany any man who is trying to do something in the world of letters. In his later years he did not want to say very much about his early and rather vagabond experiences, when he played the guitar and sang with the Wizard Oil Medicine Company, and was a journeyman sign painter, and for a while advertised himself in the small towns as a "blind sign painter." He had moss-agate eyes, and his business partners assured the public that he was stone blind; therefore when he felt his way up a ladder and painted a show sign above the entrance to some store, his feat was properly regarded with wonder and admiration.

(Right) The turn of the century saw the introduction of sports clothes for men. Playwright George Ade poses in his knickers suit.

Suited for a day of bathing and fishing leisure, three sportswomen are well protected from the elements as they display the day's catch.

Collars

(May 1828)

What an inconsistent creature is fashion. She was born in April, and has ever since exhibited the spirit of her natal month. Is it not high time for her to permit the gentlemen to disenthrall their necks from cravats and starched collars. A cravat is the most uncomfortable of all things; it restricts respiration, heats the head, and produces apoplexy. Nor does it add any charm to the appearance, while it sends comfort into exile. It hides from the eye the beautiful union of the head with the neck, brings on a premature double chin, and gives an air of clumsiness to every motion of the head. Nor is the starched collar any better. One might as well have a butcher's knife under his ears; its sharp corners stick in his cheeks every time he laughs. We pray that her highness will take these matters into consideration.

The Arrow collar man, pieced together as an ideal man by Leyendecker, received 17,000 letters the first month he appeared in magazines.

How We Looked

Hats

(October 1882)

Of all the tyrannies, the most ancient and the most universal is that of fashion. Philosophers laugh at it; but show us a philosopher who is philosophic enough to wear in broad daylight his grandfather's Sunday hat.

Is it not a good hat? It is an excellent hat. The soft and silken fur of the beaver covers it; it glistens in the sun with a resplendent gloss. The original proprietor wore it with pride. What is the matter with this superior hat? The hat is simply out of fashion; nothing more. The present owner knows that, if he were to wear it, his friends would take him for a madman. So rooted, so unconquerable is this tyranny which many of us deride yet all of us choose to obey after all.

Fashion runs endlessly in cycles. Vests, wide lapels and collar pins are back. Only spats and striking poses are waiting in the wings.

135

Life in the White House

by Julie Nixon Eisenhower

The most frequent request of visitors to the White House—and one which almost always must be denied—is "Can we see what it's like upstairs?" Upstairs are the bedrooms and private sitting rooms of the President and his family. Ever since the mansion's first First Lady, Mrs. John Adams, hung her laundry in the cavernous expanse of what is now known as the East Room, Americans have been fascinated by every aspect of life in the White House. The rich lore which records the comings and goings of the thirty-eight families provides us today with a unique microcosm of 200 years of changing fashions, furnishings, tastes and lifestyles.

Some presidents and their families were undoubtedly unaware that, with every action, they might have been setting a precedent. An amusing story is that of Calvin Coolidge's breakfast for congressional leaders at the White House. When the President poured coffee and cream into his saucer, a few of the guests immediately followed suit before they realized the saucer was intended for Coolidge's dog, who was waiting patiently under the table. Others who have lived in the White House, however, were only too keenly aware of the glare of public interest. Eleanor Roosevelt once remarked that in choosing a dress she no longer simply selected clothes for herself, but felt she was "dressing a public monument."

Each First Lady consciously or unconsciously developed an image and style all her own. I believe the official White House portraits, almost all painted from life, reveal much about the woman and her times. For example, Angelica Singleton Van Buren, painted by Henry Inman (one of the great artists of the day), was hostess to her father-in-law during his four years in the White House. The richness and elegance of her gown and jewels is worthy of a young woman whose marriage was arranged by the legendary Dolley Madison.

Grace Goodhue Coolidge and her collie, Rob Roy, were painted by a former Post *illustrator, Howard Chandler Christie.*

Henry Inman's portrait of Angelica Singleton Van Buren is considered one of the finest paintings in the White House collection.

The dress Angelica Van Buren selected to wear for her portrait is the one in which she was presented to Queen Victoria at the Court of St. James.

The portrait of Grace Coolidge, though formal, has a warm small-town flavor which reflects the unpretentious styles of the Coolidges. Mrs. Coolidge's beloved collie, Rob Roy, shares the spotlight with his mistress; and pinned to Grace Coolidge's velvet dress is her Pi Beta Phi sorority pin.

Aaron Shikler created a dreamlike mood in his portrait of Jacqueline Kennedy. The painting is the only White House portrait with a hint of impressionism. The French sculpture in the background conveys Mrs. Kennedy's love of art.

As one reads about the joys and sorrows, the likes and dislikes, the small moments and the large in the lives of those who have called the White House home, it is much easier to understand how decisions were made and history was shaped. And, in the process of studying the White House, I think we discover more about what we are like as a people.

Aaron Shikler's portrait of Mrs. J.F. Kennedy, painted in Mrs. Kennedy's New York apartment, was presented to the White House in 1970. The artist also painted, posthumously, President John Kennedy. Both pictures show a strong, French influence.

Edith and Woodrow Wilson in the procession which followed the Unknown Soldier's body to Arlington, November 11, 1921. He had insisted on a carriage though the other vehicles were motor cars. Wilson's somber clothes reflected the collapse of his dream of world peace.

CONFLICT

A NATION'S GROWING PAINS

The labor of this country's birth was mild compared to the bloodbath revolutions of Russia and France. The midwife was economic discontent, not class distinction. Taxation without representation was merely an elimination of the middleman, a catastrophe in a land that was to become a nation of middlemen. Americans like Jefferson and Franklin were forced to lobby against their own interests in alien corridors. As an indication of how little they wished to succeed in isolating the colonies, both men regarded their years abroad among their happiest.

The status quo never makes wars. America demanded the profits of its own labors, but it was with a certain social regret that the country achieved its independence.

Independence has adopted many guises in America, including civil disobedience. Men like Samuel Adams and Henry David Thoreau are perhaps the spiritual ancestors of the young people of this century who staged—drama was its essence—a minor revolution, the results of which were a lowered voting age, elimination of the military draft, and a voice in university affairs—ends which sound very much like the means of a declaration of independence.

With power has come the responsibility of leadership, a baton most Americans have been reluctant to take up. But overseas interests, growing internationalism and the necessity of keeping world trade lanes open have made it impossible for a nation to isolate itself. The United States, monolingual, its melting pot thoroughly standardized, has faced inevitable conflicts with unfamiliar ideologies and cultures. The Monroe Doctrine was perhaps as much an outpouring of the insularity of the American spirit as it was a protective device to guard the Western Hemisphere against European colonization. But the conflict within the American spirit is an ongoing examination in which faith more than confidence, right more than might, and objectivity more than subjectivity promise the continuity of the country's original ideals.

(Right) Bird watching. J.C. Leyendecker's god of war, Mars, contemplates the dove of peace, small, but like the sun, making an appearance every now and then.

Battle Cry

A whole government of our own choice, managed by persons whom we love, revere and can confide in, has charms in it for which men will fight.

—John Adams

"Almighty and most merciful Father, we humbly beseech Thee, of Thy great goodness, to restrain these immoderate rains with which we have had to contend. Grant us fair weather for battle. Graciously hearken to us as soldiers who call upon Thee that, armed with Thy power, we may advance from victory to victory, and crush the oppression and wickedness of our enemies and establish Thy justice among men and nations. Amen"

—General George S. Patton, prayer sent on card of greeting to every soldier in his 3rd Army, Christmas 1944

God forbid we should ever be twenty years without a rebellion.

—Thomas Jefferson

There is a time to preach and a time to fight; and now is the time to fight.

—John Peter Muhlenberg, 1776

We must determine, each of us, to do his or her part in spreading understanding among peoples, for while understanding is no guaranty of peace, without understanding there will be no peace. And as we strive, with the fortitude and nobility that Americans always possess in great crises, we shall experience the satisfaction that such efforts induce. We must recognize once more, as we have in the past, that happiness is often the child of sacrifice.

—Dwight D. Eisenhower

It is the united voice of America, to preserve their freedom, or lose their lives in defense of it.

—Joseph Warren, 1774

Call it independence or what you will, if it is the cause of God and humanity it will go on.

—Tom Paine, 1775

One of the difficulties we encountered with regard to gas shells was the spreading of the alarm among men in trenches. In some battalions it was the custom for men to spread the word of a gas alarm by taking off their steel helmets and beating them with their bayonets. This certainly makes good old noise, but unfortunately it is just when gas shells are coming over that shrapnel is also likely to be in the air, and to deprive a man of his tin hat at this time in order to provide him with a gas alarm is rather like robbing Peter to pay Paul.

—Major S.J.M. Auld, July 6, 1918

All wars are follies, very expensive and very mischievous ones. When will mankind be convinced of this, and agree to settle their differences by arbitration?

—Benjamin Franklin, 1783

Tyranny, like hell, is not easily conquered; yet we have this consolation with us, that the harder the conflict, the more glorious the triumph. What we obtain too cheap, we esteem too lightly; it is dearness only that gives everything its value.

—Tom Paine, 1776

It became so that there was no human relationship, however sweet, however dear, which did not, beside this one here experienced, fade into distant nothingness. The regiment displaced all our other loves. It became a glorious symposium of father, mother and sweetheart; gave, asked and received our dying all.

—A World War I soldier writing from the trenches

Before we can win the war in France we must put every idler in America to work. War is the wonder cure for idleness. There is a war job ready and waiting for every piano-pounding girl, lounge lizard, tango queen, poolroom hobo, doll and he-doll, perfect lady and imperfect gentleman in the country—all good jobs at useful work.

—1918 Saturday Evening Post *editorial*

(Right) Post *cover character Willie Gillis gives in to the battle of the bulge as waged by two USO ladies a long way from home.*

PT 109

by Robert J. Donovan

(November 1961)

PT 109, commanded by Lieutenant (j.g.) John F. Kennedy, was on night patrol, cruising in 200 fathoms of water, when the Japanese destroyer *Amagiri* rammed her. There were islands all around, but that meant nothing to the survivors struggling in the water. The nearest land was 1,200 feet, straight down. The next closest offered scarcely more of a haven. Hidden by darkness, Kolombangara Island, crowned by its extinct volcanic cone, rose from the sea a little more than two miles east. But the Japanese held it. Wherever the survivors of *PT 109* turned, there was only risk—risk of being captured and possibly tortured, risk of drowning in deep waters or amid seething coral reefs, risk of an even grimmer death from unseen sharks.

That was the outlook for John Kennedy and his shipmates early on the morning of August 2, 1943. The enemy destroyer had sped northwest to Rabaul. Two other PT's, cruising behind Kennedy's craft, launched four torpedoes but missed the destroyer. Then, with gasoline flames from the shattered *109* dancing high, the other PT's left in the night. All thirteen men on board the *109* were given up as dead.

Two were dead. Eleven, including Kennedy, managed to stay afloat through a nightmare of shock and fire. The ramming caught part of the crew on deck, part below; part awake and part asleep. In the engine room, Motor Machinist's mate Patrick McMahon—"Pop" to the younger men because he was thirty-seven years old—was checking an engine gauge when the ramming flung him sidewise and sat him flat. Mate William Johnston was asleep. He was awakened by being knocked into the sea and saw the destroyer sliding by with the Japanese sailors running on deck. Ensign George H.R. Ross was attempting to load a 37-mm antitank gun lashed to the bow when the *109* reeled and broke apart. Gasoline fumes choked him and he fainted. The other three on the bow were Lieutenant Kennedy, Radioman John E. Maguire and Seaman Edgar E. Mauer. Fearing that the bow would explode, Kennedy ordered his men into the water and jumped with them. As the flames around the derelict bow subsided, Kennedy concluded there would be no explosion. He and Maguire and Mauer swam back and climbed on board. Kennedy told Mauer to get the blinker and flash it periodically as a beacon for men who might be alive in the water. Then he stripped off his

shoes, shirt and sidearms and dived overboard in a rubber life belt to make a personal search.

On the bow Maguire and Mauer heard someone call, "Mister Thom is drowning! Bring the boat!" Maguire tied one end of a line to a torpedo tube and the other around his waist. He began paddling toward the voice. The call came from Machinist's Mate Gerard E. Zinser, who never saw the *Amagiri*. He heard a cry of "General quarters!" and then found himself flying through space. For an instant, he saw flames. Then he fainted in the water. When Zinser came to, he found Ensign Leonard Thom floating nearby. Just then Ensign Ross, who had passed out from the fumes, recovered enough to spot Zinser and Thom. All three men joined in shouting for help. Maguire, guided by the chorus, swam up and led the three toward the blinking of Mauer's light.

Kennedy's water search rounded up two more men: "Pop" McMahon and Charles Harris. When Kennedy arrived, Harris told him, "McMahon is too hurt to swim." Kennedy replied, "All right—I'll take him back—part of the boat is still floating." But McMahon mumbled feebly, "Go on, skipper, you go on. I've had it." Kennedy took McMahon in tow, finally bringing him to the *PT 109*'s bow.

Johnston called for help, retching and groggy from swallowing and inhaling gasoline. Thom swam out and towed Johnston to the wreckage. Among the last of the eleven survivors to make it safely to the bow was Torpedoman Raymond Starkey. Starkey splashed up to the floating fragment of the boat about the time that Seaman Raymond Albert also reached it safely.

Lieutenant Kennedy caught his breath and took stock. Of the eleven men, all seemed to be in good condition except McMahon and Johnston. McMahon's face and limbs were badly burned. Johnston was alternately unconscious and racked by vomiting. At intervals, Kennedy called the names of the two missing men. But there was only silence; no answer ever came. The night, moonlit and starlit early in the evening, was now as black as tar.

When dawn came, the survivors propped up on deck and took comfort from the sight of Rendova Peak, rising above the nearest United States base, thirty-eight miles to the southeast. But daylight substituted the dread of exposure for the terror of darkness. With the protection of the night gone, the drifting crew could see buildings of some kind on Kolombangara and Gizo.

"What do you want to do," Kennedy asked his men, "fight or surrender?"

"Fight with what?" someone asked.

By ten o'clock that morning, the bow seemed to be sinking. It became increasingly evident to Kennedy that if help did not come within a few hours, he would have to order the men to abandon what was left of the boat.

Kennedy made his decision. He decided that all hands should swim three and a half miles west to the small islands at the southeastern tip of Gizo Island. As these islands extended out for four or five miles, they were well away from the eyes of the Japanese on Gizo. Of the four islands in the little group, Leorava and Three Palm Islet were too small to conceal eleven men. Naru, on the other hand, was large enough to support a Japanese outpost. Kennedy pointed past them to Plum Pudding Island, an oval of green a hundred yards long and seventy yards wide. As some of the men were better swimmers than others, Kennedy hit upon a device to keep them together. Two-by-eight planks, lashed under the 37-mm antitank gun before leaving Rendova, still floated off the bow. Kennedy ordered the men, "Swim together on this plank. Thom will be in charge." There were four men on each side of the plank, holding on with one arm and paddling with the other. A ninth man, often Ensign Thom, pushed or pulled at one end. All of them kicked.

Kennedy meanwhile undertook a special mission of his own. McMahon was totally helpless. McMahon remained silent as Kennedy helped him into the water, which stung his burns cruelly. Towing McMahon in spurts, Kennedy swam vigorously for ten or fifteen minutes, then paused to rest. Kennedy would ask, "How do you feel, Mac?" and McMahon invariably replied, "I'm O.K., Mr. Kennedy. How about you?"

Even handicapped by his tow, Kennedy gradually pulled ahead of the nine men on the plank. Near sundown Kennedy and McMahon drifted onto the clean white sand of Plum Pudding Island. McMahon, his hands grotesquely swollen, crawled out of the water on his knees and tried to drag Kennedy across the exposed beach to the trees. The beach was only ten feet wide but McMahon could not make it. Kennedy began vomiting salt water and collapsed on the beach. After a while,

Kennedy saw the men on the plank approaching. Altogether it had taken the men fully four hours to swim approximately three and a half miles.

Knowing that PT's passed almost nightly through adjacent Ferguson Passage on their way to explore Blackett Strait, they decided that someone should swim out into the passage to signal the boats. Stripping down to his underwear, Kennedy hung his .38 revolver around his neck by a lanyard and bundled a ten-pound battle lantern in a life jacket to float along.

"If I find a boat," Kennedy said, "I'll flash the lantern twice."

When Kennedy failed to return at daybreak, despair gripped the survivors. As the men lay at rest, watching the gulls, Maguire suddenly exclaimed, "Here's Kirksey!"—one of the men killed in the ramming. When he looked again, he saw it was Kennedy swimming in slowly from the reef. Thom and Ross dragged their skipper across the beach into the bushes. Finally he fell asleep. He woke briefly and told Ross, "You try it tonight."

Ross obeyed Kennedy. Reaching Ferguson Passage by dusk, he waited until well after dark. After a long wait, Ross swam back to Plum Pudding Island.

On the same night that Kennedy swam alone into Ferguson Passage seeking aid for his shipmates, the enemy landed 200 to 300 troops on Gizo Island. Next to Gizo, on little Sepo Island, the "Gizo Scouts," natives serving the Allies, kept an outpost. Spotting the Japanese movement, the scouts acted at once to inform their nearest Allied contact, Lieutenant A.R. Evans, an Australian coastwatcher, stationed across Blackett Strait. The two scouts paddled through Blackett Strait on what seemed like a routine mission. Their names were Biuku Gasa and Eronit Kumana. Biuku and Gasa noticed the *109* wreck on a reef. They paddled over to take a look.

Kennedy decided the only sure way to get help would be for Biuku and Eronit to paddle all the way to Rendova. He had Biuku husk a coconut. Kennedy inscribed a message: NATIVE KNOWS POSIT. HE CAN PILOT. 11 ALIVE. NEED SMALL BOAT. KENNEDY.

Well after ten p.m., Kennedy detected the rumble of PT boat engines. "Hey, Jack!" a voice called in the night. "We've got some food for you."

"Thanks," Kennedy replied dryly. "I've just had a coconut."

Two Defeats

Paoli

[1777]

Paoli, outside Philadelphia, was Mad Anthony Wayne's birthplace. It was assumed he knew his way around but the English, under General Viscount Howe's command, delivered a surprise attack on Wayne and his men which amounted to a slaughter.

Howe had arrived by sea from New York in a fleet of ships—260 in all—that constituted a virtual armada. Before embarking, Howe had tried unsuccessfully to engage Washington in battle in New Jersey, but by this time Washington had realized his only hope was to hold his army together so that the British would have something to fight. When they had accepted the fact that his band of stragglers constituted an enemy, then the British might start making mistakes.

By the time Howe's ships landed on the northern tip of Chesapeake Bay, fifty miles from Philadelphia, a valuable month of the summer which might have been spent in routing rebels had been consumed, and Washington had moved south blocking Howe's path to Philadelphia. Howe met Washington at Brandywine Creek September 11, and, employing the traditional British military-academy maneuver of flanking, put him on the run. Washington, by now having learned the art of retreat, suffered relatively few casualties and seemed ready and willing to fight again.

General Wayne was left behind with his division to occupy a secret position near Paoli Tavern and harass Howe's troops when they advanced.

Unfortunately the British intelligence learned where Wayne's men were, and troops under Major General "No-Flint" Gray were sent to surprise them in the darkness. Gray got his nickname that night; he made his men remove the flints from their guns so they could not fire and make noise that would alarm the Americans. Bayonets only were to be used.

The Americans were taken unawares. In the dim light of the campfires they suffered casualties numbering about 150, counting captured and wounded. The neighbors found 53 mangled and bloody bodies at the site, next morning. The British lost just ten men.

Was Wayne to blame? Probably not. He was later acquitted "with highest honors" by a court-martial that investigated charges that he had failed to heed an advance warning of the British attack.

Night, September 21, 1777, the scene of General Gray's bloody attack on Anthony Wayne's men near Paoli, Pennsylvania. This picture and the one opposite were painted by Xavier Della Gatta five years later, probably for a British officer who fought in the battle and who instructed the artist as to uniforms, weapons, and the deployment of troops. Originals of the paintings hang at Valley Forge, Pennsylvania.

Germantown

[1777]

On the night of October 4, 1777, Washington with 11,000 American troops attacked the 9,000 British regulars stationed in Germantown, now part of Philadelphia. The area had been settled by German Pietists in 1683 who established small craft shops (weaving, tanning, cobbling, wagon building, and later, in 1690, printing). Because of George III's German connections and the Hessian soldiers taking part in the war, there was some sympathy for the English on the part of the Germantown residents. As a center of publishing, it was also valuable to both sides for propaganda purposes. The main reason for assaulting the city, though, was its importance as the key defense of British-occupied Philadelphia.

Washington, desperate for victory after his recent defeat at Brandywine on September 11, 1777, hit on the extraordinary maneuver of assaulting the town from all four directions simultaneously. Unfortunately, a dense fog settled in, and Washington's army, composed in the main of raw recruits, ill fed, ill equipped and generally demoralized, ended by firing on its own columns. British reticence and the strict formal tactics of the King's army worked to its advantage. The English had only to stand and hold their lines. The American losses were double those of the British (535). Philadelphia was still held by the British, but the battle had one happy result in that the French, buoyed by the American victories at Saratoga, were assured that Washington's leadership and strategy could win the war for the Americans, thus embarrassing their old enemy, Britain, and consequently weakening the English colonial structure in the shaky balance of world power.

After the engagement at Germantown the British settled into snug winter quarters in Philadelphia while the Americans faced the rigors of a long, cold winter without adequate shelter, at Valley Forge.

Much of Germantown's rich architectural heritage has been preserved, including the house where Washington lived in the summers of 1793 and 1794 (the Morris House), Wyck, a rare example of late seventeenth-century building, and Cliveden, Chief Justice Benjamin Chew's home which became the British troops' armed fortress and which is depicted, not very accurately, in this painting.

The High Street in Germantown, October 4, 1777. The redcoats at right (120 of them) are taking up their position in the Chew house. Wayne's men (left) and Sullivan's (right) are advancing along the road. The treacherous fog has not yet descended. Wounded British soldiers are being carted off at the right, while two British officers (lower left) direct the action from astride picturesquely cooperative horses.

(Top) On July 21, 1961, a group of Civil War buffs reenact the First Battle of Bull Run (called First Manassas by the South), in which 37,000 Union men clashed with 35,000 Confederates. Some 5,000 were killed or wounded. A year later (bottom, and right), Second Manassas was run out again (August 29). In the original, General Lee with 50,000 men met General John Pope with 70,000 Federal troops. Pope withdrew; casualties were 35,000, but Lee had failed to create an offensive posture.

Brother Against Brother

(March 1864)

Latest News—The rebels crossed the Rappahannock at Fredericksburg on Wednesday night, and again on Friday morning at Morton's Ford, but were repulsed in both instances.

From Chattanooga we learn that the rebels, though large in force in our front, make no demonstrations. A despatch from Meridian says that General Sherman has gone down the Mississippi with his troops, evidently for the Red river.

(June 1864)

A Touching Incident.—Mr. John Seymour's report contains many thrilling incidents. We extract the following which transpired on the battlefield of Gettysburg:

A rebel prisoner asked a clean shirt for his young comrade whose fresh, but blood-stained bandages told of a recent amputation just above the knee.

One of the Sanitary Commission gave the shirt, but said the boy must first be washed. "Who will do that?" "Oh, any of those women yonder." A kind-looking woman from Philadelphia was asked if she was willing to wash a rebel prisoner. "Certainly," was the prompt reply. "I have a son in the Union army, and I would like to have somebody wash him."

With towel and water in a tin basin she cheerfully walked through the mud to the tent. Careful not to disturb the amputated leg, she gently removed the old shirt and began to wash him; but the tenderness of a mother's heart was at work, and she began to cry over him, saying that she imagined she was washing her own son. This was more than he could bear. He, too, began to weep, and to ask God to bless her for her kindness to him. The scene was too much for the bystanders, and they left the northern mother and the southern son to their sacred grief, wishing that tears could blot out the sin of this rebellion and the blood of this unnatural war.

(December 1864)

Latest News—Hood's army is said to be totally demoralized. He is reported to have told his corps to get off the best way they could with their commands. The rebel army is now beyond Columbia. The railroad is but little injured, and the trains run to Spring Hill. The enemy has lost fifty-one cannons, eighteen general officers, and 17,000 men.

(March 1865)

Latest News—General Sheridan commenced a movement in the Shenandoah valley on Monday week, and General Grant telegraphed to the War Department on Sunday that deserters report that Charlottesville, Va., General Early, and his entire force, counting 1,800 men, have been captured.

Army of the Potomac advices report that no new movements have taken place. Deserters continue to come in large numbers.

Hon. Abraham Lincoln was re-inaugurated President of the United States on Saturday.

March Through Georgia

by Edmund Deacon

(December 1864)

The whole loss in Sherman's army is believed not to have exceeded over one thousand in both columns. They averaged twelve miles per day, and a halt was made for a day once a week.

When the two columns were passing Milledgeville, one of them on each side, five scouts penetrated through to the city, and, meeting no opposition, penetrated into the very town. They coolly gave out that a large union force was just behind them, and the mayor thereupon surrendered the town. As the scouts were leaving, they encountered a company of the Sixth Georgia, whom they turned in the other direction by giving the information that the town was full of Yankees.

The Army, in its march to the sea, sweeping over an area of territory at least sixty miles in breadth, foraged extensively on the country over which it passed, and lived in the most sumptuous manner. Not a hungry man could be found in the command. They lived on poultry almost entirely; as General Sherman observed, "They had turkey even for breakfast, and would not look at pork, but," he added, "I can't speak so well of those whom I leave in the rear."

In 1868, General Sherman (center, with arm around daughter) and General Grant (by bird cage) met at Fort Sanders, Wyoming with Union Pacific railroad vice-president Thomas C. Durant to ease friction between the Central Pacific, which had employed Chinese coolies in laying its tracks, and the Union Pacific, whose builders had been Civil War veterans. Sherman and Grant were often called upon to be peacemakers.

Drummer Boy

by Henry Peterson

(March 1870)

Abram F. Springsteen (right) was the youngest soldier in the Union army. He enlisted at the age of eleven years and two months on October 15, 1861. He was assigned to the drum corps of Company A, 35th Indiana Regiment, when his parents caught up with him and demanded that he be sent home. He was discharged, December 23, 1861, but on his twelfth birthday, with his parents' consent, he reenlisted.

Springsteen took part in seventeen engagements during the war, was captured at Spring Hill, Tennessee on November 29, 1864, but escaped during that same autumn evening.

Springsteen was one of many young people who enlisted, especially from the border states, where slavery was hated by the yeomen who could not conceive of someone else doing their work. At first both North and South counted on volunteers to fill their ranks. Eventually, both had to adopt systems of military conscription. There were just 11,000 men in the United States Army when the conflict began; before it ended 1½ million men wore the Union blue, and that many the Confederate gray.

A Mathew Brady glass negative preserves this tranquil moment as faithfully as others preserve the blood and smoke of battle. Here we see the cozy side of war: headquarters of the First Brigade Horse Artillery at Brandy Station, Virginia. A visiting wife and dog pose with unidentified officers in front of snug cabins the men have built from the materials at hand (note the barrel serving to top off the chimney).

Man for the Ages

The warm and generous sympathies of President Lincoln are well illustrated in the following extract of a private letter from Lieutenant Wise, the friend of Lieutenant Worden, commander of the *Monitor*:

"That night I left the fortress and got Worden safe home in Washington city, when, leaving him to the care of my wife, I went with the Secretary to the President, and gave him the particulars of the engagement. As soon as I had done, Mr. Lincoln said, 'Gentlemen, I am going to shake hands with that man,' and presently he walked round with me to our little house. I led him upstairs to the room where Worden was lying with fresh bandages over his scorched eyes and face, and said, 'Jack, here's the President, who has come to see you.' He raised himself on his elbow, as Mr. Lincoln took him by the hand, and said, 'You do me great honor, Mr. President, and I am only sorry that I can't see you.' The President was visibly affected, as, with tall frame and earnest gaze, he bent over his subordinate; but after a pause, he said, with a quiver in the tones of his voice, 'You have done *me* more honor, sir, than I can ever do to you.' He then sat down while Worden gave him an account of the battle, and, on leaving, he promised, if he could legally do so, that he would make him a captain."

(July 1862)

Mr. Dicey, an English gentleman, is traveling in this country and writing some lively sketches of notable men about Washington. We quote the following:

"On the occasion when I had the honor of meeting the President, the company was a small one, with most of whom he was personally acquainted. I have no doubt, therefore, that he was as much at his ease as usual. There was a look of depression about his face, which, I am told by those who see him daily, was habitual to him even before his child's death. It was strange to me to witness the perfect terms of equality on which he appeared to be with everybody. Occasionally some of his interlocutors called to him 'Mr. President,' but the habit was to address him simply as 'Sir.' It was not, indeed, till I was introduced to him that I was aware that the President was one of the company. He talked little, and seemed to prefer others talking to him to talking himself; but, when he spoke, his remarks were always shrewd and sensible. You would never say he was a gentleman; you would still less say he was not one. There are some women about whom no one ever thinks in connection with beauty, one way or the other: and there are men to whom the epithet of gentlemanlike or ungentlemanlike appears utterly incongruous; and of such Mr. Lincoln is one. Still there is about him an utter absence of pretension, and an evident desire to be courteous to everybody, which is the essence, if not the outward form, of good breeding.

"The conversation was unrestrained in the presence of strangers, to a degree perfectly astonishing. Any

This photograph, from the National Archives, shows the crowd gathering at Gettysburg on November 19, 1863. The speaker's platform is left of center, marked by a vertical flagstaff. An enlargement of this segment of the picture (right) shows Lincoln seated, hatless, waiting his turn to speak. Edward Everett gave an oration that reviewed the course of the entire war and lasted two full hours before Lincoln rose and spoke the few words of consecration that rendered the day forever memorable.

remarks that I heard made, as to the present state of affairs, I do not feel at liberty to repeat."

(June 1864)

Mr. Lincoln's Last Anecdote—A gentleman just returned from Washington relates the following incident that transpired at the White House the other day. Some gentlemen were present from the West, excited and troubled about the commissions or omissions of the Administration. The President heard them patiently, and then replied: "Gentlemen, suppose all the property you were worth was in gold, and you had to put it into the hands of Blondin to carry across the Niagara River on a rope, would you shake the cable or keep shouting out to him—Blondin, stand up a little straighter—Blondin, stoop a little more—go a little faster—lean a little more to the north—lean a little more to the south? No, you would hold your breath as well as your tongue, and keep your hands off until he was safe over. The government are carrying an immense weight. Untold treasures are in their hands. They are doing the very best they can. Don't badger them. Keep silence, and we'll get you safe across."

Four score and seven years ago our fathers brought forth upon this continent, a new nation, conceived in Liberty, and dedicated to the proposition that all men are created equal.

Now we are engaged in a great civil war, testing whether that nation, or any nation so conceived, and so dedicated, can long endure. We are met on a great battle-field of that war. We have come to dedicate a portion of that field, as a final resting place for those who here gave their lives, that that nation might live. It is altogether fitting and proper that we should do this.

But, in a larger sense, we can not dedicate — we can not consecrate — we can not hallow — this ground. The brave men, living and dead, who struggled here, have consecrated it, far above our poor power to add or detract. The world will little note, nor long remember, what we say here, but it can never forget what they did here. It is for us, the living, rather, to be dedicated here to the unfinished work which they who fought here, have, thus far, so nobly advanced. It is rather for us to be here dedicated to the great task remaining before

us — that from these honored dead we take increased devotion to that cause for which they here gave the last full measure of devotion — that we here highly resolve that these dead shall not have died in vain — that this nation, under God, shall have a new birth of freedom — and that government of the people, by the people, for the people, shall not perish from the earth.

Lincoln wrote out six copies of the Gettysburg Address. This one was made for Edward Everett, chief speaker of the day, and is now owned by the Illinois State Historical Library.

A day after the speech, Everett wrote Lincoln to say: "I should be glad if I could flatter myself that I came as near to the central idea of the occasion in two hours as you did in two minutes."

Lincoln Shot!

A Special Dispatch

(April 1865)

President Lincoln and his wife, together with Miss Harris and Major Rathburn, this evening visited Ford's Theater for the purpose of witnessing the performance of the *American Cousin*.

During the third act, and while there was a temporary pause for one of the actors to enter, the sharp report of a pistol was heard, which merely attracted attention, but suggested nothing serious, until a man rushed to the front of the President's box waving a long dagger in his right hand and exclaiming, "Sic Semper Tyrannus!" and immediately leaped from the box, which was of the second tier, to the stage beneath, and ran across to the opposite side, thus making his escape, amid the bewilderment of the audience, from the rear of the theater, and, mounting a horse, fled.

The screams of Mrs. Lincoln first disclosed the fact to the audience that the President had been shot, then all present rose to their feet, rushing toward the stage, many exclaiming, "Hang him! hang him!"

The excitement was one of the wildest possible description, and of course there was an abrupt termination of the theatrical performance.

There was a rush towards the Presidential box, when cries were heard, "Stand back!" "Give him air!" "Has anyone stimulants?"

On a hasty examination, it was found that the President had been shot through the head above and back of the temporal bone, and that some of the brain was oozing out.

He was removed to a private house opposite to the theatre, and the Surgeon General of the Army and other surgeons were sent for to attend to his condition.

An immense crowd gathered in front of it, all deeply anxious to learn the condition of the President. It had been previously announced that the wound was mortal, but all hoped otherwise. The shock to the community was terrible.

The surgeons were exhausting every possible medical skill, but all hope was gone, the blood oozing from the wound at the back of his head.

The entire city tonight presented a scene of wild excitement, accompanied by violent expressions of indignation and the profoundest sorrow. Many shed tears.

Vice-President Johnson is in the city, and his hotel quarters are guarded by troops.

We learn that General Grant received intelligence of this sad calamity soon after midnight, at Philadelphia.

Lloyd Ostendorf of Dayton, Ohio treasures the small piece of a broken glass negative that bears this excellent likeness of Abraham Lincoln, made just one year before the President's assassination.

(Left) The gun that John Wilkes Booth used to kill Lincoln, a pocket derringer, is displayed with other relics of the tragedy in the museum at Ford's Theater. It is photographed on a contemporary newspaper to show its small size. (Center left) Ford's Theater as it appeared a few days after the assassination, draped in black as were most public buildings. There were no more gay theatrical evenings at Ford's for more than 100 years. The building was used for government offices until a collapse of its overloaded floors killed 22 workers and injured 65 more, in 1893. It was later used for storage, and then as a museum. In 1968 it reopened as a careful reconstruction of the original theater, and in 1975 another president, Gerald Ford, went there to see a play. (Bottom left) This photograph, the only one made of Lincoln after his death, was discovered in the files of the Illinois State Historical Library. It was taken while the body lay in state at New York's City Hall. There were, in all, twelve funerals in twelve different cities. In each location, floral tributes were heaped upon the casket, public buildings were decorated with greenery and swags of black cloth, and people lined the streets hours before the procession was to begin. Uncounted thousands of Americans waited in long lines to view the body, or along the railroad tracks, merely to see the black-draped funeral train pass by on its slow, sad journey across half the country. (Below) The New York City funeral procession was one of the most impressive. One hundred thousand persons marched, and it took nearly four hours to pass one point along the route. This picture, half of a stereopticon view, shows spectators crowded at windows and on rooftops to see Union troops march behind the horse-drawn hearse.

Spanish-American War

by Theodore Roosevelt

(October 1911)

The King of Spain, by the way, *was* worthwhile talking to. I was much impressed by him. He at first thanked me for having behaved with such courtesy and consideration to Spain, while I was President, and I told him, of course, that I had simply done my duty, for which I deserved no thanks, and that, anyhow, it was real pleasure for me to do anything I could for Spain.

He then said, looking me straight in the face, "I am glad to meet you, Mr. Roosevelt; I have admired your public career, and I have also admired your military career—though I am sorry that your honors should have been won at the expense of my countrymen."

I bowed and said: "Your Majesty, I have always borne testimony, and I always shall bear testimony, to the gallantry and courage your countrymen showed in battle; although, frankly, I cannot speak as highly of their leadership."

To which he responded: "I should think not! I should think not! But I am glad to have you speak thus of the courage of the soldiers"; to which I answered that I could not speak too highly of the courage that the Spanish had shown under very depressing circumstances.

*   *   *

From an anecdote of the Spanish-American War, September 1898
It was recently found out that Colonel Roosevelt really possesses that which Mr. Croker says any man running for Governor this fall will need—the evidence that he was wounded in battle. The story was told by a private in Colonel Roosevelt's regiment who is now in the hospital at Governor's Island. It was at San Juan Hill. Roosevelt and some other officers were standing together in a little clearing on the slope of the hill. Bullets were whistling all about them, and finally a fragment of shell struck Colonel Roosevelt on the back of the left hand.

It was a glancing blow, and simply scraped the flesh. The wound bled profusely. Colonel Roosevelt whipped out his handkerchief, bound his hand, and said:

"Well, that's the first one. They'll have to do better than that next time."

"Just as he said that," continued the Rough Rider, "a young officer standing near him was killed by a Spaniard up in the top of one of the trees.

"About that time I was sent into the trenches. Oh, but it was hot! After I'd been there for some time I was relieved to go back to take a rest. On the way I met Colonel Roosevelt. Although I was only a private, he noticed me and asked:

" 'Where have you been, my boy? Up in the trenches? It's hot as the devil up there, isn't it? Now, I'll tell you what to do. You go back there and tell my cook to make you some good coffee and give you a bite to eat. We can't spare any good men, and they must have enough to eat. Go along, now.' I tell you, you can fight for a man like that."

Theodore Roosevelt stands with his Rough Riders after the victories of June and July which defeated the Spaniards at the Battle of Santiago, and led to the destruction of Admiral Cervera's fleet on the southern coast of Cuba. The Rough Riders had penetrated the city's defenses, thus giving support to Admiral Sampson's efforts in the harbor and establishing the strength and reputation of the U.S. Navy.

On February 15, 1898, the battleship Maine exploded mysteriously in Havana harbor, killing 260 American sailors. She had been sent to Cuba to protect U.S. interests when Cuba revolted against Spain. The Spanish offered to submit the question of its responsibility to arbitration but the U.S. chose military intervention in April, after U.S. newspapers played national emotions into a fury.

The Great War

by Gen. John J. Pershing

(November 1921)

Our plunge into the World War, in the face of all our handicaps, was extremely courageous, but quite pathetic. One hesitates to contemplate the fate of Europe, and ourselves as well, if the grave of the Almighty had not seen fit to confuse our enemies and mercifully watch over our allies for more than a year while we undertook to train five million officers and men to provide them with munitions, airplanes and transports.

Primarily, the solution of the problem of defense against enemies from within lies with the

A GI shares his tea and toast with a Bretonne, who, dressed in her native costume, appears more ready for the artist than for the hardships France was to endure during the 1914-1918 war.

upbuilding of a sane citizenship, and the Army is doing its part to encourage this work. The obligation to assist falls upon every patriotic man and woman in the nation. The slump in patriotism and the consequent increase in the dangerous elements among us must be checked.

Viewing the world conditions in the light of the past few years, it is difficult to avoid the conclusion that we can no longer regard with disinterest the gathering clouds of war in several parts of the Northern Hemisphere. In Central Europe relations involving bankruptcy or disintegration arising out of world catastrophe have become critical, while Bolshevik Russia maintains a menacing attitude.

In 1917, we had only a small regular army, and the National Guard was only partly organized. The Draft Law had to be hastily drawn to meet the demand for men. There were only 14,000 regular and partially trained National Guard officers combined.

(Top) The Lusitania *was sunk May 7, 1915, by a German sub four miles off the Irish coast. Of the 1,959 passengers aboard, 1,198 perished. The ship was carrying munitions to England and as such was fair game, but it gave America another reason to get into the war. (Bottom) Doughboys arrive in a large midwestern city for a hero's welcome while young ladies on pedestals strew rose petals in their path.*

Battle Report

by General Douglas MacArthur

(1954)

"We now dominate the Moluccas. I rejoice that it has been done with so little loss. Our campaign is entering upon its decisive stage. Japanese ground troops still fight with the greatest tenacity . . . Their officer corps, however, deteriorates as you go up the scale. It is fundamentally based upon a caste and feudal system and does not represent strict professional merit. Therein lies Japan's weakness. . . . Gripped inexorably by a military hierarchy, that hierarchy is now failing the nation. It has neither the imagination nor the foresighted ability to organize Japanese resources for a total war. Defeat now stares Japan in the face . . . That failure may mark the beginning of a new and ultimately happier era for them; their hour of decision is close at hand.

His hand already wounded, a lonely soldier maintains a steaming vigil among tropic Asian flora. Dry uniforms were unknown.

World War II Diary

by Gen. George S. Patton

(November 1947)

August 1, 1944

The first Sunday I spent in Normandy was quite impressive. I went to a Catholic Field Mass where all of us were armed. As we knelt in the mud in the slight drizzle, we could distinctly hear the roar of the guns, and the whole sky was filled with airplanes on their missions of destruction. I shall always remember very unpleasantly the time I spent in the apple orchard, because I was obsessed with the belief that the war would end before I got into it.

While the 3rd Army did not become operational until 1200 on the first of August, General Bradley appointed me to command it by word of mouth on the twenty-eighth of July.

September 24, 1944

The twenty-ninth of August was one of the critical days in the war. Everything seemed rosy, when suddenly it was reported to me that the 140,000 gallons of gas we were to get on that day had not arrived. I later found the delay was due to a change in plan implemented by General Montgomery. It was my opinion this was the momentous error of the war. It finally ended with permission to secure crossing over the Moselle and prepare to attack the Siegfried Line whenever I could get fuel to move.

Like some strange insect, a fighter pilot prepares to add more rising suns to his fuselage in Mead Schaeffer's World War II cover.

Christmas dawned clear and cold; lovely weather for killing Germans, though the thought seemed somewhat at variance with the spirit of the day. As a whole, the day was not too successful. We continued to advance, but we had not relieved Bastogne.

With a sixty-pound pack and an automatic weapon, an artillery man scans enemy targets for the gun emplacement behind him.

Conflict

The eighth of May marked exactly two and one-half years since we had landed in Africa. During all that time until midnight of May 8-9, we had been in practically continuous battle, and, when not in battle, had been under the strain of continuous criticism, which I believe is harder to bear.

I said good-bye to the war correspondents after having a final briefing with them, during which one of them said, "General, why didn't we take Prague?" I said, "I can tell you exactly why," whereupon they all got their notebooks and looked expectant. I said: "Because we were ordered not to." They were disappointed.

Had I been permitted to go all out, the war would have ended sooner.

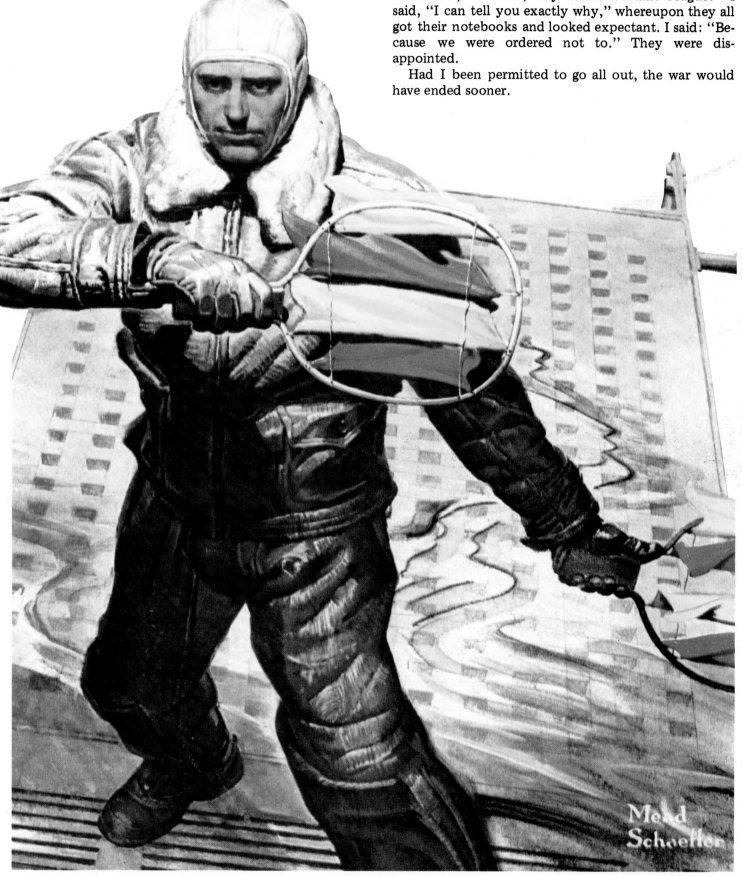

Aircraft carriers were floating cities and sometimes sitting ducks. Miraculously, when the carrier Lexington sank, all hands escaped.

A Private War

by P. G. Wodehouse

(July 1941)

It is generally agreed that at the conclusion of hostilities we shall see many changes from the old familiar conditions of the days before September 1939. Listen to any group discussing the shape of things to come and you will hear such statements as "Mark my words, after this war, things will be much altered."

It may be, of course, that these groups are discussing the future of Europe, but the probability is that they are referring to me. Since July 21, 1940, I have been a guest of the German government at a series of their justly popular internment camps. At this moment the whole world, you might say, is seeking to answer the question: "What is going to be the effect on Wodehouse of this spell in the cooler? Have we," civilization is asking, "got to go back to the same old codger we have seen puttering around these last sixty years or so, or will there emerge something new and unforeseen? In short, whither Wodehouse?"

Well, there may be some changes. Owing to my ef-

(Top) Eisenhower and Bradley take five in the European theater of operations. (Bottom) Hitler and Goering wring their hands with glee. Before the war was over, 27 million people would die.

forts, during the first few weeks of transplantation, to preserve a stiff upper lip, I have become too bright and sunny. I have developed a way of smiling dazedly at passersby and saying, "Good morning! Good morning! What a lovely morning!" with a sort of Pollyanna winsomeness which nobody outside a prison camp would tolerate.

If this habit persists at the conclusion of the hostilities, it is going to be very unpleasant for everybody. I can only hope that things will adjust and that I shall again become the grouch of the old days whose morning greeting was a growl.

Being a married man with a Pekingese and a German boxer, I am in favor of moving elsewhere if it can be arranged. The only thing I can suggest is that Germany and I get together at a round table and discuss the terms for a separate peace. The only concession I want from Germany is that she give me a loaf of bread, tell the gentleman with the muskets at the main gate to look the other way, and leave the rest to me. In return for this I am prepared to hand over India and an autographed set of my books and to reveal a secret process for cooking sliced potatoes on the radiator known only to myself. This firm offer holds good till Wednesday of next week.

(Top) MacArthur, in fulfillment of his "I shall return" prophecy, arrived dry, but repeated his performance wet for photographers. (Bottom) Hirohito announces his defeat to his ancestors.

163

SHOW
BUSINESS

THE UNIVERSAL TICKET

The Americanization of the world began with the movies. Since it was made in 1915, not a day has passed, not one single, solitary day, that Birth of a Nation *has not played in a theater somewhere on this distracted globe. "We never doubted for a moment that the film was the most powerful thing—the mind and heartbeat of our technical century," says Lillian Gish, one of the great stars of the American film. When talkies came in, Hollywood became His Master's Voice, and the voice was Liberty's, the sounding box of a free people who would as soon push a custard pie in the face of an emperor as admit to any inferiority in art or person. With the movies went music and the feeling of freedom, and young people in oppressed countries risked their very lives to hear it and dance it. Missionary patriots had always preached democracy, but it took that inverted seventh of the jazz scale to make it a reliable and credible export. Show business has entered other aspects of our American life: politics and religion, education and business. The candidate most likely is the candidate most presentable. Mass media pose a threat to intimacy which human dignity can scarcely sustain. Survival depends on the funny bone, theirs and ours. Born actors need born audiences, and America filled the bill with participation-dramas— game shows, talent shows, talk shows. Stars were one thing but what the audience liked most was seeing itself. The "housewife from Dubuque" who couldn't remember the capital of Alabama was really Everyman.*

American entertainment was English entertainment for the better part of two hundred years. The Beatles and other British groups continue a long tradition, but the music they play—and which they have reexported to the U.S.—is essentially American, the irresistible combination of tribal rhythms brought here by African slaves, and the tunes of glory emanating from the great land of promise. But that only proves the old saw about music being the universal ticket.

(Right) Gary Cooper gets made up for a role in that great American export, the Western. Invincibility could not be painted on; audiences demanded truth, Cooper supplied it.

Footlights

If the script of *Mr. Smith Goes to Washington* were submitted to producers today, they would reject it. It was too short of psychological kinks and immorality to be qualified in these times as a "promising film property."

—James Stewart on dirty movies

Rock 'n' roll music, of course, annoys most parents, which is one of the main reasons why millions of youngsters love it.

—Vance Packard

Question: How do you rate your music?
Answer: We're not good musicians. Just adequate.
Question: Then why are you so popular?
Answer: Maybe people like adequate music.

—A Beatle Press Conference

I'm just the big tough guy on the side of right. Simple themes. Save me from the nuances. All I do is sell sincerity, and I've been selling the hell out of that ever since I started.

—John Wayne

When America dances, it pays its pipers well. And yet, despite that I earn close to five thousand dollars a week, I'd think twice before advising anyone to follow in my footsteps. The one-night stands, the long brutal jumps from town to town in rainstorms and blizzards, the bottles of aspirin I had consumed to keep going and blowing. What for? To die at twenty-eight?

—Artie Shaw on "The Road"

His heroic drinking scenes, like many of his other reprehensible activities on screen, are highly autobiographical. Three years ago, his physician said, "Unless you stop drinking, you won't live six months." "Why, that's exactly what a doctor in Berlin told me twenty years ago," said Fields. "He must have been right."

—Alva Johnston on W.C. Fields

The price of Indians is way up. I used to get a whole tribe for practically nothing. Now they have a union.

*—William "Hopalong Cassidy" Boyd,
on the high cost of moviemaking*

He's a right guy, Ed. He's *America*. He will never be destroyed. The way I feel about my country is the way I feel about Ed.

—A bartender on Ed Sullivan

In 1935, I was working on *Lives of a Bengal Lancer*. Director Henry Hathaway wanted realism. When bullets were to be zinging overhead, he wanted to hear them zinging. But bullets flying past the microphone merely whispered. If parents will forgive me, I was the one who hit upon the trick of placing a microphone by a rock, and then ricocheting a high-velocity bullet off the rock and past the mike. The resulting sound has had the small fry shouting "pee-yow" ever since.

—Gary Cooper

The thing the public remembers about *Public Enemy* is the scene in which I shoved a half a grapefruit into Mae Clarke's face. That grapefruit has become a piece of Americana. It was the first time a woman had been treated like a broad on the screen, instead of a delicate flower.

—James Cagney

That novel was one of the all-time best-sellers. People didn't just read it, they lived it. They had a preconceived idea of the Rhett Butler they were going to see. All of them had already played Rhett in their minds. Suppose I came up empty?

—Clark Gable on Gone With the Wind

The poet says the eyes are "the windows of the soul," and your mother's soul came through those windows and made her truly beautiful.

*—Catherine Hayes Brown addressing
her granddaughter about her
mother, Helen Hayes—the first lady
of the stage*

Hello Sucker!

*—Texas Guinan's greeting to
nightclub patrons*

(Right) The Beatles return to London after colonizing the United States. The group appeared on the Post *cover five times.*

The trombonist son of a trombonist father, Sousa had bigger things in mind when he concocted the sousaphone and wrote three novels.

'76 Trombones

by John Philip Sousa

(November 1925)

We had received an offer to go to San Francisco for an indefinite period. That meant the company would be in California for the summer of 1876, or longer, and that didn't suit me. I had set my heart on going to Philadelphia and viewing the first great exposition this country had ever held.

I went to the manager, explained my desire, adding that he would find thoroughly capable conductors in San Francisco. So I left the company and returned to Washington. As soon as friends of mine in Washington heard I was going to Philadelphia, in the kindness of their hearts, they wrote letters of introduction to the musical people of the town.

When I reached Philadelphia I stopped at a modest little hotel on Filbert Street called The Smedley, and went out two or three days in succession, taking in the sights of the Centennial, and there heard the first really good and well-equipped band, which was the famous Gilmore aggregation. After three or four days, I took one of the letters of introduction from the pile I had and proceeded to call on the gentleman to whom it was addressed. I found him to be the prime minister of the joy-killers of the world.

He read the letter and said, "My advice to you is to get out of Philadelphia as quickly as you can. There is not enough work here for local musicians without our helping anyone else who is a rank outsider like yourself. If you stay here you'll starve to death."

I shook hands with him most cordially, thanked him for his advice, went back to the hotel and destroyed my other letters of introduction.

As I had no desire to starve to death, I thought I'd call on Mr. Simon Hassler, who was one of the most popular conductors of Philadelphia and a most genial and pleasant man.

"I've been commissioned to recruit the extra men for the Offenbach orchestra," he said. "Offenbach doesn't take but half of the men from Paris to come here and I have been deputized to engage the rest of the orchestra. I would like to have you in the orchestra if you can pass the examination."

I played over five minutes and then Mr. Hassler said, "I'll put you down with Offenbach."

Notwithstanding the terrible prediction of the joy-killer, I didn't starve to death.

Sousa set the nation marching, wrote 140 high steppers including "Stars and Stripes Forever," "Washington Post" (written for a picnic sponsored by the newspaper), and "Semper Fidelis." Sousa did for the brass industry what Henry Ford did for wheels. Every kid from Kansas City to Keokuk was tooting a sousaphone and selling magazine subscriptions to finance it.

Stage Struck

by A Child Actress of the 1880's

(March 1926)

Helen Hayes grew up in greasepaint, sharing backstage adventures not unlike those of another young actress of an earlier period who wrote her memoirs for the Post *in 1926. Miss Hayes's career has made her the First Lady of the Stage.*

The first memory that I have of the stage and its environment is of my mother in her dressing room, and of myself sitting beside her on a long shelf, watching her make up before her mirror. This was in Boston, in the spring of 1882, I think, when she played Henriette in *The Two Orphans*.

Associated, too, with this early memory is the mingled fragrance from the trunk the moment the lid was raised, a curiously fascinating blend—her favorite powder, her favorite perfume, heliotrope, the leather odor of her Rosalind jerkin and high boots of soft, leaf-brown suede laced at the sides, her black-lacquered makeup box filled with greasepaint, with trays beneath for wigs, and layers of costumes with sachet bags of faded satin filled with down from milkweed pods.

I liked the trunk better than anything else in her dressing room. It was like a magician's trunk for me, from which my mother produced all of that paraphernalia of home life behind the scenes. It had two large deep tills. My baby sister used to be nursed and put to sleep in the top one when my mother went on the stage.

There were long silk stockings of varied colors which I could pull on and pin to my waist for make-believe tights. Best of all, I liked to try on her long, blond wig, the one she wore in *Ophelia*.

She was twenty-two and I was four, but at anytime I can easily shut my eyes and bring back the sweet, vivid memory of her.

From the time I was four until the time I was thirteen, I played with her either in stock or with traveling road companies, mostly dramatic repertoire.

East, west and south we journeyed, covering the same routes year after year. It always surprised me when people we met were sorry for me. They could not conceive of the thrill and charm the roving life of the stage held for a child.

With the post-Civil War prosperity, Americans began to feel the heat, and retreated to seaside and mountaintop. The theater accompanied them.

Norman
Rockwell

Laughs Unlimited

by Paul Frederickson

(June 1972)

There is some debate about where Chaplin got his idea for the tramp character. Winston Churchill thought it came from an ancient cabman whom the teenage Chaplin encountered in London's Kensington Road; the poor fellow suffered from bad feet and, to compensate, wore oversized boots and splayed down the road in a ludicrous walk. One of Chaplin's several biographers has an eclectic theory: that he took Mack Swain's moustache, French comedian Max Linder's cane and bowler, and Fatty Arbuckle's baggy trousers. But Chaplin himself, in *My Autobiography*, describes the creation as simple and sudden inspiration:

"I was in my street clothes and had nothing to do, so I stood where Sennett could see me—'We need some gags here,' he said, then turned to me. 'Put on a comedy makeup, anything will do.' I had no idea what makeup to put on . . . However, on the way to the wardrobe, I thought I would dress in baggy pants, big shoes, a cane and a derby hat . . . I had no idea of the character. But the moment I was dressed, the clothes and makeup made me feel the person he was. I began to know him, and by the time I walked onto the stage he was fully born. Gags and comedy ideas went racing through my mind."

Whatever the source, there can be no doubt of the influence. Since the Twenties, international screen comedians have owed a piece of their art to that creation: Harpo Marx, to his pantomime; Laurel and Hardy, to his pratfalls; Cantinflas, to his unconquered spirit.

The one thing we need ever say about Charlie Chaplin, then, is this: that we can't forget the character he created even if we wanted to. We may confuse plots and forget the titles of his movies, but what remains preserved like a jewel under glass are the antics of a battered little man with a pair of outsized shoes, a bamboo cane and a bowler perched on his head like a bird cage.

Sir Charles Chaplin in his halcyon and baggy-pantalooned days.

A celery stalk endures the torments of Stan Laurel and Oliver Hardy as they endure the torments of a formal dinner. The pair could turn a stalk of celery—or thin air—into sheer bedlam.

Ambassadors

by Mary Pickford

(August 1930)

The screen of the picture theater lets in the light of romance. It illuminates the eyes of the world.

Douglas and I—I refer of course to my husband, Douglas Fairbanks—were concluding our seventh trip abroad. We decided to roam through Egypt, India, China and Japan, and back to Los Angeles, over the Pacific.

On previous trips we had had some hectic and thrilling experience with street mobs—particularly in London and Moscow. Somehow we counted on this trip as one on which we could go as we pleased, unobserved and free-willed. But it was not to be so. It turned, increasingly, into the most remarkable reception we ever had. I shall never forget the indignation of Karl Kitchen, newspaper writer, who happened to be with us when our train pulled into Kyoto and the mob at the station engulfed us. I was rescued just in time and

sat perched on Douglas's shoulders until the mounted police, with drawn sabres, cleared a lane for us. Poor Mr. Kitchen was thrown down and trampled over. When, after a violent struggle, we reached our rooms in the hotel by way of a rear elevator, the disheveled Mr. Kitchen exclaimed: "This is outrageous. How can you keep taking it with a smile?" "This is cordiality," I said. "It becomes violence only because there is a mob that cannot control itself. Stop and think—what a remarkable tribute it is to the motion picture."

The cheering crowds were not shouting for me but the American motion picture and the American people and the world of make-believe. The American motion picture is indeed a tremendous influence abroad. It has in the most forceful and direct manner introduced American life to millions who could not possibly have understood us.

Mary Pickford, America's sweetheart, a keen businesswoman and an expert comedienne, assured her future by buying most of her films.

Good Guys

John Wayne

(August 1965)

John Wayne is not a good actor as perhaps sequoias aren't good trees to plant in your backyard. Like the great American West, which he portrays with sheer and enduring grandeur, truth becomes merely an insignificant fact. The American version of truth is performance, getting the job done, not philosophizing about it, *working*, i.e., John Wayne personified. There are even movies where the Duke, through errors in judgment, gets his fellow workers/soldiers/cowboys slaughtered, but they don't die from idleness. The devil would never find a workshop at the end of John Wayne's rangy arms.

He has tackled everything, including the big C. And flattened it. When he got the Oscar for *True Grit*, the applause welled up with the satisfaction of something long overdue, of a *job* well done, of an aspect within ourselves that was the best of us.

John Wayne is not a glamorous star. He's bigger than that. Even though he began as a glamour boy back in the Thirties he overcame the image and with it put Hollywood into perspective. It doesn't seem nearly so remote now because the Duke closed up the gap between your house and 20th Century-Fox. "Acting?" he seems to say, "Who's acting?"

(Top) Splendor in the grass. The Duke relaxes during the filming of The Sons of Katie Elder. *(Bottom) Buckskinned and brazen-faced, he protects the heroine of a 1930 epic,* The Big Trail, *from unknown dangers. Wayne never played a villain.*

Gary Cooper

(February 1956)

Gary Cooper was different. It was never "You're dead where ya sit," but "I wouldn't be a-doin' that if'n I was you." It was friendly persuasion, with a firm hand on the holster. He came from The Real West and would not sacrifice his principles for a movie camera. Arriving in Hollywood in 1920, he ran into some friends who made money by falling off horses for the cameras. "You guys aren't—*movie actors*?" Back in Montana, "actors" was fightin' words. But Cooper became an actor and in a forty-year career including two Oscars, he still managed to answer most queries with a "yep" or a "nope."

James Stewart

(March 1961)

He was believable. Hollywood never changed him. He always looked and talked as if he were still behind the counter of his father's hardware store in Pennsylvania. Though he lived in Hollywood, his Oscar was on display in the knife case above the checkout counter back home. A Princeton graduate, he came west to study architecture and stayed to become a Hollywood legend. He carved a niche for himself in the Hall of Fame by drawling and stuttering his way through forty years of films, many of them regarded as movie classics. He wasn't perfect and he never claimed to be. He was the guy next door, only better.

(Top) Cooper strides out to the showdown in the 1952 classic High Noon. *(Bottom) Mr. Smith goes to Washington. In those days, Americans believed a junior Senator could change the world. Stewart, in director Frank Capra's picture, almost did it.*

Fallen Stars

by Marilyn Monroe

(May 1956)

When I showed up in divorce court to get my divorce from Joe, there were mobs of people there asking me questions. "Are you and Joe still friends?" and I said, "Yes, but I still don't know anything about baseball." And they all laughed. I don't see what was so funny. I'd heard that he was a fine baseball player, but I'd never seen him play.

I'm beginning to understand myself now. I can face myself more. I spent most of my life running away from myself. I never got a chance to learn anything in Hollywood. They worked me too fast. They rushed me from one picture into another. You're just banging your head against a wall. If you can't do what they want you to do, the thing is to leave. One newspaper had an editorial about me. It said, "Marilyn Monroe is a very stupid girl to give up all the wonderful things the movie industry has given her to go to New York to learn how to act." That was supposed to scare me, but it didn't, and when I read it and realized it wasn't frightening me, I felt strong. If I have the same things I had before I started to go to the Actor's studio and I've added more—well, how can I lose?

People say it's chic to have separate bedrooms. That way a man can have a place for his fishing equipment and a woman can have a fluffy, ruffly place with rows and rows of perfume bottles. The way I feel, separate bedrooms are lonely. I think people need human warmth.

(Top) The Dish appears in Some Like It Hot. *(Bottom) The mix of innocence and sexiness seemed to make her two persons.*

Humphrey Bogart

(August 1952)

Humphrey DeForest Bogart, who will be fifty-three years old come Christmas morning and doesn't care who knows it, is a whiskey-drinking actor who has been hooting at Hollywood for twenty-three years. One day last year, John Huston, the director, called Bogie on the telephone.

"I have a great story," Huston said. "The hero is a low-life. You are the biggest low-life in town and therefore suitable for the part."

Enchanted by this approach, Bogart suggested that the two of them drink lunch. The upshot of this encounter was that they hurried over to call on Katharine Hepburn and reveal to her the enticements of a story about a skinny missionary spinster and a gin-swizzling clown floating down an African river to fire a homemade torpedo at a German gunboat. This strange tale, *The African Queen*, has been despaired of by every studio in town, but Huston, Hepburn and Bogart saw the fun in it. They went all the way to Africa. By all accounts, the boys treated Miss Hepburn like dirt, which she liked enormously. She lectured them sharply about whiskey-drinking, without which both Huston and Bogart found Africa unendurable, but responded happily when Bogart gave his usual command: "Ah, get yourself a chair, Katie, and pull up one for me. And fix the drinks."

Bogie, here with Ingrid Bergman, was always as rumpled as his trench coat, made no concessions to life, love or liquor. Leading ladies found him irresistible precisely because he found them so resistible. His utterances—when he made them—were like epitaphs in marble.

Screen Sirens

Their faces flicker with a quality of perfect beauty and man-made character which made celluloid seem as though it were eternal. They devoured leading men like primeval arachnids; they became their lines. Garbo's "I want to be alone," Bette Davis's "I'd love to kiss you but I just washed my hair," Dietrich's "Men cluster to me like moths around a flame," Joan Crawford's "I love gardenias but I have too much body heat to wear them," Harlow's snapping at Clark Gable, "Whaddya mean, ya don't like Gorgonzola?" Katharine Hepburn's enigmatic "The calla lillies are blooming" cast a powerful spell of glamour that amounted to a kind of independence. If Marlene felt like lighting up a cigar she proceeded to. Hepburn stood on her head when

Time cannot dim the luster of these legendary ladies of the silver screen: Katharine Hepburn, Greta Garbo and Joan Crawford. For them searchlights pierced the sky above Grauman's Chinese Theatre while police lines held back fans with outstretched autograph books.

the questions got personal. Jean Harlow had something to say about the restrictive covenants of underwear. When Garbo spoke (for the first time in movies), "Git me a viskey and don't be stingy, baby," the words were as monumental as Cortez's when he saw the Pacific, or those of the first GI's upon landing in France.

A lot of it was makeup. But you can't paste bones on a face with a powder puff, nor can a public relations agent build guts into a spineless personality. Seeing these women today, one is aware of a class and style that have vanished but which is not the least bit dated. Except for Harlow, they are all alive (much more than most of their successors) and well (Hepburn is still standing on her head), and they remind us that beauty is truth, even if it is a business.

Marlene Dietrich, Jean Harlow and Bette Davis. "Glamour" was the special word for their special quality—one the dim, grim Thirties badly needed. For twenty-five or fifty cents the moviegoer could forget his troubles for two hours; longer if there was a double feature.

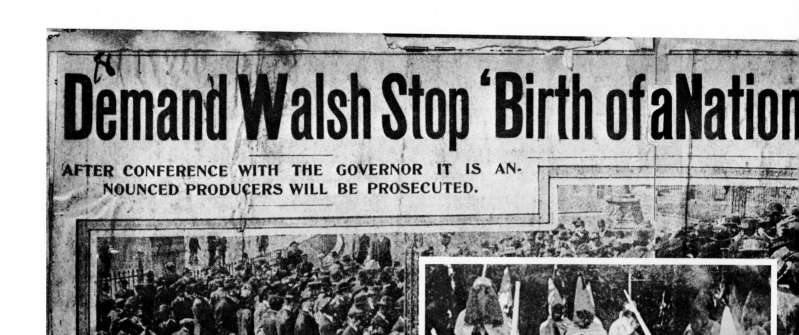

Demand Walsh Stop 'Birth of a Nation

AFTER CONFERENCE WITH THE GOVERNOR IT IS AN-NOUNCED PRODUCERS WILL BE PROSECUTED.

As a result of a protest made at the State House today by a crowd of more than 1,000 ne-groes, Governor Walsh and a ittee of the protesting peo-

The colored delegations began to ar-rive singly and in groups from all points of the compass an hour earlier. It was hot in the sun, but they stood close. Women and chil-dren squatted on the stone steps. They were good-natured, but terribly n earnest. They talked about Satur-lay night's trouble and the ringing sentiments expounded by the ght in the

BIG MI

Protest

Birth of a Nation *was criticized most frequently for its treatment of blacks. Here a lynch mob manhandles an alleged rapist.*

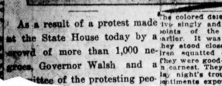

Birth of a Nation

(March 1926)

After Mr. Edison and his followers "got the bugs out," movies became a public novelty and nothing else. It wasn't until 1915, when David Wark Griffith made *Birth of a Nation*, that movies became something more than Brownie snapshots strung together in a nonsensi-cal line. Griffith made the movies into the art form of the twentieth century. His movies had characters, they told a story and they moved the audience. *Birth of a Nation* was the Civil War and Reconstruction from a Southern point of view, and it was symbolic of the South casting off the shroud of subservience it had worn since 1865. Consequently, it raised a great deal of controversy. But it remains a milestone. It pioneer-ed in film techniques. The battle scenes had a Mathew Brady quality to them. Though only a few extras were used, Griffith made the battlefields look as if they were strewn with thousands. A cameraman turned away from his machine and by accident the fadeout was invented. *Birth of a Nation* is still considered con-troversial, but it holds its place in history simply be-cause it was the first real "movie."

The controversy over Griffith's film, released on the fiftieth anniversary of Appomattox, showed the wounds had not healed.

After a grueling two-year talent search for the right Scarlett, MGM found an English girl to play the Southern Belle. Vivien Leigh was perfect.

Gone With the Wind

(July 1940)

Based on a monumental best-seller ingrained in the minds of millions of Americans, *Gone With the Wind* was destined to be a hit long before the camera started rolling. The public demanded that Clark Gable play Rhett Butler and put up with a two-year-long talent search to find the "right" Scarlett O'Hara. It took two directors and dozens of screenwriters (among them F. Scott Fitzgerald), but when *Gone With the Wind* hit the screen in its three-hour-long glory in 1939, it became an instant film classic. For years afterward, we would measure other films in relation to it, always coming back to *Gone With the Wind* in droves when it came to our local cinemas every five years or so. Other films may have had more "redeeming social value" and other films (albeit only a few) may have made more money, but no other film has endured like *Gone With the Wind*. It is Clark Gable at his peak, forceful and romantic. It is Vivien Leigh in her Academy Award-winning role, beautiful and hard-headed as Scarlett. The story, from Margaret Mitchell's book, is again the South during the Civil War and Reconstruction. But it is a personal story as well, of a determined young woman and the man she loves. It resists television, sallying forth now and then to relieve our cinemas of "modern" moviemaking, to bring back the times when movies were movies.

Clark Gable as Rhett in a romantic scene that caused women to faint in the aisles and submit bids for Gable's used hotel linen.

Citizen Kane

(February 1942)

He was a millionaire who influenced an entire generation and made them think "what I tell them to think!" He was Charles Foster Kane, sultan of the media, in Orson Welles's fictionalization of the life of William Randolph Hearst, *Citizen Kane*. The film is, in the strictest sense, a mystery. Kane dies uttering the word "rosebud." Using a variety of techniques, Welles shows Kane's life from different angles, trying to get behind the headlines into the real story of this man's life.

It is a tale of power and the effect power has upon men and their ability (or lack of same) to love. Welles, who shocked the nation in 1938 with his radio broadcast of *War of the Worlds* (millions of listeners mistook it for a news bulletin), made *Citizen Kane* when he was twenty-four. He delivered a virtuoso performance as Kane, portraying him from a young, rambunctious lad who inherits a fortune, to a bitter, dying man searching for something he lost long ago as a boy—happiness.

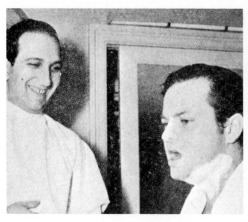  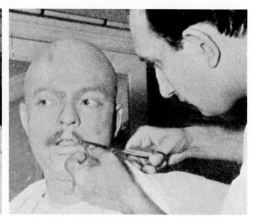

Makeup man Maurice Seiderman transforms the 24-year-old whiz kid, Orson Welles, into the aging publishing tycoon Charles Foster Kane.

Citizen Kane introduced many new techniques to a Hollywood still floundering before cameras. Welles *moved* the camera, held it at odd angles, overlapped dialogue between scenes and devised a way of getting both foreground and background elements in focus. It is considered by most film critics to be the most innovative movie ever made.

Kane uses his tremendous influence to advance himself politically. Here, he campaigns unsuccessfully for governor of New York.

Kane's second wife, portrayed by Dorothy Comingore, dabbles with a jigsaw puzzle in Kane's enormous, lonely mansion, Xanadu.

Shane

(August 1956)

Shane, released in 1953, has taken its place as the classic Western of the American film. Director George Stevens made sure of it. In the climactic fight scene, he used real furniture (not the usual flimsy balsa wood) and when Alan Ladd hit evil Jack Palance with that chair, the chair didn't break but Jack Palance did. Bones were broken, eyes were blackened and fingers were smashed. *Shane* was as close to a mirror of nature as any mid-twentieth-century filmmaker could get, right down to the lonely, desolate location Stevens chose for the town. And the town itself is one muddy street with only enough buildings for one side, visible from any point in the valley, from any scene in the film. The action literally *centers* around the town and its people—a small group of farmers trying to hold onto their land while being threatened by a large landowner who hires gunslingers to keep the homesteaders in line.

Shane has been called a perfect film in composition and color; each scene is suitable for framing, a complete emotion in itself.

The movie opens with a young boy, playing in the river near his father's modest Wyoming farm. In the distance he sees a man on a horse crossing the river upstream. The boy watches him all the way up the river and across the field toward the farm. From these opening moments of *Shane*, a myth is in the making. A gunfighter, trying to escape his past, hires on as a ranch hand for a poor farmer, his wife, and his son, and defeats the evil land baron trying to steal the homesteader's land. But he has to resort to his guns, and, considering himself a failure, he leaves the farm and the town he has helped to rebuild.

Filming the fight scene was an engrossing experience. Alan Ladd became too involved and had to be told to pull his punches.

The boy, Brandon DeWilde, and Ladd, the stranger he loves and respects more than his father, share a tender moment.

183

Two Troubadours

Woody Guthrie

(July 1966)

Woody Guthrie came from nowhere in particular and went nowhere in particular, living a hobo's life for most of his years, catching freights, thumbing rides and walking. He moved along the backroads, far from the big highways, absorbing and re-creating a nation's music and folklore.

He hit the road while still a teenager and traveled through the nation's heartland, in the dark days of the Great Depression of the 1930's. He witnessed the great Okie migration from the Dust Bowl to the Promised Land of California. He saw dreams shattered. He saw a disillusioned nation of people struggling to survive.

This is what Woody Guthrie wrote about. He made up his songs as he traveled—songs about the people he met, the people he heard about, the stories he read in the papers.

He said he hated songs that made men feel they were no good. His songs were to make people proud of what they were and where they came from and happy for what little they had. Music was the best way in the world to fight hate; on his guitar were carved the words "This machine kills fascists."

As I was walking
That ribbon of highway,
I saw above me
That endless skyway,
I saw below me
That golden valley,
This land was made
For you and me ©

FAUST

Bob Dylan

(June 1974)

It is true that Bob Dylan was the pied piper of a generation of young people who changed America. Like most great poets, he was both a thermometer of the political climate and a barometer of the cultural changes constantly going on around him and inside him. In many ways, Bob Dylan's story is like an American odyssey. He grew up in Hibbing, Minnesota, a small mining town a hundred miles from the Canadian border. He was born Bob Zimmerman in May 1941, but as a freshman at the University of Minnesota, he began calling himself Bob Dylan.

In January 1960, Dylan decided to drop out of school and hitchhike east. He bummed around and began to meet people and make friends, including the legendary Woody Guthrie. When Bob Dylan made his debut at a New York folk club, he wore an old jacket which had once belonged to Guthrie and a pair of Brooks Brothers slacks he had borrowed from a friend.

It was almost miraculous how this boy who had spent years learning other people's songs suddenly began to write his own. In 1962 he wrote a song which may rank with "The Battle Hymn of the Republic" in terms of its impact on America. It was called "Blowin' in the Wind."

A whole new stratum of young Americans were entering college. They were impulsively impatient about solving all of America's problems. Dylan saw things the way they did and wrote about it. He was the new voice for the new generation. His songs were like mirrors held up to America during the 1960's.

How many roads must a man walk down
Before you call him a man?
How many seas must a white dove sail
Before she sleeps in the sand?
How many times must the cannonballs fly
Before they're forever banned?
The answer, my friend,
Is blowin' in the wind.
The answer is blowin' in the wind. ©

Swooners and Crooners

Rudy Vallee

(April 1962)

By 1928, Rudy Vallee and his Connecticut Yankees had become the darlings of high society and the major attraction at New York's Heigh-Ho Club. In February of that year, when the Heigh-Ho Club agreed to air a few programs, Rudy gratefully plugged the club with his first words on the air—"Heigh-Ho, everybody." Within minutes, the switchboard was swamped. Within days, the mail was ceiling-high with fan letters. By 1932, *Variety* could report he'd made his first million.

Bing Crosby

(March 1953)

I had something to do with another song, "White Christmas," which became a modern Christmas Carol. In the trade, "White Christmas" is known as a standard. Anywhere I go, I have to sing it. It's as much a part of me as my floppy ears.

Frank Sinatra

(September 1946)

Frank Sinatra proved that the knack of causing young ladies to shriek and swoon is a highly profitable art. His is the most spectacular

success story of our time—how a skinny kid from Hoboken, New Jersey, went from $15 a week to $25,000 a week in five years. One night, he took his girl, Nancy, to hear Bing Crosby in person. They saw Bing open his mouth and tear the house down. That night, as the

Crosby's perfect pitch and Elvis's perfect adaptations of black rhythms were mirrored in the harmonic rock triumphs of the Beatles.

skinny kid with the Adam's apple walked her home, he told Nancy he had decided to be a crooner. "I bet I could sing like that with more practice. I bet I could. Do you think I could, Nancy?" "Yeah, Frankie. Sure you could."

Elvis Presley

(September 1959)

On a hot day in 1953, a slim high school boy fidgeted with a guitar below the windows of the newly opened Sun Studios in Memphis, Tennessee. He got his courage up and walked into the small studio. When Sam Phillips, the owner, approached, the boy gulped and said, "Please, mister, I'd like to make a record for my mother." Phillips made a few tapes of him singing. He said, "I like what I hear, son—you'll be hearing from me." The boy's name was Elvis Presley.

The Beatles

(March 1964)

Their plane had just landed. Amid a fanfare of screeches, there emerged four young Britons in Edwardian suits. These are the Beatles, who brought America a phenomenon known as Beatlemania. While the Beatles toured the United States, Beatle wigs were selling at three dollars apiece, boys were combing their forelocks forward and hairdressers were advertising Beatle cuts for women. "I think everyone has gone daft," said John Lennon.

Frank Sinatra's career spanned 30 suave years in the pop world. Rudy Vallee emerged as a successful character actor 40 years after his debut.

187

Television

(November 1968)

Television's greatest moments have been those in which it brought the viewer an image of reality that he had never seen before—the Army-McCarthy hearings, the Kennedy-Nixon debates, the launching of astronauts into space, the shooting of Lee Harvey Oswald, or, for that matter, Jerry Kramer opening the hole for Bart Starr's championship touchdown.

There is no doubt that the televising of great events has had a major effect on our social and political lives. Television certainly helped to elect Jack Kennedy. It has been estimated that the televising of civil rights clashes in the South advanced the timetable of racial integration by several years. And Vietnam has become our most unpopular war because of the way some brave TV cameramen have shown it—more closely than any war has been seen by civilian America in this century.

Milton Berle's success as a comic was a hard act to follow. He himself had trouble duplicating his early avuncular popularity.

Ed Sullivan updated vaudeville, stoically walking a reinforced concrete tightrope between grand opera and the three-ring circus.

Lucille Ball wide-eyed her way through years of viewers who found her reruns more watchable than the movies downtown.

Senator McCarthy discovered television as a political medium as well as communists lurking behind innocent government façades.

Dave Garroway mixed news, reviews, weather, chimps, and entertainment into an alarm clock called the "Today" show.

Mouseketeers were inexorably cheerful. Many of the kids, including Annette Funicello and Tommy Kirk, went on to stardom.

Steve Allen was the original "Tonight" show. His clever routines, solid music and engaging chattiness made his show a TV classic.

Elsa Maxwell socializes with the urbane Jack Paar who made the talk show an end in itself, a style that was later to go out of style.

The assassination of Lee Harvey Oswald confronted America with the doubts of its own eyes and a week of unbearable drama.

Martin Luther King's non-violent "I have a dream" stirred the country. King died tragically before his dream could be realized.

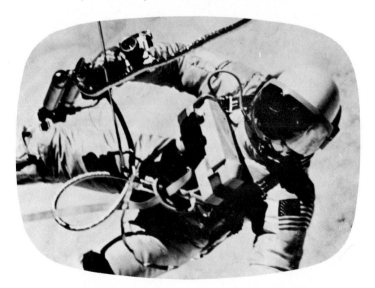

Man walks in space, free from the constraints of gravity, on his way to the moon. Even television could not make it believable.

INNOVATION

THE LITTLE ENGINE THAT COULD

America invented its progress, tamed its surroundings with machinery. Cyrus McCormick, not the pioneers, planted the prairies with gold. Eli Whitney created the feudal system in the South, and when it was eliminated, helped the area survive. Henry Ford put industry on an assembly line. Cyrus Field, Alexander Graham Bell and Samuel F.B. Morse let everybody know about it.

The great expansion west was made possible by George Westinghouse's invention of the air brake (1869) which enabled locomotives to carry the huge pay loads of finished products out and the raw materials back. Eighteen years before, Donald McKay had built a flying machine, the clipper ship. This fragile cloud had the velocity of a bullet, hit Liverpool from New York with a good wind in twelve days, eighteen hours, and introduced the world to the power of American know-how. Europe realized a daring and aggressive competitor had emerged who was closer to world markets via brain and elbow grease than it was geographically.

Many of America's inventions and scientific advancements came from the unlettered and unknown, fueling the American dream which opened up the realm of possibility to all people. Universal education and health care improved the level upon which the country based its hopes, and such spurs to competition as the missile gap narrowed the distance between now and the future. "I think I can" became "I know I can"; solving the practical problem became an abstraction amounting to an American philosophy. The corporations these inventions gave birth to wielded such enormous power the nation in a sense became a giant company town. One of the most efficient organisms man has ever invented, the corporation, has solved as well as created problems beyond a single man's comprehension. The close connection between pure science and profitable industry, however, has made the suggestion box and the laboratory twin gateposts to financial success.

(Right) The careful cure. The standardization of measurement, uniform sanitary conditions, and a large dosage of heart have made America the healthiest nation in the world.

One Giant Step

Williams performs every operation on the teeth complete for one dollar. Filing, extracting and plugging a single tooth for 25 cents, if plugged with gold, 50 cents. He saves teeth in the same way his own were saved, the least painful of any of the English ways. B. Williams, Dentist. 161 Vine Street, near Fifth, Philadelphia.

—1822 dentist's advertisement

Trying to do the impossible makes about one-half the impossible easy.

—Thomas Alva Edison

The incredible American believes that if something has not been accomplished, it is because he has not yet attempted it.

—Alexis de Tocqueville

Fireplaces with small openings cause draughts of cold air to rush in at every crevice and 'tis very uncomfortable as well as dangerous to set against any such crevice. . . . Women, particularly from this cause (as they sit so much in the house) get colds to the head, rheums and defluxions, which fall into their jaws and gums, and have destroyed early, many a fine set of teeth in these northern colonies.

—Benjamin Franklin, from his account of the Newly Invented Pennsylvania Fireplaces

An inventor has at last succeeded in making a machine that will lay eggs—or, at least, he believes he has succeeded; he has backed his opinion by paying the fees necessary to secure protection for his cogwheel hen, and, it is said, has placed the contract for a manufactory where eggs are to be made at the rate of a hundred thousand per day. The inventor not only claims that his machine will lay good eggs, cheap eggs, and eggs guaranteed to be fresh, but is prepared to bet that a connoisseur will find it difficult to distinguish his artificial eggs from the prime product of a Plymouth Rock or Leghorn.

—1893 news report

Today, as always, there are those who believe that the mental, as well as the physical map has been completed—that we know all we are ever going to know and that our job is henceforth to rearrange and reorder what we already have. That is the Old World spirit. That is the surrender of those who fear to think, to plan and to try.

—Henry Ford

The risk in flying is far smaller than nervous terrestrians imagine—riding in an airplane with a competent driver is about as safe as any other mode of locomotion. Scientific students of the subject confidently predict regular mail and passenger routes immediately after the war. New York to London in twenty-four hours is just around the corner.

—1918 editorial

We find a very ingenious receipt for bringing to life a man who is dead drunk. Observing such a one lying in the street, on his back, with his mouth wide open—all you have to do is to pop a handful of salt into his mouth and immediately he will come to life and spring to his feet. But you must get out of the way as soon as you have administered the remedy, for he will make battle like a madman, and knock you down for your pains.

—1836 remedy for drunkenness

A Philadelphia surgeon, who was on his way to perform an operation on a patient, had his carriage robbed and lost his surgical instruments while making a temporary stop, "Whereby," adds the reporter, "the operation was prevented and the patient's life saved."

—A Civil War era anecdote

Some inventions slip quietly into the American consciousness and are put to practical use long before the man in the street realizes their significance. Others, as witness the dramatic arrival of the talkies, drop bomb-like into our startled midst. Still others are preceded by a vast amount of public speculation and with such great expectations that when they finally step from the laboratories into the full view of the audience there is danger of an anti-climax. Television is among the latter.

—The Post *introduces TV, 1929*

Man on the moon represents the culmination of the space war, a competition between the U.S. and Russia which began with Sputnik.

Artist Samuel F.B. Morse painted the old senate chambers as the lights were being lit for an evening session in which the north and south were desperately trying to work out a compromise.

Samuel F. B. Morse

by Starkey Flythe, Jr.

Samuel F.B. Morse's life caught America at the flood. Born in 1791, he painted portraits more in an attempt to capture his own talents than the likenesses of his sitters. A fascination with electricity led him to study Franklin's experiments and eventually, in 1835, to construct a working model of a telegraph. Plagued by financial difficulties, he finally persuaded Congress to appropriate money for a telegraph line between Washington and Baltimore. After a year of false starts he sent his first message, "What hath God wrought?"

In 1838, he developed the Morse Code. A supreme court decision established his patent rights in 1854.

In France, while painting *Masterpieces of the Louvre*, a huge canvas in which Morse planned to sum-total Western civilization, Morse met Henri Daguerre and studied the process of capturing images on light-sensitive plates. Thus Morse became the father of American photography. When he died in 1872, the country, partly due to his inventions, had been bound together into an active response to world markets and a national image satisfactorily nourishing to the emotional yearnings of an industrious people.

Photographed with his telegraph in 1854, Morse still affected the flowing cloak and poet's tie of his younger days as a painter.

The Doctor Poet

by Cory SerVaas, M.D.

Better known as a poet than a doctor—"The Autocrat at the Breakfast Table"—Oliver Wendell Holmes (right) brought urbanity and jocosity to American medicine along with serious efforts to educate his colleagues about the contagiousness of childbed fever and the need for antisepsis in delivery rooms. As head of the Harvard Medical School with which he was associated for thirty-five years, he profoundly influenced the education of doctors well into the twentieth century. Also trained as a lawyer, he urged his son, who became the country's greatest Supreme Court Justice, not to enter law school, saying, "What's the use of that, Wendell? A lawyer can't be a great man."

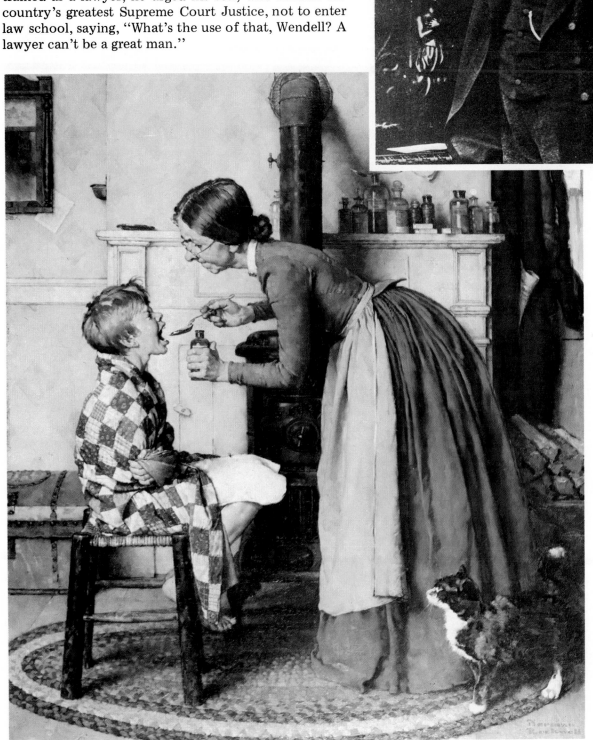

Holmes is credited with separating medicine from patent medicine, and raising standards for training doctors.

Widow's walks adorned many houses in American seaports. Here, Rockwell's young tar has just told his bride the sea's blue is more bewitching than her eyes. After 1860, America's marine energies went into the Civil War, leaving the waves to English supremacy.

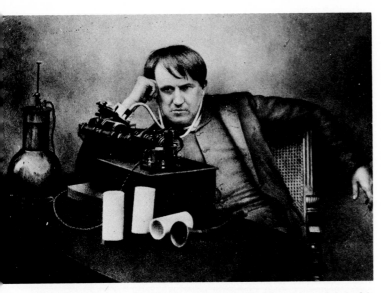

The young inventor with the phonograph. He set up a lab in his father's basement when he was ten, was working as a roving telegrapher by the time he was fifteen. His early work on Wall Street led to the Edison Universal Stock Printer which helped put American businesses in the hands of millions of shareholders.

That suggests an educational use of the motion picture for brain quickening. But that is another subject. The point here is that it has already had an educational value distinct from the value of the matter presented.

One of the effects of machinery has been to increase the general intelligence. As more machinery is introduced, that general intelligence will be further quickened. As our intelligence rises, we shall use still more machines, but we have no reason to bother about men turning into automatons. The machine age has caused our intelligence to rise and requires less work to earn a decent living. Through further use of power and machinery the amount of work a man will need to do to support his family will measurably decrease. There will not be widespread involuntary unemployment by reason of automation—the machinery has to be made and kept in condition.

It is necessary to have more leisure or more consuming time—whatever one likes to call it. The universal five-day week will step up consumption in much the way that the electric light and the eight-hour day have stepped it up.

We have not yet begun to realize the possibilities of automatic machinery. For instance, I see no reason why any handiwork should be necessary in the manufacture of a garment. The automatic machine should cut the price of manufactured articles very nearly in half.

A machine could be devised to take in cloth at one end and drop out finished trousers at the other. The principle of the Jacquard loom, which is one of the greatest principles of all time, has scarcely been utilized except in the manufacture of silk and in the player piano. It is the principle of bringing into action the various parts of a machine in accordance with a pattern traced on a steel card by perforations or as on the paper roll of a player piano. This principle gives us a control which can be applied to any kind of machine. It is a great reserve principle for the future.

In the old days a man spent most of his life getting ready to die. Now, a family thinks more of living than dying. If the cost of living goes down—and invention and engineering are bound to drive it down—and wages go higher—and they are bound to go higher with more efficient production—then still more attention can be paid to living rather than dying.

We shall steadily require more power, but a great deal more fuss is being made over hydroelectric power than its intrinsic value warrants. The first and best source of power is coal. We can probably use coal at our present rate for a thousand years or so without exhausting our supply.

I have been working with Henry Ford and Harvey Firestone to discover some home source for a rubber supply. There is no money in this for any of us. That is not the object of our work. I want to find a rubber supply that we can turn to in the emergency of war, for then cost will not matter. I do not know when this work will end.

Nature has many great surprises left for us and it is great fun to dig into the unknown and pull something out of it. Some of these surprises include motion pictures, telephones, electric railways, cars, lighting, power supplies and fixtures. Also phonographs, dynamos, motors, storage batteries, cement, telegraph and wireless telegraphy. My assistant for many years, Mr. W.H. Meadowcroft, has estimated that about fifteen billion dollars was invested in industries founded on these inventions.

Edison had over a thousand patents. Some were accidental discoveries like the "Edison effect," the basis of the electron tube.

Thus Man Learned to Fly

by Orville Wright

(July 1928)

When we left Kitty Hawk in the fall of 1901, we knew that many problems remained to be solved. Wilbur did not intend to come back to Kitty Hawk for more experiments. He was convinced that we had not been able to accomplish enough to warrant further tests. Wilbur predicted that one day men would fly, but that it would not be in our day.

We had taken up flying as a sport. We reluctantly entered upon the scientific side of it and soon found the work so fascinating that it drew us in deeper and deeper. Wilbur did not feel it would pay us to go back to Kitty Hawk. But he finally agreed to go.

Wilbur took this picture of an early flight with Orville at the controls. The brothers ran a bicycle shop in Dayton, Ohio.

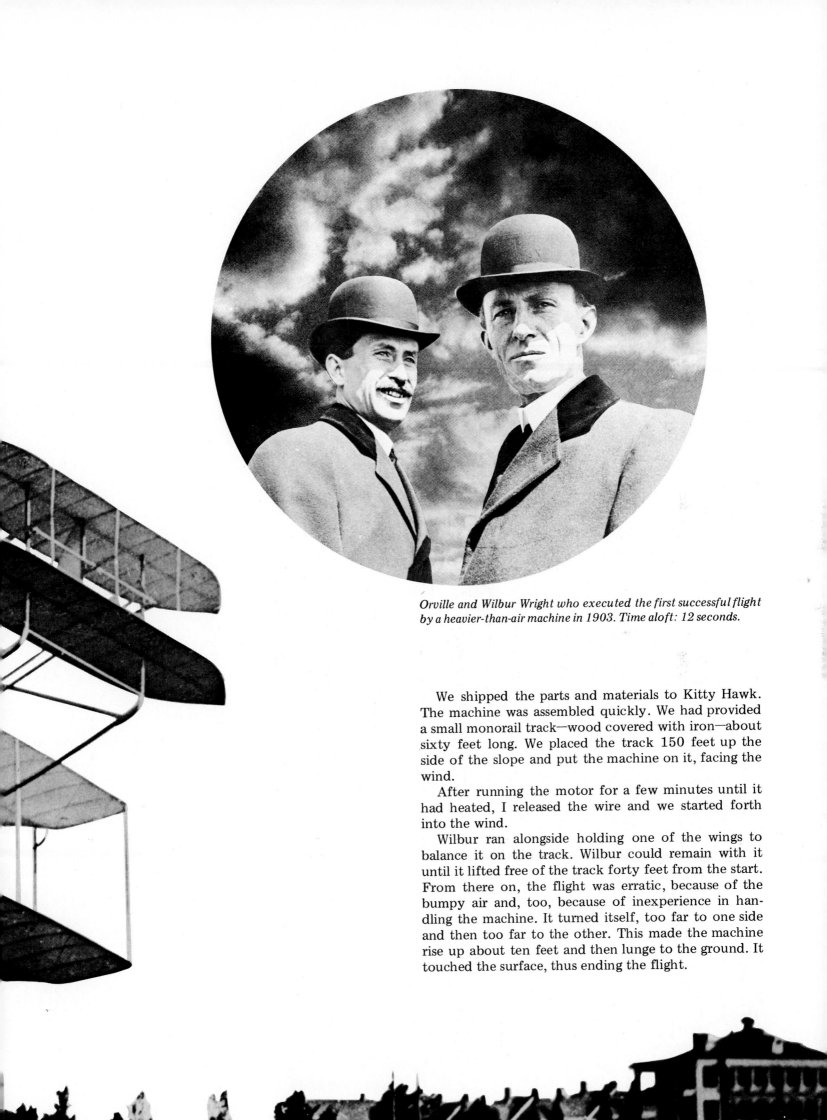

Orville and Wilbur Wright who executed the first successful flight by a heavier-than-air machine in 1903. Time aloft: 12 seconds.

We shipped the parts and materials to Kitty Hawk. The machine was assembled quickly. We had provided a small monorail track—wood covered with iron—about sixty feet long. We placed the track 150 feet up the side of the slope and put the machine on it, facing the wind.

After running the motor for a few minutes until it had heated, I released the wire and we started forth into the wind.

Wilbur ran alongside holding one of the wings to balance it on the track. Wilbur could remain with it until it lifted free of the track forty feet from the start. From there on, the flight was erratic, because of the bumpy air and, too, because of inexperience in handling the machine. It turned itself, too far to one side and then too far to the other. This made the machine rise up about ten feet and then lunge to the ground. It touched the surface, thus ending the flight.

Our Job

by Henry Ford

(October 1936)

The big thing for the country to keep its mind on is production. There is talk of prices, of restrictions and controls, but not about production, and yet it is only production that can cure the conditions of which these discussions are the symptoms. Plenty means production and still more production; production means wealth, and scarcity means poverty, and the entire social problem is poverty.

Production and the effects of production give the answer to practically all the things that trouble us. They answer the question of supply; you can't give the people what they need except by production. They answer the question of progressive efficiency; such national resources as we have today in industry are in the large-production industries.

We are going forward but not so quickly and so surely as we would if so many people were not trying to live off money instead of off production. We have not only the moneychangers trying to both make money out of money and to manage business at the same time, but we have also strange and unworkable theories introduced in such a way as to slow up the process.

Three Ford heirs—William, Benson and Henry Ford II—show off an Edsel, the famous model named for their father, Henry Ford's son.

Innovation   202

Henry Ford at work in his little shed behind his Michigan home. While his wife Clara darned socks in the lamplight, Ford designed and built the parts he needed for his "gas engine that will do the work of the horse." He completed his small car in 1896, road-testing it in the alley near his home at two o'clock in the morning. Later, Ford delighted in the imaginative uses farmers made of his "Tin Lizzies."

Ideas Worth Millions

by Frank Parker Stockbridge

(April 1939)

If you are an average American and haven't yet invented anything, the chances are that you've got an idea in your head for some sort of gadget that you're going to work out someday and get a patent on.

Maybe you'll make a million. It's been done and it's still being done. Inventors, working on their own, are still making money out of patents, despite the widely propagandized belief that the corporations grab off every valuable invention and cheat the little fellow.

The Franklin stove put heat in the living room instead of sending it up the chimney.

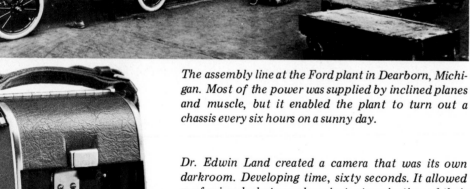

The assembly line at the Ford plant in Dearborn, Michigan. Most of the power was supplied by inclined planes and muscle, but it enabled the plant to turn out a chassis every six hours on a sunny day.

Dr. Edwin Land created a camera that was its own darkroom. Developing time, sixty seconds. It allowed professional photographers instant projection of their work and amateurs unlimited fun.

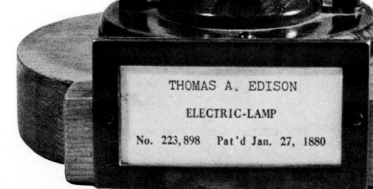

THOMAS A. EDISON

ELECTRIC-LAMP

No. 223,898   Pat'd Jan. 27, 1880

Edison's incandescent bulb doubled the working day in 1879.

(Left) George Eastman perfected a cheap camera which produced amazingly accurate results. He made his invention, the Kodak, a household noun for small cameras. (Top) This 1930's television set uses a mirror to reflect its screen, because the early cathode ray tubes would work only in a vertical position.

Charles Kettering's inventions—the electric starter, anti-knock fuel, the high-compression engine—helped build General Motors.

Apprentice

by Walter P. Chrysler

(June 1937)

A Union Pacific shop apprentice! You can bet that I was proud! I had a badge to show that I was a cadet of that vast loom for weaving the Western half of the continent into the nation. Railroading, the entire art as we knew it, held my imagination in focus.

My opinion of myself expanded tenfold when I became an apprentice. Everybody in Ellis knew that any apprentice had been required to pass an examination—a stiff one. Some boys failed to make the grade.

When I began to work at my trade, tools were crude, so that is probably why I see that mainly we owe the tremendous advances of the physical aspects of our civilization to new and better tools. Electric lights are a tool; the telephone is a tool; so are the motion picture, the radio and the automobile, to mention just a few. In a world that offers not only new and wonderful tools but likewise astonishing new materials, each of which is a fresh challenge to everything that men have made before, new human needs and bigger human problems are being revealed faster than a single human mind can even count them.

Young Walt Chrysler, photographed in Ellis, Kansas, alone, in hat, and with members of his baseball club (standing, second from right).

Breakthrough

by **Richard Carter**

(December 1965)

On April 2, 1955, the world learned that a vaccine developed by Jonas Edward Salk, M.D., could be relied upon to prevent paralytic poliomyelitis. This news consummated the most extraordinary undertaking in the history of science, a huge research project led by a Wall Street lawyer and financed by the American people through hundreds of millions of small donations. More than a scientific achievement, the vaccine was a folk victory, an occasion for pride and jubilation. A contagion of love swept the world. People observed moments of silence, rang bells, honked horns, blew factory whistles, fired salutes, kept their traffic lights red in brief periods of tribute, took the rest of the day off, closed their schools or convoked fervid assemblies therein, drank toasts, hugged children, attended church, smiled at strangers, forgave enemies. It seemed that this Salk, a somewhat withdrawn figure during the months preceding his announcement, had worked seven days a week, sometimes twenty-four hours at a stretch, lest the vaccine be delayed for one needless minute and one child be crippled for lack of it.

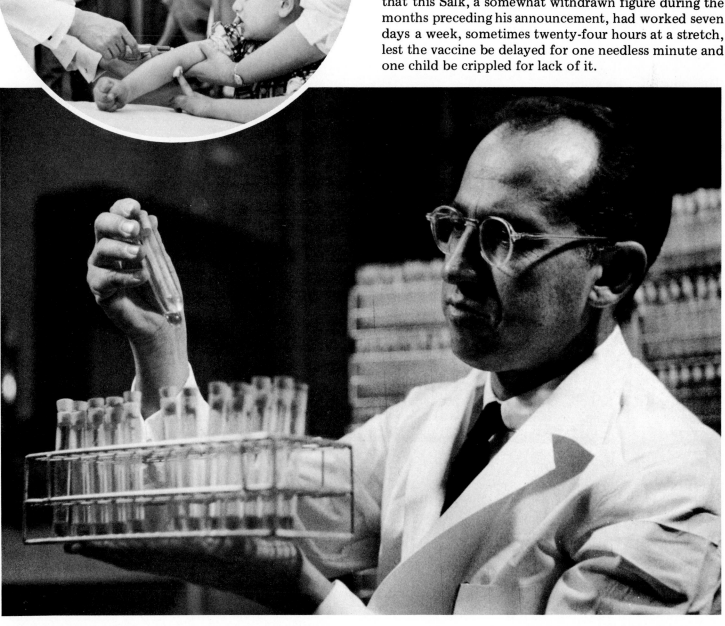

The controversy between the vaccines developed by Dr. Salk and Dr. Sabin still simmers but poliomyelitis has been all but eliminated.

Don't Let Them Die

by Richard E. Byrd

(May 1928)

"We are going into a tailspin."

Out of the night came this voiceless cry by radio last August. Eagerly waiting journalists in San Francisco pictured the possibility of another front-page story. Fellow aviators felt their hearts beat faster for the peril they knew their brother flyers faced. Some businessmen shrugged and wondered what was the sense of it all. A few fathers and mothers, one or two in particular, whose own flesh and blood was out there in that plane bound for Hawaii——

"Belay that! We are out of the spin."

A sigh of relief around the big newspaper's radio desk; in one or two clubs where hushed men were gathered; in a big room of a private mansion where several tense and silent people huddled over a special line to follow the progress of this valiant effort to find the missing in the great transpacific race. Then, once more, the trickle of words out of the vast darkness that had followed the setting sun: "SOS. We are in the spin agai——"

Silence. The world "again" was never finished. That broken message was the last ever heard of the airplane *Dallas Spirit*, en route by air from San Francisco to Honolulu. In her perished Captain Erwin, her pilot, a war flyer and as gallant an airman as ever drove aloft. Indeed, he was searching for other victims when he died.

It is superb that a man should give his life to science. By so doing he is making the greatest possible sacrifice for the benefit of future generations. He is following in the footsteps of human benefactors of the past; heroes who have been burned, frozen, inoculated, tortured and blown up that man's knowledge might be increased.

But when, abruptly, scientific research resolves itself largely into emotionalism, and the gain is naught as compared with the loss of precious lives, then the spectacle casts doubt upon the moral soundness of the project that invites it.

Since January 1, 1927, about thirty-five young pilots, mechanics and passengers have lost their lives in connection with ocean flying. The percentage of mortality has been far higher than that in the trenches on the Western Front in 1918.

There is good reason to believe that as I write there are scores of similar transoceanic flights being planned for this summer, many of which will actually be attempted, unless public opinion stops them before they start.

There is no case against the properly prepared flights. These are not only feasible and desirable but necessary to bring about regular flights. The next step forward, it seems to me, is to make the flight with a multi-engined seaplane that has a pontoon or a boat for landing.

It is safe to say that the men—and women, for there are many such this year—who propose these daring flights are the cream of our civilization. I found the ones I knew brave, enterprising, resourceful and imaginative.

Are we going to sit idly by and watch these young Americans go to their deaths, as so many are bound to, and never raise a hand to try to stop them?

I personally and with the greatest reluctance venture to protest, because so many of us suffered last summer, seeing plane after plane get ready and go when we felt their chances of success were so pitiably slight. Yet whenever I undertook to point out the lack of planning and equipment in some of the other flyers I was met with: "Well, you took big chances, didn't you?"

The trouble was that in the confusion of that wild and unforgettable summer of 1927 we were all lumped together as a sort of fraternity, of which the members were heroes in public and clowns in private; idols if they lived and quickly forgotten if they died.

I have been urged strongly to speak. For months I have wondered if it were my place to do so. I can no longer remain silent. I feel that the lives of splendid people are perhaps involved.

I hope this is not presumption on my part. It simply happens that I have given many years of time and thought and investigation to the problem of long-distance flights, ever since 1918, when I began flying out of sight of land to test the possibility of navigating an airplane as a ship is navigated.

This is nothing to boast about. It simply shows I have had a hobby, just as another man might play golf or shoot clay pigeons. And I say this merely as my credentials in being so bold as to raise my voice against the tragedies sure to come if feverish, inadequately prepared ocean flights are made this summer.

There was my good friend Lloyd Bertaud, who was lost on the *Old Glory*. He and the others with him took off just before noon on September sixth. At four a.m. next morning *Old Glory*'s radio whispered the last desperate words of that brave little group:

"SOS. Five hours out of Newfoundland east."

This message was caught by three liners that happened to be in the vicinity.

For weeks previously Bertaud had been coming frequently into my New York office. I was discussing navigation with him.

"It's a big chance you're taking, old man, with your single engine," I once told him. He shrugged his shoulders but did not reply.

I think that, like so many others, he was caught up in the fever of it all.

Then there was my friend Lieutenant Omdahl, whom my shipmate Bernt Balchen had brought over from Norway on the chance that he might be able to go to the South Polar regions with me. Omdahl was a typical Viking, a strong, fearless fellow who had proved his worth with Amundsen on the Polar Sea in 1925, and again in the Norge in 1926. When I greeted him in New York I told him I hoped he wouldn't get the fever and try to cross the Atlantic.

"No danger of that," he said.

I believed him, because I couldn't picture a rock of a man like Omdahl being swept off his feet.

But even this calm Nordic succumbed. He accepted a job in Mrs. Grayson's ill-fated plane. Knowing that the season was late and this plane unlikely to succeed, I tried to talk Omdahl out of his ambition to fly the Atlantic. Failing to move him, I urged his intimate friend Balchen to do something to save him.

"I do something!" cried Balchen. "I can do nothing. He is a changed man since he took this disease to fly the ocean."

And so Omdahl died.

It is with a feeling of helplessness that one tries to combat an emotionalism of this sort. Logic fails. I have tried it.

"Yes," the ones I knew retorted, "you are right. We probably shan't make money. We may not become famous. We shall make no scientific observations. But

we're going just the same."

Mrs. Grayson is reported to have said, "I dreamed that I should go. I am going."

A will-o'-the-wisp.

I believe that the only effective argument against this state of mind is public opinion. It does not seem practicable for the government to step in.

After Roosevelt had talked me out of trying to fly the Atlantic in 1921, using a single-engined plane, we determined to do the job in a multi-engined plane. A plane with three engines, but capable of being kept aloft on any two, would have an enormous factor of safety compared with the single-engined machine.

The answer to this theory came last summer when 100 percent of three-engined transoceanic planes that started reached their destination—the big army plane, the *Bird of Paradise*, piloted to Hawaii by Maitland and Hegenberger, and our plane, the *America*.

Only about one-fourth of the single-engined planes that started succeeded.

One could be built or bought at short notice. Usually there was one around that could be adapted to a long flight.

"Why don't you make the flight in a three-engine plane?" I asked Lieutenant Tully sometime before he went to his death.

"There isn't one available," was his laconic reply.

Like some of the others, he recognized the chance he was taking, but simply did not see his way clear to avoid it. At the same time his excited state of mind would not let him give up the rash flight at hand.

Most of those lost disappeared without the slightest trace. But one plane was picked up at sea—that of Ruth Elder and Haldeman. Their single engine was failing from a broken oil lead.

In 1919 Hawker and Grieve landed by a ship in mid-Atlantic from engine failure. How many of the lost single-engined planes came down in the ocean from engine failure?

In fairness to Lindbergh and others, I should point out that if the long flight is to be made with a single-engined plane, then probably it is better for the pilot to go alone. Without the added weight of a companion, he can fly lighter and go faster and farther, besides taking off more easily and with less risk.

Country Doctor

by Norman Rockwell

(April 1947)

Dr. George Russell's office witnessed the woes and ailments of two generations of patients. His usual prescription was rest and fresh air, soap and water. The office had once been his living room.

A young doctor opened his first office in northern Vermont and had to journey to Poughkeepsie, New York in 1911. Overnight, he stopped in Arlington, Vermont, putting up in a pre-Revolutionary War inn. Arlington was an old town flourishing long before Ethan Allen and his Green Mountain Boys were born, as Early American as pewter. The traveler liked the looks of the place so well that he resolved to stay there.

So goes the story of George Russell, American institution. He is a family doctor, just one of a legion of hard-working men who have kept the nation healthy for two centuries. Their fame is not horizontal and national, but vertical and local. They are expected to battle everything from appendicitis to zonilitis, which,

(Right) House calls were easier for Dr. P.L. Marble of Marshalltown, Iowa, after he bought this Reo four-seater in 1907. The whole family participated in the test drive around the homestead.

along with being a handy example of an ailment beginning with z, is an eye trouble affecting the "zone of Zinn."

The family doctor is a hometown's man of miracles. The people want him when they need him, and he is usually there. His office resembles a den more than an examining room. The doctor himself is a kindly, tolerant man with a reassuring manner and a good disposition, with friendly advice stemming beyond the field of medicine. "My old man," Damon Runyon once wrote, "said that whenever his faith in humanity commenced to falter, he just contemplated the character and works of the doctors he knew, and that bolstered him up right away."

THE AMERICAN SPORTING SCENE

FROM SANDLOT TO SUPERDOME

"Give me a ball-park figure." "Game plan." "Run with it." "Teamwork." Our whole life is permeated with sports figures. If the Battle of Waterloo was won on the playing fields of Eton, the corporate strength of America, the ability of men to lead men, the satisfaction of fair play rose from the dust of back lots and high school stadiums. The endless tracks, the long afternoons, the stretched and battered muscles which make up the state of being called "in shape" take the athlete only so far. Beyond, is the game of the mind, as attested by Bobby Jones's immortal dictum that "golf is played on a three-inch course between the ears."

Sports have been a path to glory open to all, cheering the American imagination, which always delights in rags-to-riches stories. "The caddy who became a great golfer," "The little man from Middletown, U.S.A. who went on to fame and fortune in the Olympic games" are a standard broadcast line any Saturday afternoon.

The instinct of play is as basic in the human spirit as that of preservation or perpetuation of the species. Our first American sports were rural contests—greased-pig chases, flagpole climbs, farm-horse races. The essence of these tilts was participation. The prize—at least in the movies and fictional accounts—seemed always to be a pretty girl. Now the guerdon is endorsement of profitable products and the giving of vicarious pleasure to millions of Monday-morning quarterbacks. American front yards may well return to jungle because of the weekend habits of the American male. He wears sports injuries almost like badges of honor, and the initiation of the young on the playing field amounts almost to a puberty rite, especially for those past adolescence. The feats of the body, unlike the accomplishments of the mind, are impermanent. Big new frames break old small records. Sports are health, and health success, the paradise of the American mind. Bobby Jones, Babe Ruth, Red Grange, Bill Tilden, Babe Didrikson Zaharias. Would they change their state with kings?

(Right) To commemorate the 100th anniversary of baseball, Rockwell painted this old-time howitzer and his hairline sighter. The picture hangs in the Baseball Hall of Fame in Cooperstown, New York.

Running With It

Pal, all you got to do is remember three things: keep your guard up, your chin down and your seat off the canvas.

—*Jack Dempsey*
to a young fighter

The first thing to remember is never to read the papers when our team loses.

—*Yankee Johnny Lindell*
to rookie

Bob, no matter how much money you make, or games you win, or clubs you belong to, the size of your funeral depends on one thing—the weather.

—*Undertaker friend*
to Bob Devaney, award-winning
coach at Nebraska

The fans said we couldn't pass, couldn't run, couldn't dribble and didn't hustle. They're just like fans everywhere—picky, picky, picky.

—*Gary Hulst, head*
basketball coach at Montana
State after team had won four
and lost twenty-two in his first
season at the helm

During my eighteen years, I came to bat almost 10,000 times. I struck out about 1,700 times and walked maybe 1,800 times. You figure a ball player will average about 500 at-bats a season. That means I played seven years in the major leagues without even hitting the ball.

—*Mickey Mantle*

Trainer: "Yog, what time is it?"
Yogi Berra: "You mean now?"

—*Dugout anecdote about*
former New York Yankee Yogi Berra

In the old days, I had trouble finding people who could afford to pay me for golf lessons. Now everyone wants lessons from me. A few years ago, I had no car. Now I have five cars. I lived in a trailer. Now I have a five-bedroom house. I had no phone. Not only do I have a phone now, but the number is unlisted. Boy, that's progress.

—*Lee Trevino*

I have seen men, and women too, in the football and boat race and polo crushes guilty of discourtesy that they would never dream of under ordinary circumstances; pushing, jostling, elbowing, snatching, and talking in a way that would probably bring the blush of shame to their cheeks did they reflect on the matter afterward.

—*Damon Runyon*

Winning isn't everything; it is the only thing.

—*Green Bay Packer Coach*
Vince Lombardi

The way I sees it, braggin' is where you do a lot of poppin' off and you ain't got nothing to back it up. But I ain't braggin'. I know me and Paul is gonna win four games in this here series—if Detroit is good enough to win a couple when we ain't pitchin'.

—*Dizzy Dean on how he and*
his brother Paul would overwhelm
the Detroit Tigers in the World Series

Don't look back, something may be gaining on you.

—*Ageless pitcher*
Satchel Paige

All right—so I think I'm one helluva hitter. Well, all I'm asking is, suppose I stop thinking it, then who do you suggest is going to?

—*Boston Red Sox star*
Ted Williams

Tennis, anyone?

—*Humphrey Bogart's*
first spoken lines as an actor

When the Great Scorer comes to write against your name, he marks not that you won or lost, but how you played the game.

—*Sportswriter*
Grantland Rice

Thanksgiving, 1628 glares at Thanksgiving, 1928 as gridiron threatens meeting house as the proving ground for the American male.

Board meetings stop, the President has been known to turn down a crisis in order to watch, and spectators line up as much as a week ahead to get tickets. The day of $1.10 seats has long since passed but not the anticipation, though the Dodgers and Giants have moved west.

The Bad Old Days

by Connie Mack

(April 1912)

In 1883, when I was going on twenty-one, the manager of the East Brookfield team, for which I caught, felt cocky enough to write to Pop Anson's Chicago Colts and suggest that they stop off on their way back from a series in Boston and take us on an exhibition game. Our ball yard was just a vacant lot filled with Irish confetti—tin cans, plug tobacco tags, and shoe-finding scraps—but we got there during our hour off for lunch from the shoe factory and kicked most of the debris into far corners, where it wouldn't put a cockeyed hop on a ground ball.

The Colts were something to see. When they stepped on a baseball diamond, their air of devil-may-care force and vigor and skill inspired confidence and admiration among their followers and appreciation and awe in the breasts of their opponents. Above their white-stockinged legs they sometimes wore short but wide Dutch pants of dark hue; then they would appear the next day in the tightest kind of black tights. They affected bathrobes of loudly colored checks which they wore not only in the locker room, but on every possible occasion.

Baseball was mighty exciting and glamorous to me, but there is no use in blinking at the fact that at the time the game was thought, by solid, respectable people, to be only one degree above grand larceny, arson and mayhem. The late A.G. Spaulding estimated that about 5 percent of the players were crooks in the early days of professional baseball.

The first professional ball club, The Cincinnati Reds, was organized in 1868. Amateur clubs had been around since the 1830's. A 1907 commission found baseball was a purely American sport.

Gate crashers at the first World Series, 1903, between Boston and Pittsburgh, demonstrate the athletic prowess that made watching baseball the national sport. Abner Doubleday, pacing out the bases in the Elysian fields, Cooperstown, N.Y., would have been amazed.

Sports and Pastimes

by Irvin S. Cobb

(April 1936)

As I understand it, sport is hard work for which you do not get paid. If, for hire, you should consent to go forth and spend eight hours a day slamming a large and heavy hammer at a mark, that would be manual toil and you would belong to the union and carry a card, and have political speeches made to you by persons out for the labor vote.

But if you do this without pay, and keep it up for more than eight hours on a stretch, it becomes a sport of a very high order—and if you continue it for a considerable period of time, at more or less expense to yourself, you are eventually given a neat German-silver badge, costing about two dollars, which you treasure devotedly ever after.

A man who walks twenty-five miles a day for a month without getting anything for it—except two lines on the sporting page—is a devotee of pedestrianism, and thereby acquires great merit among his fellow athletes. A man who walks twenty-five miles a day for a month and gets paid for it is a letter carrier.

Also, sport is largely a point of view. A skinny youth who flits forth from a gymnasium attired in the scenario of a union suit, with a design of a winged Welsh rabbit on his chest, and runs many miles at top speed through the crowded marts of trade, is highly spoken of and has medals hung on him. If he flits forth from a hospital somewhat similarly attired, and does the same thing, the case is diagnosed as temporary insanity—and we hang a straitjacket on him and send for his folks. Such is the narrow margin that divides marathon and mania; and it helps to prove that sport is mainly a state of mind.

We in America have a range of sports and pastimes that is as wide as our continent, which is fairly wide as continents go. In using the editorial "we" here, I do not mean, however, to include myself. At sport I am no more than an innocent bystander. One time or another I have tried many of our national diversions and found that those which are not strenuous enough are entirely too strenuous for a person of fairly settled habits. It is much easier to look on, and less fatiguing to the system. I find that the best results along sporting lines are attained by taking a comfortable seat up in the grandstand, lighting a good cigar and leaning back and letting someone else do the work.

Reading about it is also a very good way.

Take fishing for example. What can be more delightful on a bright, pleasant afternoon than to take up a standard work on fishing, written by some gifted traveling passenger agent, and with him to snatch the elusive finny tribe out of their native element, while the reel whirs deliriously and the hooked trophy leaps high in the air, struggling against the feathered barb of the deceptive lure, and a waiter is handy if you press the button? I have forgotten the rest of the description; but any railroad line making a specialty of summer resort business will be glad to send you the full details by mail, prepaid. In literature, fishing is indeed an exhilarating sport; but so far as my experience goes, it does not pan out when you carry the idea farther.

To begin with, there is the matter of tackle. Some people think collecting orchids is expensive—and I guess it is, the way the orchid market is at present; and some say matching up pearls costs money. They should try buying fishing tackle once. If J. Pierpont Morgan had gone in for fishing tackle instead of works of art he would be now in the hands of a receiver. Any self-respecting dealer in sporting goods would be ashamed to look at his dependent family in the face afterward if he suffered you to escape from his lair for even the simplest fishing expedition unless he had sawed off about ninety dollars' worth of fishing knickknacks on you.

Let us say, then, that you have mortgaged your home and acquired enough fishing tackle to last you for a whole day. Then you go forth, always conceding that you are an amateur fisherman who fishes for fun as distinguished from a professional fisherman who fishes for fish—and you get into a rowboat that you undertake to pull yourself and that starts out by weighing half a ton and gets half a ton heavier at each stroke. You pull and pull until your spine begins to unravel at both ends, and your palms get so full of water blisters you feel as though you were carrying a load of hothouse grapes in each hand. And after going about nine miles you unwittingly anchor off the mouth of a popular garbage dump and everything you catch is secondhand. The sun beats down upon you in unabated fervor and the back of your neck colors up like a meerschaum pipe; and after about ten minutes you begin to yearn with a great, passionate yearning for a stiff collar and some dry clothes.

Suppose you do catch something! You cast and cast, sometimes burying your hook in submerged debris and sometimes in tender portions of your own person. After a while you land a fish; but a fish in a boat is rarely so attractive as he was in a book.

Camping is highly spoken of, and I have tried camping a number of times. When I go camping it rains. It begins to rain when I start and keeps on raining till I come back. It never fails. I have often thought that drought sufferers in various parts of the country who seek to attract rain in dry spells make a mistake. They try the old-fashioned Methodist way of praying for it, or the new scientific way of shooting dynamite bombs off and trying to blast it out of the heavens; when, as a matter of fact, the best plan would be to send for me to go camping in the arid district. It would rain copiously and without cessation.

It is a fine thing to talk about the perfumed, restful bed of balsam boughs and the dip in the mirrored bosom of the pellucid lake at dawn—old Emerson Hough does all that to perfection; but these things assume a different aspect when it rains. I remember camping with a man who appeared to be all that one could ask in the way of a comrade; after four days together, I could think of seven thousand things about that man I cordially disliked.

Coming now to aquatic sports as distinguished from pastimes ashore, I feel that I am better qualified to speak authoritatively, having had more experience in that direction.

Let us start with canoeing. Canoeing is a sport fraught with constant surprises. A canoeing trip is rarely the same trip twice in succession; and particularly is this true in streams where the temperature of the water is subject to change. It is comparatively easy to paddle a canoe if you only remember to scoop toward you. Even if you never master the art of paddling, you may still get along fairly well if you know how to swim. On the whole, I would say that one is liable to enjoy a longer career as a canoeist where one swims but can't paddle, than where one paddles but can't swim.

Approaching the subject of motorboating as compared with sailboating, we find the situation becoming complicated and growing technical. In sailing you depend on the wind, and there are only two things the wind does—one is to blow and the other is not to blow. But when you begin to figure up the things a motorboat will do when you don't want it to, you are face to face with one of the most complicated mathematical jobs known to the realm of mechanical science. A motorboat undoubtedly has a larger and fancier repertoire of cute tricks and unexpected ways than anything on the nature of machinery.

Motorboating for an amateur has certain advantages over sailboating. A motorboater—even the most reckless kind—knows enough to stay ashore when a West Indian hurricane is romping along the coast, playfully chasing its own tail like a young puppy; but that kind of situation is just pie for your seasoned sailboater.

Only last summer I had a very distressing experience with a sailboat, which was owned by a friend of mine— or perhaps I should say he was a friend of mine until this matter came up. From the clubhouse porch I had often admired his boat skimming gracefully over the bay, with its sail making a white gore against a blue background; and one day he invited me to go out with him for a sail. Before I had time for that second thought which is so desirable under such circumstances.

We cast off, as he called it, and almost immediately I was struck by several disconcerting facts. The first one was that his boat, which had looked moody and commodious when viewed from shore, appeared to shrink up when you were aboard her. Really, she was not much larger than a soap dish and not nearly so reliable. Another thing I noticed was the angriest looking clouds that anybody ever saw, piling up on the horizon. As I recall now, I said something about waiting until the typhoon was over; but my friend grinned in an annoying, superior kind of way and said he doubted the wind would blow more than half a gale.

When I came to, I decided to give up sailboating. This leaves the field of outdoor sport considerably circumscribed. I am too peaceful for baseball and not warlike enough for football. The doctor says I need exercise and I think I will go in for golf. I have chosen my caddie. He is a deaf and dumb caddie who has never been known to laugh at anything.

A Ballpark Figure

by Mrs. Babe Ruth

(March 1959)

In World Series competition he pitched twenty-nine and two-thirds scoreless innings. He batted in 1,495 runs to add to his own 714, and pitchers were so afraid of him he was walked 2,056 times. Ruth divided friends into "good guys" and "bad guys."

We had a matinee the next day, and when I arrived at the National Theater a little gnome was waiting. He was Eddie Bennett, bat boy for the Yankees. He had a note for me: "I don't know what hotel you're at, so I'm sending you this note. Will you have dinner with me this evening?" It was signed "Babe Ruth."

*   *   *

He was the first-born of George Herman and Katie Ruth. George Herman Ruth, Sr., owned a struggling barroom at 426 West Camden Street. His son George was hanging around it when he was five years old. He was chewing tobacco at seven, and drinking whiskey before he was ten! He was committed to St. Mary's at the request of his parents.

Everything that happened to my husband in his childhood was bad except one thing. This was the fact that a certain six-and-a-half-foot man saw something in Babe that no one else could see. He saw that Babe was inherently a decent human being, although outward appearances were to the contrary. The six-and-a-half-foot giant was a Xaverian Brother named Matthias. He was a teacher at Mary's Industrial School in Baltimore when Babe and he crossed paths.

"Brother Matthias was the greatest man I ever knew," the Babe said often. The Brother taught Babe to read and write; the difference between right and wrong (and there was a job); and he taught Babe a game called baseball.

*   *   *

The 1927 Yankees were the greatest baseball team that ever played and my husband was the greatest player on that team. The pennant race was over by the first of September, but Babe was fighting to break his home-run record of fifty-nine. He did it, of course. The sixtieth was made in the Yankee stadium against Washington. Tom Zachary, a left-hander, was the pitcher, and the homer came in the final game of the season.

*   *   *

Babe Ruth and kids went together. Babe was bluff and blunt, but he could reduce the shyest of kids to the status of a bosom companion in three minutes or less. I think Babe's own childhood gave him an affinity and an understanding with children, particularly with a child in distress. I believe he went to see more sick kids than any other man who ever lived.

*   *   *

On the "silly feud" that separated Ruth and Lou Gehrig:

Lou Gehrig was a shy, handsome giant of only twenty-two when he joined the Yankees in 1925. The Babe and Lou had ten years as teammates. They were to become fast friends, and bitter enemies—and friends again.

Ruth was adjudged a "hopeless incorrigible" at seven by the Maryland courts. When he wooed his wife, an actress, he asked her to come to his hotel room for dinner. Weren't there any restaurants, asked the future Mrs. Ruth. "Lord, Miss Hodgson," he replied, "I can't go into any restaurant. I get mobbed every time. You won't have to worry though, my suite'll be lousy with people." Then, sadly, "It always is." (Top) In an early Wheaties ad, two kids demonstrate that familiarity does not necessarily breed contempt. Everybody called George Herman Ruth Babe. (Bottom) Lou Gehrig, Number Four, greets Ruth, Number Three, as he crosses the plate on one of his frequent trips home.

The Babe's face was a square. Ditto his trunk. Six feet two, he weighed 215. His arms were short and seemed powerless, but when he came to bat and the ash stripling cracked with his might, he could make a whole forest sorry it had ever sprouted.

One day, the Babe and Lou met in the clubhouse. There was no Ruthian outburst. He simply told Gehrig, "Never speak to me again off the ball field."

And so it went until 1939, several years after the Babe had retired. Lou, the man of iron, was dying of amyotrophic lateral sclerosis. In May of 1939 he asked Joe McCarthy not to start him in a game. It ended the longest playing streak in history—2,130 consecutive games.

On July 4, 1939, the Yankees sent for all the great stars who had been part of the Gehrig saga to pay tribute to Lou. The spectacle of a man who is going to die, talking to 60,000 people, is an awe-inspiring one. Lou was up to it. He spoke of his mother and father, of his wife and of being a Yankee—the four things he loved the most on earth. Then he said, "I consider myself the luckiest man in the world."

I was conscious of movement in the deathly-still infield, and realized it was Babe. He walked over to Lou and threw his arms around him. Lou returned the greeting and smiled. Later Babe told me, "Damn it, I went over there because I had to, I wanted to cheer him up. I wound up crying like a baby."

He was to make one more appearance at the stadium. On June 13, 1948, the Yankees celebrated the silver anniversary of "The House That Ruth Built."

He stood there near home plate, so very thin and bent. He had a bat in his hand. Now the bat was no longer a weapon of destruction. It was a thinly disguised support for his trembling body. They cheered and cheered. He took off his hat, his head hung low.

Thirteen days later Doctor MacDonald took the Babe to a hospital. At the hospital on the evening of August fifteenth I kissed my husband good night and he said, "Don't come back tomorrow. I won't be here." I did come back the next morning, and he was there, but only for a little while. He died that morning at 8:01.

Ruth connects. He not only announced his plans to blast home runs but even pointed to the spot where the ball would disappear, sending it out for a sick child by a radio somewhere.

The Babe stands for the last time in Yankee Stadium, "The House That Ruth Built." Within two months he would be dead of cancer.

The Homerun King

by Bob Collins

(July 1972)

How could a soft-spoken, easygoing fellow destined to drudge through his career in Milwaukee and Atlanta possess the combativeness of a Ty Cobb, the swagger of a Babe Ruth, the apple-pie good looks of a Mantle or the grace of a Mays? Answer: no way. So Henry Aaron became Henry Afterthought as Mantle and Mays took up the chase to the mountain. It cannot be reached by ropes, it must be climbed one home run at a time. It's Ruth's mark of 714 home runs.

Mantle retired with 536 home runs. Mays began this season with 646, but Willie (is it possible?) is forty-one and slowing rapidly.

The new idol of the sporting public is a thirty-eight-year-old outfielder with a bum knee. On the subject of records, Aaron says: "They are made to be broken, and if I don't break Babe Ruth's record, I hope someone else comes along and breaks it."

Aaron heads for home after blasting his 715th. His modest lifestyle suggested hitting the ball meant more than hitting the headlines. "The records that I am setting—for that matter the records any players are setting—I think someone will shatter all of them."

Homestretch

by Eddie Arcaro

(June 1958)

The pressure is easier on a jockey. Even men who play on teams are on their own, more or less. The pitcher or the hitter in baseball has got to be good in his own right. Nobody is up there helping a boxer. A jockey has a horse going for him, and I have to believe the horse is at least 90 percent of the battle.

The best horse I ever rode was Citation. I wasn't any asset to him. Anybody who knew the elements of riding could have won with him. Citation was so good you could make two or three mistakes in a race and still win. On the other hand, the best jockey in the world can't help a plug that's outclassed by superior horses.

I may get kicked out as president of the Jockeys' Guild for saying this, but I think our importance is overrated. Any one of two dozen top jocks does a good job if he makes a horse run up to its potential, because 70 percent of them don't want to win.

That's right. Horses are like people. Everybody doesn't have the aggressiveness or the ambition to knock himself out to make a success. Most horses will dog it and goof off if you let them get away with it.

Too much junk is written about a sense of pace. Every good new boy who comes up is described as a "jock with a clock in his head." It's ridiculous. There isn't one rider in the country who knows how fast a race is run. Track conditions vary so much there can be a difference of three seconds in a mile from one day to the next.

I've never set goals for myself. I treat riding as a business and try to win each race as it comes along.

(Top) Arcaro himself posed for Rockwell's 1958 cover of a jockey weighing in. (Bottom) Derby day at Churchill Downs in Louisville attracts a hundred thousand fans to watch the ninth race for a purse as large as the audience. 1974 was its hundredth run.

Golden Gloves

by Jack Dempsey

(October 1934)

A number of factors went to make me the greatest money fighter of all time. One was the fact that everybody wants to see the champion licked.

In the eight years and two months between July 4, 1919, when I won the heavyweight championship of the world from Jess Willard at Toledo, Ohio, to, and including, September 22, 1927, when Gene Tunney was given the decision in our second fight for the championship in Chicago, 576,213 people paid $9,255,848 to see me fight nine opponents.

In only three of the nine were the crowds with me. They were the Willard fight, into which I carried the crowd's wish that the champion be whipped; the Sharkey fight, in which I, a beaten champion, was trying to make my comeback, and the second fight with Tunney, into which again I carried the crowd's wish that the champion be beaten out from under his crown. In the other six the customers were pulling for my opponents to knock my head off.

The first Tunney fight was a real "natural." Tunney's record from the time he started fighting was that of a champion. He was one of the best boxers of all time and a better fighter than I was when we met in Philadelphia—a fact he proved by beating me.

Being human, I would like to have won my second fight against Gene Tunney, but losing it brought certain compensations. I was no longer a champion, so people could like me again. They said—and believed—that I was one of the greatest that ever lived, and that's a pretty nice thing to hear.

Jack Dempsey was considered one of the great fighters of all time, in the ring and in the business world. He never pulled punches.

by Gene Tunney

(February 1940)

I did six years of planning to win the championship from Jack Dempsey. I said to myself that he had his weakness, that Dempsey could be hit by a straight right and hurt. This was confirmed by what I saw in subsequent Dempsey battles. The next pertinent factor was Dempsey's ring mentality. If you were to ask me: "Who is the most intelligent fighter you have ever known?" I should reply: "Jack Dempsey out of the ring." I doubt if he ever planned anything in the ring, or thought about it much. But what a fighting instinct he had.

I was cocky about flying. A great deal too cocky. I got airsick. It was one of the worst airplane rides anyone ever had, and I almost passed out, airsick. When I got to Philadelphia, I was shaking and pale, green. And I had to go at once to weigh in. The illusion created by my airsickness put the finishing touch to the psychological background. The Dempsey camp believed more that the champ needed only to go in for a quick kill.

When the bell rang, he came charging. I fended him off and backed away. He made a second rush, and I repeated the maneuver of elude and clinch. Then, when he rushed a third time, I waited for the inevitable opening, the wide left hook that he was throwing at me. I stepped in with the straight right I had so long been practicing for that moment. He was dropped in his tracks and his knees sagged. I could see he was hurt. That blow won the fight.

The way to know about championship quality is to learn from champions; and that I did.

With Tunney down, Dempsey is waved to the corner before the count is begun. The extra seconds gave Tunney a break.

Gene Tunney was a well-educated, literate man, who happened to beat up people for a living. He helped change the fighter's image.

Winning

by **Red Grange**

(November 1933)

For forty-five minutes I held smelling salts under my nose, and with ten minutes of the fourth quarter remaining, the game still a scoreless tie, Coach Jones sent me back in.

Bronko received the ball from center and took two steps forward. The Spartan secondary closed in, expecting to stop Nagurski. Luke Johnsos, our end, had drawn in the secondary-defense man in that territory back in the end zone. Bronko threw a short, low pass to me. Any school boy could have caught that ball, but I wrapped both arms around it and held on for dear life as I fell. I have the football I caught under lock and key. Maybe they're right when they say football is an emotional game.

The "Galloping Ghost" disappears in his own dust to the despair of a grounded opponent. The empty-handed rival was one of many Grange left behind him in his brilliant career at the University of Illinois and as a professional with the Chicago Bears from 1923 to 1934.

by Elmer Layden

(November 1937)

Homesick expressions ran rampant among freshman faces, mine included. Oh, to be home again. By coincidence or by chance I found myself in Rock's office. Knute Rockne—the greatest teacher of football the game ever developed.

It was a casual conversation at first. He drew me out about my football aspirations and laughed at my notion that I was too small to play for Notre Dame—I weighed only 150 pounds. Suddenly, he said: "Layden, what's this I hear about your going home?"

"Well," I said sheepishly. "I've thought about it."

"That would be too bad!" he said crisply. "Too bad indeed. If you do go home though, you'll have one distinction! You'll be the first freshman Notre Dame ever lost because of homesickness!"

For a moment I was mad. Then I decided to stay.

When Stuhldreher, Miller, Crowley and I came along, Rock drilled us, hour after hour. If there are any benefits in football, there are some in the practice as well as in the actual playing of the game.

(Top) Notre Dame's Four Horsemen, Miller, Layden, Crowley and Stuhldreher. (Bottom) Layden, the undefeated fullback.

229

Basketball Players Make Good Dancers

by Justin M. Sam Barry

(January 1937)

My team, for the most part, was composed of boys who were fast but short, only one or two running more than six feet. Reach in basketball is just as important as in a boarding house. That extra few inches sometimes means the gravy. Nature had given me a squad of small boys to work with, but out of the slow-breaking offense I learned a great deal about coaching basketball.

I learned that I could take a boy who was not better than a twelve-second man running the hundred, and make a good basketball player out of him with the right training. I discovered that, with rope-skipping, boxing and an attempt at ballet dancing technique, I could develop skillful players. I say that modestly but sincerely. I insist that in basketball, under the rules today, there is more finesse, skill and athletic technique than in any other sport. Look at it the way I see it: You are in a dimly lit theater. Under the shimmering lights of the stage, the skillful toe dancer glides gracefully, rhythmically across the boards. To the measured beat of a 100-piece orchestra, the star of the dance steps lightly, deftly through her routine, her artistry holding the great audience breathless, silent. Then,

suddenly, the tempo changes. The orchestra leader flips his baton, the music swings into a faster time. The toe dancer whirls into a fast, difficult routine, her intricate steps coming faster and faster. To thousands of folks, that sends chills up their spines.

Now, in a high-ceilinged auditorium two basketball teams face each other. One team gets possession of the ball, the other team sets up a quick defense. The offensive team moves toward scoring territory. Back and forth, they pass the ball slowly. The forwards, from positions near the basket, suddenly start a play. They move into pre-arranged spots; the center takes the ball from a guard and bounces it to a forward. That man, running like a deer, flips it to the other forward, who in one motion flips it to the ring and the ball slips through. *That* sends chills up my spine!

Wilt Chamberlain, alias Wilt the Stilt, alias "Big Dipper," former genius on the court, goes up for points. Author, millionaire, high liver, Chamberlain was one of the first sports heroes to constructively criticize his professional association, both as a coach and a player.

Hard Harrys
of Hockey

by Dink Carroll

(January 1938)

The first time James J. Johnston, ex-matchmaker at Madison Square Garden, ever saw a major-league hockey game was at the end of a long day's wrangling, in which he had tried unsuccessfully to match fighters who wanted a first mortgage on the building for their services. It was so late when he emerged from his office that a New York-Toronto Maple Leaf game was in progress, and he stopped a while to watch it.

The player who caught his eye at once was Red Horner, the husky on the Toronto defense, who is known as the league's "bad man." Horner was dishing out the body checks that night, and every time he would throw a flying block into an oncoming forward, Johnston's enthusiasm moved up another notch.

"That Horner's the only guy I've ever seen," he said afterward, "who fights for nothing and doesn't care who he meets or how fast they come."

Boxing promoter Johnston did not have to know anything about hockey to realize that the game's biggest thrill is the terrific body clash it provides. His enthusiasm for Horner was the instinctive appreciation of the promoter for the man who stirs big crowds, and to the hockey mobs Horner personifies body clash. Every time the Toronto redhead appeared on ice that night, there was a sudden tightening in the 15,000 fans who jammed the Garden from rail to roof; and the moment he hurled his muscular body in the path of a speeding attacker, promoter Johnston could see the crowd come suddenly and galvanically alive, the vibrant relationship between the crowd and what was happening down there on the ice.

There is seldom any damage done in those fights you see on ice, because fighting on skates is not conducive to exact timing, and wild swings predominate.

The most hilarious battle in some years took place last year in a Toronto Maple Leaf-Montreal Maroons game, with the Conacher brothers in the leading roles and Red Horner and a policeman acting as stooges. Lionel Conacher resented Horner's method of checking. Charlie Conacher was only a few feet away and hurried to separate the embattled pair. In that process, he was roughed up, which made him sore at his brother, and he threw a couple of heavy punches in his direction. The referee appeared on the scene and put all three of them off. Lionel and Charlie continued to argue as they were going through the gate and they suddenly grappled again. It was at this juncture that an innocent cop appeared. He picked on Lionel, only to find Charlie on his back in a twinkling. It was a family fight, and the Conachers were prepared to offer a united front against outsiders.

There are other reasons, of course, besides this spectacular body contact, for the surprising hold hockey has secured on the American sport public in the last ten years. It is played at such blazing speed that it is called "the fastest game in the world." It has the color and exhilaration of football and the beauty and rhythm of tennis. It calls for quick thinking and accurate puck handling. Playmaking requires the smoothness and delicate precision of baseball. All are pleasing, but it's body clash alone that stirs the crowds. For the emotion he shows, it might be ice water, not blood, that flows in a hockey player's veins.

Bobby Orr (right) was rookie of the year, outstanding defenseman five years in a row, and the National Hockey League's most valuable player for three years. "Because of his great speed he's always got the split second to do something extra," lamented an opposing goalie.

Helen Wills demonstrates her famous serene return. Unflustered by the competition, Miss Wills announced plans for a comeback at age 70.

My Life on the Courts

by Helen Wills

(June 1933)

Looking back on my early days of tennis, I can see that I accepted my wins with the calmness that takes all for granted. My defeats served to make me determined to win the next time. I never bumped my head on the clouds when I won, because I seriously felt that my wins were deserved, or rather that they were matter-of-fact events. Such is the faith of the very young.

Peace of mind is so valuable that the game of tennis is hardly worthwhile if the player is to become upset by what he reads. My advice to young players is: Forego the sports page. Delusions of grandeur have spoiled more than one player's game, and the heart has been often stabbed by adverse criticism. Strangely enough, it is much easier to recover from the latter than the former.

I have been asked, "What degree of skill did you display in your first tournament match?" It is rather difficult to answer such a question. I did well enough so that my father was surprised and pleased. The local sportswriters said that my game held a great deal of promise. As for myself during the match, I was so busy running after balls and returning them when possible that I was unaware whether I was playing well or badly. A tennis game is formed within the player. He learns by contact with the games of other players. This is reality in tennis, perhaps, as it is in life.

In tournament play, or in club play, there are players who have more power, more strength and more pace than other players. The tempo of their game is faster. Taking part in tournaments, I was continually trying to play better than I was able to play. Had anyone told me that I was going to be champion, I would have thought I would be so full of joy that life itself would have been painful to live. Things didn't feel differently at all. I was delighted, but the universe hadn't changed.

Secrets for Winning

by Billie Jean King

(March 1975)

Tennis is my thing and I love it. There are few thrills in life for me that compare with hitting a particular shot just right at a given moment—knowing that my balance is perfect, that the ball has hit the pocket of the racket and that it has taken me fifteen years of steady practice and playing to make the right shot at the right time. Although I play tennis competitively to win, I don't like to beat men. I've beaten them in practice and they were crestfallen. I beat Bobby Riggs and felt badly about it because the match was publicized as a battle between the sexes. It wasn't that at all. It was a competition between a young athlete and an aging athlete. I am younger and at this stage of our careers, I am the better player and that's all there is to it.

A good man can beat a good woman if they are more or less of equal age. There's no way I could beat Rod Laver, Stan Smith or Pancho Gonzales. But I think that at some time in the future we may have a woman win the world championship of tennis.

Many people think that because I am an athlete and like to compete I must be tough. To my surprise, this attitude even exists among some of the so-called women's libbers.

The woman champion of the future will probably be one who has been brought up differently from most of today's women. She will not have to face discrimination in sports and will probably be a woman who has been a good all-around athlete since childhood, accustomed to competing against men without any mental hangups.

That was not my case. I was brought up to be a wife, to consider men physically superior, and to look at sports strictly as a man's occupation. When I was in junior high school, and turned down invitations to slumber parties and girls' homes in favor of tennis tournaments, my friends thought I was an oddball. But I loved tennis and as the daughter of parents with a low income (my father was a Long Beach fireman) I felt that if I could become proficient at tennis I could travel and meet people—a notion the other girls laughed at.

I soon learned it was not a good idea to beat a boy I liked. It's amazing how losing to a girl can turn a guy off. Most fellows consider the girl who is a better athlete a threat. The only men who don't think this way are, in my view, the real men; these are the men who have their own thing, too, and no one can take that away from them.

I persisted, however, and learned that if a woman wants to make sports a career she has to be strong-willed because most everyone will try to discourage her. It's a tough psychological battle for the girl who wants to be an athlete, but I think it's getting easier.

Billie Jean King pours the laser beam of her concentration on her opponent's return at a match in St. Louis. Her widely publicized contest with Bobby Riggs made her a women's liberation heroine.

Net Results

by Jimmy Connors

(February 1975)

My mom and grandma taught me until I was sixteen. We had a court in our backyard. And then they said I needed more than two women could give me. "The only one we'd give you to is Pancho Segura," whom mom had played mixed doubles with years ago. So, when we moved out to California, I was fortunate enough to live about ten minutes from the country club where he was. It was hard for Pancho to change my game. I had more or less my own strokes. What he taught me was strategy and percentage tennis, which is mostly mental. Then there was Pancho Gonzales. The two Panchos tried to teach me a little bit the way each played. On the hard courts, I mixed up the Gonzaleslike attack with Segura's strategy.

Tilden was only six feet one but he seemed nine feet tall. The angle of his returns was often adjudged "impossible" by admiring fans.

by Bill Tilden

(January 1934)

What's wrong with our Davis Cup policy? Well, there's a new method of coaching—known, I guess, as the semaphore, or the stop-and-go-traffic method. Unfortunately, this theory of coaching violates the first great fundamental of tennis: "Keep the eye on the ball at all times." Let me state that the less one is forced to concentrate on tennis off the court, the more one can concentrate on it while playing.

I am forty years old, and for the past three years since I turned professional I have averaged four hard matches a week without vacation. It is time that tennis grew up to manhood.

Whiz kid Connors promises to become one of tennis's greats. His brashness and daring had him on the pro circuit at 19.

Eye on the Birdie

by Bobby Jones

(April 1958)

Golf is played at such a slow pace that you don't have an opportunity to work off steam in physical activity. Playing around that golf course in four hours, you get so weighted down by the strain and the responsibility and the difficulty of concentrating that you just wish to goodness that you could hit a careless shot—just hit the ball without thinking. And if you ever yield to that temptation you'll always pay for it.

It was like the time Sam Snead was talking to me in Augusta two or three years ago. Sam said to me, "Bob, tell me, which one of the championships that you won did you want to win the most?" I said, "Sam, it was always the one I was playing in at the time. And if I hadn't felt that way, I never would have won any."

Nicklaus has won more money in professional golf than any player in history. His legendary concentration triumphs over par.

by Jack Nicklaus

(April 1963)

Everybody says we make a lot of money. Well, we do. But we have to spend so darn much. Traveling with your kids, you have to spend, oh, $35 a night for two rooms if you're lucky.

The other day, I was paired with Dave Ragan and Al Baldwing. All three of us putted to within two feet of the hole, and then all three of us missed the cup with our next putts. As I walked off the green, some guy comes up to me and says, "Boy, you sure make me feel good missing those short putts. Are the greens really that bumpy?" Why, it was like trying to putt on peanut brittle!

The present way of playing was pioneered by Ben Hogan. Hogan perfected every shot except the putter, but somebody's going to perfect the putter too. Ben perfected the drive, the fairway woods, the irons, the pitch, the chip—everything.

Golf is still a gentleman's game.

Atlanta's Jones won golf's triple crown, was greeted by "Marching Through Georgia" played by a New York welcoming band.

Lapping It Up

by Johnny Weissmuller

(March 1930)

You may not believe it, but my championship life has not been all parade and no work. I had to do my stuff every day, whether anybody was looking or not. To keep in shape, once I arrived, required more work from me than from any other athlete who ever flipped a fin.

My workouts were a daily affair. Regularity was most important. I was swimming a quarter of a mile each time. This calls for twenty-two lengths of our sixty-foot tank. During this quarter-mile swim, I studied the purchase power I got on the water with my hands and forearms. Water is elusive, but you can get a hold of it if you know how to go after it.

Form and not fight results in good swimming. We are not machines of muscle and bone and blood alone. And we are not mentalities alone. We are a combination of both.

When I set out to break a record, I begin training a week or two ahead to swim exactly the time I expect to make. I don't do it every day, but three or four times a week. And I swim it in the very course where I plan to break the record.

Johnny Weissmuller, known to younger generations as Tarzan, is remembered by others as a great Olympic swimmer and model for the 1932 Games poster. Weissmuller's records stood intact until 1972 when a man with a moustache went all the way from Indiana to Munich to win seven gold medals. Mark Spitz took it all (including the money from television endorsements) in stride, shrugging off the credit to his coach and mentor, James "Doc" Counsilman: "He's one of the biggest inspirations of my career. He's just like a friend—a father. He's the best."

Freestyle

by Paul Gallico

(September 1931)

On August 6, 1926, Miss Gertrude Ederle swam the English Channel in fourteen hours and thirty-one minutes. Six women have swum it since and none has approached her time. No one but Trudy, blonde, sweet-faced daughter of an Amsterdam Avenue butcher in New York, will ever know what she went through in the exhausting struggle against the worst body of water in the world. It had never been done before by a woman. Sometimes, for every 100 yards she swam toward England, the tide whirled her 200 toward France. Sick, dizzy, tired, chilled, she kept on, and when she seemed at the end of her endurance and was asked whether she wanted to quit, she merely said, "What for?"

Two great swimmers of the Golden Decade of American sport, Annette Kellerman (left) and Gertrude Ederle (above). Miss Kellerman followed her swimming career with a stint with the Ziegfeld Follies—a hit in Broadway's famous Hippodrome pool.

THE AMERICAN STORY

A NEW ART FORM IS BORN

In 1843 Edgar Allan Poe wrote a story, "The Black Cat," for The Saturday Evening Post, then under the editorship of Thomas Cottrell Clarke. The other stories that were appearing in the Post and literary magazines of the period were in reality abbreviated novels. Length was strength. People bought magazines primarily "for the next installment," even when there was only one, i.e. a short, watered-down version of a novel posing as a tale. Poe's theory was that a story should be read at a sitting, its mood should overwhelm and startle, it should establish an intense and intimate relation between the reader and the word, and it should expose, like a nerve, a dark facet in the reader's own character which empathized with the dark character in the story. "The Black Cat" was of course not the first short story—telling a story is as elemental as human speech itself—but as a saleable object of entertainment it was the prototype for magazine stories for the next 100 years. Magazines changed; first they were fiction, then the article made its appearance, accompanied by the photograph. There was even a term for stories that were told mainly in pictures, photojournalism. But the eyes cannot supply all the bread of life; the mind hungers for wisdom and exercise, demands a store of useful goods for dark and lonely times, and the ages become the book on which it relies for sustenance. The most successful articles are largely fiction and vice versa. Fiction reveals to man his possibilities and his limits. Poe was followed by a flock of great American writers, most of them closely connected with the development of magazines. These writers worried first about making a living, second about producing literature. They worked with such ferocity that in some of their stories printed serially, they would kill off a character only to bring him back in a later installment, alive and well. "Pulp" was a familiar and apt description of many magazines; immortality is usually made of sterner stuff. But the tales that entertained endured, surviving in back pockets as well as libraries.

(Right) The association of the artistic with the anemic plagues the capricious world of American letters, but here, the outcome of a whodunit enables matter to triumph over mind.

Storytellers

You make it up out of everything you've ever learned, out of everything you've ever seen, out of everything you've ever felt. And then you put it down on paper, simply, as if you're telling the story to yourself or to a child. That's how to write a novel.

—*Ernest Hemingway*

That's seven schools and one apartment center named after me by now. I'm not sure about these honors to living poets.

—*Carl Sandburg*

"You must remember two things, Artie," said Lewis. "First, convince yourself that the book will never be finished. And, second, pretend that you really don't care."

—*Sinclair Lewis advising*
Artie Shaw on writing

I'm a storyteller. That, I guess, is my addiction.

—*Jacqueline Susann,*
author of Valley of the Dolls

You are the only man alive that can read your poems exactly right. There are poets who can't read their works worth shucks; and if they should offer to read their poems to me I should easily have the grit to say, "Oh, gimme the book and lemme show you *how!*— You just make me tired!" But I should never say that to you; no, I take my hat off to you, my boy; you *do* know how."

—*Mark Twain to James*
Whitcomb Riley

They ask me if I have a favorite (poem), but if a mother has a favorite child, she has to hide it from herself, so I can't tell you if I have a favorite.

—*Robert Frost*

James Thurber once met a young lady at a cocktail party who assured him that his books were even funnier in French. "Ah, yes," said Thurber, "I lose something in the original."

—*Jean Kerr's account of*
a Thurber anecdote

All the wisdom of the ages, all the tales that have delighted mankind for generations, are there at your fingertips, at negligible cost, to be picked up, savored, digested, and laid down exactly as your fancy dictates. That's why more good books will continue to be sold every year, despite all gimmicks and distractions.

—*Bennett Cerf*
on his publishing philosophy

I am a student of literature. The more knowledge a man has, the better prepared he is to lead. As I sit some time and ponder upon a word, I am lost for information.

—*A letter to*
President Roosevelt from
an admirer

The best style a man can hope for is a free, unconscious expression of his own spontaneity.

—*Oliver Wendell Holmes on*
style of writing in a letter to
Dr. John C.H. Wu

Mostly, we authors must repeat ourselves—that's the truth. We have two or three great and moving experiences in our lives—experiences so great and moving that it doesn't seem at that time that anyone else had been so caught up and pounded and dazzled and astonished and beaten and broken and rescued and illuminated and rewarded and humbled in just that way ever before. Then we learn our trade, well or less well, and we tell our two or three stories—each time in a new disguise—maybe ten times, maybe a hundred, as long as people will listen.

—*F. Scott Fitzgerald*

No one can tell what this nation will be like one hundred years from now. But one prediction is pretty safe: that, if we as a people have lost the habit of reading, if we have become a passive people, a society of viewers rather than thinkers, we will have lost our intellectual and moral vitality; and when these are gone, everything else will be about ready to go too.

—*Arthur Schlesinger, Jr.*

American stories tend to be more realistic than European tales, but the romance is there, and the dreams of Walter Mitty lurk in all of us.

Why Do We Read Fiction?

by Robert Penn Warren

(October 1962)

Why do we read fiction? The answer is simple. We read it because we like it. And we like it because fiction, as an image of life, stimulates and gratifies our interest in life. But whatever interests may be appealed to by fiction, the special and immediate interest that takes us to fiction is always our interest in a story.

A story is not merely an image of life, but of life in motion—specifically, the presentation of individual characters moving through their particular experiences to some end that we may accept as meaningful. And the experience that is characteristically presented in a story is that of facing a problem, a conflict. To put it bluntly: No conflict, no story.

It is no wonder that conflict should be at the center of fiction, for conflict is at the center of life. But why should we, who have the constant and often painful experience of conflict in life and who yearn for inner peace and harmonious relation with the outer world, turn to fiction, which is the image of conflict? The fact is that our attitude toward conflict is ambivalent. If we do find a totally satisfactory adjustment in life, we tend to sink into the drowse of the accustomed. Only when our surroundings—or we ourselves—become problematic again do we wake up and feel that surge of energy which is life. And life more abundantly lived is what we seek.

So we, at the same time that we yearn for peace, yearn for the problematic. The adventurer, the sportsman, the gambler, the child playing hide-and-seek, the teenage boys choosing up sides for a game of sandlot baseball, the old grad cheering in the stadium—we all, in fact, seek out or create problematic situations of greater or lesser intensity. Such situations give us a sense of heightened energy, of life. And fiction, too, gives us that heightened awareness of life, with all the fresh, uninhibited opportunity to vent the rich emotional charge—tears, laughter, tenderness, sympathy, hate, love, and irony—that is stored up in us and short-circuited in the drowse of the accustomed. Furthermore, this heightened awareness can be more fully relished now, because what in actuality would be the threat of the problematic is here tamed to mere imagination, and because some kind of resolution of the problem is, owing to the very nature of fiction, promised.

The story promises us a resolution, and we wait in suspense to learn how things will come out. We are in suspense, not only about what will happen, but even more about what the event will mean. We are in suspense about the story in fiction because we are in suspense about another story far closer and more important to us—the story of our own life as we live it. We do not know how that story of our own life is going to come out. We do not know what it will mean. So, in that deepest suspense of life, which will be shadowed in the suspense we feel about the story in fiction, we turn to fiction for some slight hint about the story in the life we live. The relation of our life to the fictional life is what, in a fundamental sense, takes us to fiction.

Even when we read, as we say, to "escape," we seek to escape not from life but to life, to a life more satisfying than our own drab version. Fiction gives us an image of life—sometimes of a life we actually have and like to dwell on, but often and poignantly of one we have had but do not have now, or one we have never had and can never have. The ardent fisherman, when his rheumatism keeps him housebound, reads stories from *Field and Stream*. The baseball fan reads *You Know Me, Al*, by Ring Lardner. The little co-ed, worrying about her snub nose and her low mark in Sociology 2, dreams of being a debutante out of F. Scott Fitzgerald; and the thin-chested freshman, still troubled by acne, dreams of being a granite-jawed Neanderthal out of Mickey Spillane. When the Parthians in 53 B.C. beat Crassus, they found in the baggage of Roman officers some very juicy items called *Milesian Tales*, by a certain Aristides of Miletus; and I have a friend who, in A.D. 1944, supplemented his income as a GI by reading aloud *Forever Amber*, by a certain Kathleen Winsor, to buddies who found that the struggle over three-syllable words somewhat impaired their dedication to that improbable daydream.

And that is what, for all of us, fiction, in one sense, is—a daydream. It is, in other words, an imaginative enactment. In it we find, in imagination, not only the pleasure of recognizing the world we know and of reliving our past, but also the pleasure of entering worlds we do not know and of experimenting with experiences which we deeply crave but which the limitations of life, the fear of consequences, or the severity of our principles forbid to us. Fiction can give us this pleasure without any painful consequences, for there is no price tag on the magic world of imaginative eneactment. But fiction does not give us only what we want; more importantly, it may give us things we hadn't even known we wanted.

Play, when we are children, and fiction, when we are growing up, lead us, through role-taking, to an awareness of others. But all along the way role-taking leads us, by the same token, to an awareness of ourselves; it leads us, in fact, to the creation of the self. For the individual is not born with a self. He is born as a mysterious bundle of possibilities which, bit by bit, in a long process of trial and error, he sorts out until he gets some sort of unifying self, the ringmaster self, the official self.

Fiction brings up from their dark, forgotten dungeons our shadowy, deprived selves and gives them an airing in, as it were, the prison yard. They get a chance to participate, each according to his nature, in the life which fiction presents. When in Thackeray's *Vanity Fair* the girl Becky Sharp, leaving school for good, tosses her copy of Doctor Johnson's *Dictionary* out of the carriage, something in our own heart leaps gaily up, just as something rejoices at her later sexual and pecuniary adventures in Victorian society, and suffers, against all our sense of moral justice, when she comes a cropper. When Holden Caulfield, of Salinger's *Catcher in the Rye*, undertakes his gallant and absurd little crusade against the "phony" in our world, our own nigh-doused idealism flares up again for the moment without embarrassment. When in Faulkner's *Light in August* Percy Grimm pulls the trigger of the black, blunt-nosed automatic and puts that tight, pretty little pattern of slugs in the top of the overturned table behind which Joe Christmas cowers, our trigger finger tenses, even while, at the same time, with a strange joy of release and justice satisfied, we feel those same slugs in our heart.

F. Scott Fitzgerald and Hemingway did not merely report a period, they predicted it in that they sensed a new mode of behavior and feeling. Fiction, by seizing on certain elements in its time and imaginatively pursuing them with the unswerving logic of projected eneactment, may prophesy the next age. We know this

from looking back on fiction of the past. More urgently we turn to fiction of our own time to help us envisage the time to come and our relation to it.

The story, in the fictional sense, is not something that exists of and by itself, out in the world like a stone or a tree. The materials of stories—certain events or characters, for example—may exist out in the world, but they are not fictionally meaningful to us until a human mind has shaped them. We are, in other words, like the princess in one of Hans Christian Andersen's tales; she refuses her suitor when she discovers that the bird with a ravishing song which he has offered as a token of love is only a real bird after all. We, like the princess, want an artificial bird—an artificial bird with a real song. So we go to fiction because it is a *created* thing.

Because it is created by a man, it draws us, as human beings, by its human significance. To begin with, it is an utterance, in words. No words, no story. This seems a fact so obvious, and so trivial, as not to be worth the saying, but it is of fundamental importance in the appeal fiction has for us. We are creatures of words, and if we did not have words we would have no inner life. Only because we have words can we envisage and think about experience. We find our human nature through words. So in one sense we may say that insofar as the language of the story enters into the expressive whole of the story we find the deep satisfaction, conscious or unconscious, of a fulfillment of our very nature.

The style of a writer represents his stance toward experience, toward the subject of his story; and it is also the very flesh of our experience of the story, for it is the flesh of our experience as we read. Only through his use of words does the story come to us.

And with language, so with other aspects of a work of fiction. Everything there—the proportioning of plot, the relations among the characters, the logic of motivation, the speed or retardation of the movement—is formed by a human mind into what it is, into what, if the fiction is successful, is an expressive whole, a speaking pattern, a form.

In recognizing and participating in this form, we find a gratification, a pleasing imitation of an imagined and longed-for order, though often an unconscious one, as fundamental as any we have mentioned.

The Black Cat

by Edgar Allan Poe

(August 1843)

For the most wild, yet most homely narrative which I am about to pen, I neither expect nor solicit belief. Mad indeed would I be to expect it, in a case where my very senses reject their own evidence. Yet, mad am I not—and very surely do I not dream. But tomorrow I die, and today I would unburthen my soul. My immediate purpose is to place before the world, plainly, succinctly, and without comment, a series of mere household events. In their consequences, these events have terrified—have tortured—have destroyed me. Yet I will not attempt to expound them. To me, they have presented little but Horror—to many they will seem less terrible than *baroques*. Hereafter, perhaps, some intellect may be found which will reduce my phantasm to the commonplace—some intellect more calm, more logical, and far less excitable than my own, which will perceive, in the circumstances I detail with awe, nothing more than an ordinary succession of very natural causes and effects.

From my infancy I was noted for the docility and humanity of my disposition. My tenderness of heart was even so conspicuous as to make me the jest of my companions. I was especially fond of animals, and was indulged by my parents with a great variety of pets. With these I spent most of my time, and never was so happy as when feeding and caressing them. This peculiarity of character grew with my growth, and, in my manhood, I derived from it one of my principal sources of pleasure. To those who have cherished an affection for a faithful and sagacious dog, I need hardly be at the trouble of explaining the nature or the intensity of the gratification thus derivable. There is something in the unselfish and self-sacrificing love of a brute, which goes directly to the heart of him who has had frequent occasion to test the paltry friendship and gossamer fidelity of mere *Man*.

I married early, and was happy to find in my wife a disposition not uncongenial with my own. Observing my partiality for domestic pets, she lost no opportunity of procuring those of the most agreeable kind. We had birds, goldfish, a fine dog, rabbits, a small monkey and *a cat*.

This latter was a remarkably large and beautiful animal, entirely black, and sagacious to an astonishing degree. In speaking of her intelligence, my wife, who at heart was not a little tinctured with superstition, made frequent allusion to the ancient popular notion, which regarded all black cats as witches in disguise. Not that she was ever *serious* upon this point—and I mention the matter at all for no better reason than that it happens, just now, to be remembered.

Pluto—this was the cat's name—was my favorite pet and playmate. I alone fed him, and he attended me wherever I went about the house. It was even with difficulty that I could prevent him from following me through the streets.

Our friendship lasted, in this manner, for several years, during which my general temperament and character—through the instrumentality of the Fiend Intemperance had—(I blush to confess) experienced a radical alteration for the worse. I grew, day by day, more moody, more irritable, more regardless of the feelings of others. I suffered myself to use intemperate language to my wife. At length, I even offered her personal violence. My pets, of course, were made to feel the change in my disposition. I not only neglected but ill-used them. For Pluto, however, I still retained sufficient regard to restrain me from maltreating him, as I made no scruple of maltreating the rabbits, the monkey, or even the dog, when by accident, or through affection, they came in my way. But my disease grew upon me—for what disease is like Alcohol?—and at length even Pluto, who was now

becoming old, and consequently somewhat peevish—even Pluto began to experience the effects of my ill temper.

One night, returning home, much intoxicated, from one of my haunts about town, I fancied that the cat avoided my presence. I seized him; when, in his fright at my violence, he inflicted a slight wound upon my hand with his teeth. The fury of a demon instantly possessed me. I knew myself no longer. My original soul seemed, at once, to take its flight from my body; and a more than fiendish malevolence, gin-nurtured, thrilled every fibre of my frame. I took from my waistcoat pocket a penknife, opened it, grasped the poor beast by the throat, and deliberately cut one of the eyes from the socket! I blush, I burn, I shudder, while I pen the damnable atrocity.

When reason returned with the morning—when I had slept off the fumes of the night's debauch—I experienced a sentiment half of horror, half of remorse, for the crime of which I had been guilty; but it was, at best, a feeble and equivocal feeling, and the soul remained untouched. I again plunged into excess, and soon drowned in wine all memory of the deed.

In the meantime the cat slowly recovered. The socket of the lost eye presented, it is true, a frightful appearance, but he no longer appeared to suffer any pain. He went about the house as usual, but, as might be expected, fled in extreme terror at my approach. I had so much of my old heart left, as to be, at first, grieved by this evident dislike on the part of a creature which had once so loved me. But this feeling soon gave place to irritation. And then came, as if to my final and irrevocable overthrow, the spirit of PERVERSENESS. Of this spirit philosophy takes no account. Phrenology finds no place for it among its organs. Yet I am not more sure that my soul lives, than I am that perverseness is one of the primitive impulses of the human heart—one of the indivisible primary faculties, or sentiments, which give direction to the character of Man. Who has not, a hundred times, found himself committing a vile or silly action, for no other reason than because he knows he should *not*? Have we not a perpetual inclination, in the teeth of our best judgment, to violate that which is *Law*, merely because we understand it to be such? This spirit of perverseness, I say, came to my final overthrow. It was this unfathomable longing of the soul *to vex itself*—to offer violence to its own nature—to do wrong for the wrong's sake only—that urged me to continue and finally to consummate the injury I had inflicted upon the unoffending brute. One morning, in cool blood, I slipped a noose about its neck and hung it to the limb of a tree;—hung it with the tears streaming from my eyes, and with the bitterest remorse at my heart;—hung it *because* I knew that it had loved me, and *because* I felt it had given me no reason of offence;—hung it *because* I knew that in so doing I was committing a sin—a deadly sin that would so jeopardize my immortal soul as to place it—if such a thing were possible—even beyond the reach of the infinite mercy of the Most Merciful and Most Terrible God.

On the night of the day on which this cruel deed was done, I was aroused from sleep by the cry of fire. The curtains of my bed were in flames. The whole house was blazing. It was with great difficulty that my wife, a servant, and myself made our escape from the conflagration. The destruction was complete. My entire worldly wealth was swallowed up, and I resigned myself thenceforward to despair.

I am above the weakness of seeking to establish a sequence of cause and effect, between the disaster and the atrocity. But I am detailing a chain of facts—and wish not to leave even a possible

FAUST

link imperfect. On the day succeeding the fire, I visited the ruins. The walls, with one exception, had fallen in. This exception was found in a compartment wall, not very thick, which stood about the middle of the house, and against which had rested the head of my bed. The plastering had here, in great measure, resisted the action of the fire—a fact which I attributed to its having been recently spread. About this wall a dense crowd was collected, and many persons seemed to be examining a particular portion of it with very minute and eager attention. The words "strange!" "singular!" and other similar expressions, excited my curiosity. I approached and saw, as if graven in *bas relief* upon the white surface, the figure of a gigantic *cat.* The impression was given with an accuracy truly marvelous. There had been a rope about the animal's neck.

When I first beheld this apparition—for I could scarcely regard it as less—my wonder and my terror were extreme. But at length reflection came to my aid. The cat, I remembered, had been hung in the garden adjacent to the house. Upon the alarm of the fire, this garden had been immediately filled by the crowd—by some one of whom the animal must have been cut from the tree and thrown, through an open window, into my chamber. This had probably been done with the view of arousing me from sleep. The falling of other walls had compressed the victim of my cruelty into the substance of the freshly spread plaster; the lime of which, with the flames, and the *ammonia* from the carcass, had then accomplished the portraiture as I saw it.

Although I thus readily accounted to my reason, if not altogether to my conscience, for the startling fact just detailed, it did not the less fail to make a deep impression upon my fancy. For months I could not rid myself of the phantasm of the cat; and, during this period, there came back into my spirit a half-sentiment that seemed, but was not, remorse. I went so far as to regret the loss of the animal, and to look about me, among the vile haunts which I now habitually frequented, for another pet of the same species, and of somewhat similar appearance, with which to supply its place.

One night as I sat, half stupefied, in a den of more than infamy, my attention was suddenly drawn to some black object, reposing upon the head of one of the immense hogsheads of Gin, or of Rum, which constituted the chief furniture of the apartment. I had been looking steadily at the top of this hogshead for some minutes, and what now caused me surprise was the fact that I had not sooner perceived the object thereupon. I approached it, and touched it with my hand. It was a black cat—a very large one—fully as large as Pluto, and closely resembling him in every respect but one. Pluto had not a white hair upon any portion of his body; but this cat had a large, although indefinite splotch of white, covering nearly the whole region of the breast.

Upon my touching him, he immediately arose, purred loudly, rubbed against my hand, and appeared delighted with my notice. This, then, was the very creature of which I was in search. I at once offered to purchase it of the landlord; but this person made no claim to it—knew nothing of it—had never seen it before.

I continued my caresses, and, when I prepared to go home, the animal evinced a disposition to accompany me. I permitted it to do so; occasionally stopping and patting it as I proceeded. When it reached the house it domesticated itself at once, and became immediately a great favorite with my wife.

For my own part, I soon found a dislike to it arising within

me. This was just the reverse of what I had anticipated; but—I know not how or why it was—its evident fondness for myself rather disgusted and annoyed. By slow degrees, these feelings of disgust and annoyance rose into the bitterness of hatred. I avoided the creature; a certain sense of shame, and the remembrance of my former deed of cruelty, preventing me from physically abusing it. I did not, for some weeks, strike, or otherwise violently ill use it; but gradually—very gradually—I came to look upon it with unutterable loathing, and to flee silently from its odious presence, as from the breath of a pestilence.

What added, no doubt, to my hatred of the beast was the discovery, on the morning after I brought it home, that, like Pluto, it also had been deprived of one of its eyes. This circumstance, however, only endeared it to my wife, who, as I have already said, possessed, in a high degree, that humanity of feeling which had once been my distinguishing trait, and the source of many of my simplest and purest pleasures.

With my aversion to this cat, however, its partiality for myself seemed to increase. It followed my footsteps with a pertinacity which it would be difficult to make the reader comprehend. Whenever I sat, it would crouch beneath my chair, or spring upon my knees, covering me with its loathsome caresses. If I arose to walk, it would get between my feet and thus nearly throw me down, or, fastening its long and sharp claws in my dress, clamber, in this manner, to my breast. At such times, although I longed to destroy it with a blow, I was yet withheld from so doing, partly by a memory of my former crime, but chiefly—let me confess it at once—by absolute *dread* of the beast.

This dread was not exactly a dread of physical evil—and yet I should be at a loss how otherwise to define it. I am almost ashamed to own—yes, even in this felon's cell, I am almost ashamed to own—that the terror and horror with which the animal inspired me had been heightened by one of the merest chimeras it would be possible to conceive. My wife had called my attention, more than once, to the character of the mark of white hair, of which I have spoken, and which constituted the sole visible difference between the strange beast and the one I had destroyed. The reader will remember that this mark, although large, had been originally very indefinite; but, by slow degrees—degrees nearly imperceptible, and which for a long time my Reason struggled to reject as fanciful—it had, at length, assumed a rigorous distinctness of outline. It was now the representation of an object that I shudder to name—and for this, above all, I loathed, and dreaded, and would have rid myself of the monster *had I dared*—it was now, I say, the image of a hideous—of a ghastly thing—of the GALLOWS!—oh, mournful and terrible engine of Horror and of Crime—of Agony and of Death!

And now was I indeed wretched beyond the wretchedness of mere Humanity. And *a brute beast*—whose fellow I had contemptuously destroyed—*a brute beast* to work out for *me*—for me a man, fashioned in the image of the High God—so much of insufferable woe! Alas! neither by day nor by night knew I the blessing of Rest anymore! During the former the creature left me no moment alone; and, in the latter, I started, hourly, from dreams of unutterable fear, to find the hot breath of *the thing* upon my face, and its vast weight—an incarnate Nightmare that I had no power to shake off—incumbent eternally upon my *heart*!

Beneath the pressure of torments such as these, the feeble remnant of the good within me succumbed. Evil thoughts became my sole intimates—the darkest and most evil of thoughts. The moodiness of my usual temper increased to hatred of all things and of all mankind; while, from the sudden, frequent, and ungovernable outbursts of a fury to which I now blindly abandoned myself, my uncomplaining wife, alas! was the most usual and the most patient of sufferers.

One day she accompanied me, upon some household errand, into the cellar of the old building which our poverty compelled us to inhabit. The cat followed me down the steep stairs, and, nearly throwing me headlong, exasperated me to madness. Uplifting an axe, and forgetting, in my wrath, the childish dread which had hitherto stayed my hand, I aimed a blow at the animal which, of course, would have proved instantly fatal had it descended as I wished. But this blow was arrested by the hand of my wife. Goaded, by the interference, into a rage more than demoniacal, I withdrew my arm from her grasp and buried the axe in her brain. She fell dead upon the spot, without a groan.

The hideous murder accomplished, I set myself forthwith, and with entire deliberation, to the task of concealing the body. I knew that I could not remove it from the house, either by day or by night, without the risk of being observed by the neighbors. Many projects entered my mind. At one period I thought of cutting the corpse into minute fragments, and destroying them by fire. At another, I resolved to dig a grave for it in the floor of the cellar. Again, I deliberated about casting it in the well in the yard—about packing it in a box, as if merchandise, with the usual arrangements, and so getting a porter to take it from the house. Finally, I hit upon what I considered a far better expedient than either of these. I determined to wall it up in the cellar—as the monks of the middle ages are recorded to have walled up their victims.

For a purpose such as this the cellar was admirably adapted. Its walls were loosely constructed, and had lately been plastered throughout with a rough plaster, which the dampness of the atmosphere had prevented from hardening. Moreover, in one of the walls was a projection, caused by a false chimney, or fireplace, that had been filled, or walled up, and made to resemble the rest of the cellar. I had no doubt that I could readily displace the bricks at this point, insert the corpse, and wall the whole up as before, so that no eye could detect anything suspicious.

And in this calculation I was not deceived. By means of a crowbar I easily dislodged the bricks, and, having carefully deposited the body against the inner wall, I propped it in that position, while, with little trouble, I relaid the whole structure as it originally stood. Having procured mortar, sand, and hair, with every possible precaution, I prepared a plaster which could not be distinguished from the old, and with this I very carefully went over the new brickwork. When I had finished, I felt satisfied that all was right. The wall did not present the slightest appearance of having been disturbed. The rubbish on the floor was picked up with the minutest care. I looked around triumphantly, and said to myself—"Here at least, then, my labor has not been in vain."

My next step was to look for the beast which had been the cause of so much wretchedness; for I had, at length, firmly resolved to put it to death. Had I been able to meet with it, at the moment, there could have been no doubt of its fate; but it appeared that the crafty animal had been alarmed at the violence of my previous anger, and forbore to present itself in my present mood. It is impossible to describe, or to imagine, the deep, the blessful sense of relief which the absence of the de-tested creature occasioned in my bosom. It did not make its appearance during the night—and thus for one night at least, since its introduction into the house, I soundly and tranquilly slept; aye, *slept* even with the burden of murder upon my soul!

The second and the third day passed and still my tormenter came not. Once again I breathed as a freeman. The monster, in terror, had fled the premises forever! I should behold it no more! My happiness was supreme! The guilt of my dark deed disturbed me but little. Some few inquiries had been made, but these had been readily answered. Even a search had been instituted—but of course nothing was to be discovered. I looked upon my future felicity as secured.

Upon the fourth day of the assassination, a party of the police came, very unexpectedly, into the house, and proceeded again to make rigorous investigation of the premises. Secure, however, in the inscrutability of my place of concealment, I felt no embarrassment whatever. The officers bade me accompany them in their search. They left no nook or corner unexplored. At length, for the third or fourth time, they descended into the cellar. I quivered not a muscle. My heart beat calmly as that of one who slumbers in innocence. I walked the cellar from end to end. I folded my arms upon my bosom and roamed easily to and fro. The police were thoroughly satisfied and prepared to depart. The glee at my heart was too strong to be restrained. I burned to say if but one word, by way of triumph, and to render doubly sure their assurance of my guiltlessness.

"Gentlemen," I said at last, as the party ascended the steps, "I delight to have allayed your suspicions. I wish you all health, and a little more courtesy. By the bye, gentlemen, this—this is a very well-constructed house." [In the rabid desire to say something easily, I scarcely knew what I uttered at all.]—"I may say an *excellently* well-constructed house. These walls—are you going gentlemen?—these walls are solidly put together"; and here, through the mere phrensy of bravado, I rapped heavily, with a cane which I held in my hand, upon that very portion of the brickwork behind which stood the ghastly corpse of the wife of my bosom.

But may God shield and deliver me from the fangs of the Arch Fiend! No sooner had the reverberation of my blows sunk into the silence, than I was answered by a voice from within the tomb!—by a cry, at first muffled and broken, like the sobbing of a child, and then quickly swelling into one long, loud and continuous scream, utterly anomalous and inhuman—a howl—a wailing shriek, half of horror and half of triumph, such as might have arisen only out of hell, conjointly from the throats of the damned in their agony and of the demons that exult in the damnation!

Of my own thoughts it is folly to speak. Swooning, I staggered to the opposite wall. For one instant the party upon the stairs remained motionless, through extremity of terror and of awe. In the next, a dozen stout arms were toiling at the wall. It fell bodily. The corpse, already greatly decayed and clotted with gore, stood erect before the eyes of the spectators. Upon its head, with red extended mouth and solitary eye of fire, sat the hideous beast whose craft had seduced me into murder, and whose informing voice had consigned me to the hangman. I had walled the monster up within the tomb!

Poe's exact logic—ratiocination—walls the reader in his own emotions the way the narrator immures his unfortunate victims. The black cat becomes the conscience from which neither reader nor narrator can escape.

Washington Irving made the name of Diedrich Knickerbocker, the phlegmatic old Dutchman, a permanent journalist's byline.

Washington Irving

From "The Contented Man," June 1821

In the garden there is a sunny corner under the wall of a terrace which fronts the south. Along the wall is a range of benches commanding a view of the walks and avenues of the garden. This genial nook is a place of great resort in the latter part of autumn, and in fine days in winter, as it seems to retain the fine flavor of departed summer. On a calm, bright morning it is quite alive with nursery maids and their playful little charges. Hither also resort a number of ancient ladies and gentlemen, who, with laudable thrift in small pleasures and small expenses, come here to enjoy sunshine and save firewood. Here may often be seen some cavalier of the old school, when the sunbeams have warmed his blood into something like a glow, fluttering about like a frostbitten moth before a fire, putting forth a feeble show of gallantry among the antiquated dames, and now and then eyeing the buxom nursery maids with what must have been mistaken for an air of libertinism. He seldom kissed a child without, at the same time, pinching the nursery maid's cheek.

James Fenimore Cooper

From "The Last of the Mohicans," March 1828

The warning call of the scout was not uttered without occasion. The roar of the falls had been unbroken by any human sound whatever. It would seem that interest in the result had kept the natives on the opposite shores in breathless suspense, while the quick evolutions and swift changes in the positions of the combatants effectively prevented a fire that might prove dangerous alike to friend and enemy.

A yell arose, as fierce and savage as wild and revengeful passions could throw into the air. It was followed by the swift flashes of the rifles, which sent their leaden messengers across the rock in volleys, as though the assailants would pour out their impotent fury on the insensible scene of the fatal contest.

"Let them burn their powder," said the scout. "There will be a fine gathering of lead when it is over, and I fancy the imps will tire of the sport afore these old rocks cry out for mercy!"

Cooper used American landscapes, and created distinctly new world characters in The Deerslayer *and* Leatherstocking Tales.

Hawthorne's 17th-century ancestors took part in the Salem witch trials. Guilt overwhelmed his exploration of the nature of sin.

Nathaniel Hawthorne

From "David Swan," October 1837

While he lay sound asleep, in the shade, other people were awake, and passed to and fro, afoot, and on horseback, and in all sorts of vehicles, along the sunny road by his bedchamber. Some looked neither to the right nor to the left and knew not that he was there; some merely glanced that way, without admitting the slumberer into their busy thoughts; some laughed to see how soundly he slept; and several, whose hearts were brimming full of scorn, ejected their venomous superfluity on David Swan. A middle-aged widow, when nobody else was near, thrust her head a little way into the recess, and vowed that the young fellow looked charming in his sleep. A temperance lecturer saw him, and wrought poor David into the texture of his evening's discourse, as an awful instance of dead drunkenness by the roadside. But censure, praise, merriment, scorn, and indifference, were all one, or rather, all nothing to David Swan.

John Greenleaf Whittier

From "Cypress Tree," May 1841

They sat in silent watchfulness,
   The sacred cypress tree about,
And from the wrinkled brows of age,
   Their failing eyes looked out.

Gray age and sickness waiting there,
   Through weary night and lingering day;
Grim as the idols at their side,
   And motionless as they.

Unheeded in the boughs above,
   The song of Ceylon's birds was sweet,
Unseen of them, the island flowers
   Bloomed brightly at their feet.

O'er them the tropic night storm swept,
   The thunder crashed on rock and hill;
The lightning wrapped them like a shroud,
   Yet there they waited still.

An ardent abolitionist, Whittier, without much formal education, excelled with Snow-Bound, *in the rural poetic genre.*

Henry Wadsworth Longfellow

From "The Goblet of Life," January 1842

Filled is Life's goblet to the brim;—
And though my eyes with tears are dim,
I see its sparkling bubbles swim,
And chaunt this melancholy hymn,
     With solemn voice and slow.
No purple flowers—no garlands green
Conceal the goblet's shade or sheen,
Nor maddening droughts of Hippocrene,
Like gleams of sunshine flash between
  The leaves of mistletoe.
This goblet, wrought with curious art,
Is filled with waters that upstart,
When the deep fountains of the heart,
By strong convulsions rent apart,
    Are running all to waste;
And, as its mantling passes round,
With fennel is it wreathed and crowned,
Whose seeds and foliage sun-imbrowned,
Are in its water steeped and drowned,
    And give a bitter taste.

Henry W. Longfellow made facts into legends and did so with believable rhythm to become America's most memorized author.

Lincoln said to Harriet Beecher Stowe, author of Uncle Tom's Cabin *(1853), "So this is the little lady who started the big war."*

Harriet Beecher Stowe

From "The Tea Rose," March 1842

There it stood, in its little green vase, on a light ebony stand, in the window of the drawing room. The rich satin curtains with their costly fringes swept down on either side of it, and around it glittered every rare and fanciful trifle which wealth can offer to luxury, and yet that simple rose was the fairest of them all. So pure it looked—its white leaves just touched with that delicious creamy tint, peculiar to its kind, its cup so full, so perfect, its head bending, as if it were sinking and melting away in its own richness. Oh, when did man make anything like the living perfect flower! But the sunlight that streamed through the window revealed something fairer than the rose. Reclined on an ottoman, in a deep recess, and intently engaged with a book, lay what seemed to be the human counterpart of that so lovely flower. That cheek so pale, so spiritual, the face so full of high thought, the fair forehead, the long, downcast lashes, and the expression of the beautiful mouth, so sorrowful, yet subdued and sweet—it seemed like the picture of a dream.

Mark Twain wrote the great American novel in Huckleberry Finn *unleashing realism on a reading public used to flowery romantic prose. His white suit was a sure draw on lecture tours.*

Mark Twain

From "Twain's Last," July 1869

The Wilson trial came to an end yesterday. In some aspects this was the most remarkable case that has ever had a place upon the criminal records of the country. It excited great interest in this part of the state, and during the last ten days the courtroom has been pretty generally crowded with eager listeners. The facts of the Wilson case were simply these: On the 17th of February last, George L. Roderick provoked a quarrel with Dr. R. Wilson in front of the Union Hall in this place. Wilson put up with a good deal of abuse before he even showed temper. He tried to pacify Roderick, but to no purpose. Roderick called him a thief, a liar, a swindler; yet, Wilson bore it all calmly. Roderick grew more excited, and heaped one opprobrious epithet after another upon Wilson, and finally called him a member of the New York Legislature. At this Wilson sprang to his feet, and remarking to Roderick that he would not take that from any man, shot him dead with an axe handle. Such was the evidence elicited upon the trial. The court acquitted Wilson upon the ground that the provocation was sufficient.

William Cullen Bryant

From "The Waning Moon," June 1844

I've watched too late; the morn is near,
  One look at God's broad, silent sky!
Oh, hopes and wishes vainly dear,
  How in your very strength ye die!
Even while your glow is on the cheek,
  And scarce the high pursuit begun,
The heart grows faint, the hand grows weak,
  The task of life is left undone.
See, where, upon the horizon's brim,
  Lies the still cloud in gloomy bars,
The waning moon all pale and dim,
  Goes up amid the eternal stars.
Late, in a flood of tender light,
  She floated through the ethereal blue,
A softer sun, that shone all night
  Upon the gathering beads of dew.
And still thou wanest, pallied moon!
  The encroaching shadows grow apace:
Heaven's everlasting watchers soon,
  Shall see thee blotted from thy place.

Bryant's Calvinist views contrasted sharply with his knowledge of classical rhymes and meters. He translated the Iliad *in 1870.*

251

William Dean Howells

From "Pioneer Days in the West," April 1898

Life was hard in those days, but it was sweet, too, and often it was gay and glad. The homes were at first of the rude and simple sort, which a thousand narratives and legends have made familiar, and of which every Ohio boy and girl has heard. It would not be easy to say where or when the first log cabin was built, but it is safe to say that it was in the English colonies of North America, and it is certain that it became the type of the settler's house throughout the whole middle west. It may be called the American house, the Western house, the Ohio house. Hardly any other house was built for a hundred years by the men who were clearing the land for the stately mansions of our day.

As long as the forests stood, the log cabin remained the woodman's home; and not fifty years ago, I saw log cabins newly built in one of the richest and most prosperous regions of Ohio. They were, to be sure, log cabins of a finer pattern than the first settler reared. They were framed of round logs, untouched by the ax except for notches at the end where they were fitted into one another.

William Dean Howells warned of the dangers of pervasive business in the nation's culture, influenced Crane and Henry James.

Stephen Crane's twenty-nine-year life immeasurably enriched American literature with The Red Badge of Courage *and* Maggie.

Stephen Crane

From "The Sergeant's Private Madhouse," September 1899

The moonlight was almost steady blue flame, and all this radiance was lavished out upon a still, lifeless wilderness of stunted trees and cactus plants. The shadows lay upon the ground, pools of black and sharply outlined, resembling substances, fabrics, and not shadows at all. From afar came the sound of the sea coughing among the hollows in the coral rocks. The land was very empty; one could easily imagine that Cuba was a simple, vast solitude; one could wonder at the moon taking all the trouble of this splendid illumination. There was no wind; nothing seemed to live.

Hamlin Garland

From "The Eagle's Heart," July 1900

Roseville had only one street, and it was not difficult to learn that Pratt had not yet appeared on the scene. It was essentially a prairie village; no tree broke the smooth horizon line. A great many emigrants were in motion, and their white-topped wagons suggested the sails of minute craft on the broad ocean as they came slowly up the curve to the East and fell away down the slope to the West. To all of these Harold applied during the days that followed, but received no offer which seemed to promise so well as that of Mr. Pratt, so he waited. At last he came, a tall, sandy-bearded fellow, who walked beside a four-horse team drawing two covered wagons tandem. Behind him straggled a bunch of bony cattle, herded by a girl and a small boy.

Harold said, "Pay me what you can," and Pratt replied: "Wal, throw your duds into that hind wagon."

As Harold was helping to unhitch the team the girl came around and studied him with care.

"Say what's your name?"

"Moses," he instantly replied.

"Moses what? Hain't you got no other name?"

"I did have but the wind blew it away."

Hamlin Garland's Main-Travelled Roads *emphasized the hardships of dirt farmers in the Middle West. He dubbed his style "veritism."*

"The Luck of Roaring Camp" and other sketches established Bret Harte as a colorful authority on ruffians with hearts of gold.

Bret Harte

From "Mermaid of Lighthouse Point," September 1900

It was a bright summer morning, remarkable even in the monotonous excellence of the season, with a slight touch of warmth, which the invincible Northwest Trades had not yet chilled. There was still a faint haze off the coast, as if last night's fog had been caught in the quick sunshine, and the shining sands were hot, but without their usual dazzling glare. A faint perfume from a quaint lilac-covered beach flower, whose clustering heads dotted the sand like bits of blown spume, took the place of that smell of the sea which the odorless Pacific lacked. A few rocks, half a mile away, lifting themselves above the ebb tide at varying heights as they lay in the trough of the swell, were crested with foam by a striking surge, or altogether erased in the full sweep of the sea. Beside and partly upon one of the higher rocks a singular object was moving.

253

Willa Cather

From "Jack-A-Boy," March 1901

We were not prepared to give Jack-A-Boy a very cordial welcome when his parents moved into number 324. It put us all in an ugly humor when we saw a hobby horse lifted out of the moving van. Of course there would be children, we said; we might have known that. Other people's children are one of the most objectionable features attendant upon living in terraces. We had more than enough of them already, and we resented a single addition. When he came we all eyed him sourly enough, and if looks could kill, the florist would have been sending white roses up to Number 324. I am quite unable to say just why we were all so fond of him, or how he came to mean so much in our lives. He was a trifle girlish in his ways, and, as a rule, I do not like effeminate boys.

Willa Cather, a teacher and newspaperwoman, found the background for her finest works in Nebraska, where she grew up.

A hobo, sailor and an adventurer, Jack London was an illegitimate child who became the best paid and best known writer in America.

Jack London

From "The Call of the Wild," June 1903

Hunters there are who fail to return to camp, and hunters there have been whom their tribesmen have found with their throats slashed cruelly open with wolf prints about them in the snow. Each fall when the Yeehats follow the movement of the moose, there is a certain valley which they never enter. And women there are who become sad when the word goes over the fire of how the evil spirit came to select that valley for an abiding place. In the summers there is one visitor, however, to that valley, of which the Yeehats do not know. It is a great, gloriously coated wolf, like, and yet unlike, all other wolves. He comes down into an open space among the trees; here he muses for a time, howling once, long and mournfully, ere he departs.

O. Henry

From "The Ransom of Red Chief," July 1907

There was a town down there, as flat as a flannel-cake, and called Summit, of course. It contained inhabitants of as undeleterious and self-satisfied a class of peasantry as ever clustered around a Maypole. Bill and me had a joint capital of about six hundred dollars, and we needed just two thousand dollars more to pull off a fraudulent town-lot scheme in Western Illinois with. We talked it over on the front steps of the hotel. . . . A kidnapping project ought to do. . . . We knew that Summit couldn't get after us with anything stronger than constables and, maybe, some lackadaisical bloodhounds and a diatribe or two in the *Weekly Farmer's Budget*. So, it looked good.

Often associated with New York City, the setting of The Four Million, *O. Henry published his first stories while in prison.*

Booth Tarkington received a Pulitzer Prize for The Magnificent Ambersons *and another for* Alice Adams. *He wrote twenty-five plays, served in the Indiana House of Representatives and feelingly portrayed childhood and adolescence in Middle America.*

Booth Tarkington

From "Talleyrand Penrod," June 1913

The cotillion loomed dismally before Penrod now; but it was his duty to secure a partner and he set about it with a dreary heart. The delay occasioned by his fruitless attempt on Marjorie and the altercation with his enemy at her gate had allowed other ladies ample time to prepare for callers—and to receive them. Sadly he went from house to house, finding he had been preceded in one after the other. Altogether, his hand for the cotillion was declined eleven times that afternoon on the legitimate ground of previous engagement. One lady alone remained; he bowed to the inevitable and entered this lorn damsel's gate at twilight with an air of great discouragement. The lorn damsel was Miss Rennsdale, aged eight. Miss Rennsdale was beautiful; she danced like a premiere; she had every charm but age. On that account alone had she been allowed so much time to prepare to receive callers that it was only by the most manful efforts she could keep her lip from trembling. The decorous maid announced him composedly as he made his entrance.

"Mr. Penrod Schofield!"

Miss Rennsdale suddenly burst into sobs. "Oh!" she wailed. "I just knew it would be him!"

Sinclair Lewis

From "The Other Side of the House," November 1915

He saw her nearly every time the train passed the farm; saw her reading books in the willow, or making believe as few girls still dare to do at fifteen. Once she was sitting on a wooden kitchen chair, wearing a pasteboard crown and languidly waving a scepter, which must recently have been the plunger in a patent washing machine. Though he waved his hand at the children who came out to watch the train go by, he dared not wave at the girl of the Farm of Windmills. She was sacred; he identified her with dreams and put her in a place apart. Someday, he felt certain, he should miraculously meet her; he would speak to her in a highflown, antiquated manner. He would not say Gee! to her; nor Gosh!—not once.

Sinclair Lewis, who satirized the smug and provincial businessman in Babbitt *and* Main Street, *was the first American to win the Nobel Prize. Earlier, he had refused the Pulitzer Prize.*

Ring Lardner

From "Alibi Ike," July 1915

His right name was Frank X. Farrell, and I guess the X stood for "Excuse me." Because he never pulled a play, good or bad, on or off the field, without apologizin' for it. "Alibi Ike" was the name Carey wished on him the first day he reported down South. O' course we all cut the "Alibi" part of it right away for the fear he would overhear and bust somebody. But we called him "Ike" right to his face and the rest of it was understood by everybody on the club except himself.

He ast me one time, he says:

"What do you call me Ike for? I ain't no Yid."

"Carey give you the name," I says. "It's his nickname for everybody he takes a likin' to."

"He mustn't have only a few friends then," says Ike. "I never heard him say 'Ike' to nobody else."

Irvin S. Cobb

From "Speaking of Operations," November 1916

For years I have noticed that persons who underwent pruning or remodeling at the hands of a duly qualified surgeon and survived, like to talk about it afterward. In the event of their not surviving, I have no doubt they still liked to talk about it, but in a different locality. Of all the readily available topics for use, whether among friends or among strangers, an operation seems to be the handiest and most dependable. It beats the weather, or Roosevelt, or Bryan, or when this war is going to end, if ever, if you are a man talking to other men; and it is more exciting than even the question of how Mrs. Vernon Castle will wear her hair this winter if you are a woman. Wherever two or more are gathered, it is certain somebody will bring up an operation.

Ring Lardner (above) spoke with the tongues of boxers, baseball players, chorus girls, songwriters and stockbrokers. Irvin S. Cobb (below) was the Post's *prime producer of belly laughs.*

Zelda, Scott and Scottie, archetypal expatriates, take a spin in France. Fitzgerald wrote 58 Post *stories.*

F. Scott Fitzgerald

From "Babylon Revisited," February 1931

They were gay, they were hilarious, they were roaring with laughter. For a moment Charlie was astounded; then he realized they had got the address he had left at the bar.

"Ah-h-h!" Duncan wagged his finger roguishly at Charlie. "Ah-h-h!"

They both slid down into another cascade of laughter. . . .

Again the memory of those days swept over him like a nightmare—the people they had met traveling; the people who couldn't add a row of figures or speak a coherent sentence. The little man Helen had consented to dance with at the ship's party, who had insulted her ten feet from the table, the human mosaic of pearls who sat behind them at the Russian ballet and, when the curtain rose on a scene, remarked to her companion: "Luffly; just luffly. Zomebody ought to baint a bicture of it." Men who locked their wives out in the snow, because the snow of twenty-nine wasn't real snow. If you didn't want it to be snow, you just paid some money.

Gertrude Stein

From "Money," June 1936

Once upon a time there was a king and he was called Louis the Fifteenth. He spent money as they are spending it now. He just spent it and spent it and one day somebody dared say something to the king about it. Oh, he said, after me the deluge, it would last out his time, and so what was the difference. When this king had begun his reign he was known as Louis the Well-beloved; when he died, nobody even stayed around to close his eyes.

Gertrude Stein, surrounded by modern masterpieces, including Picasso's portrait of her, takes a breather in her Paris cozy corner.

Secure behind tweeds, Marquand, Boston Brahmin, contemplates the American scene from the vantage point of Beacon Street.

J.P. Marquand

From "Pull, Pull Together," July 1937

"Take off your hat," I said to my son. "Do you think you're in a synagogue?"

My remark had been unintentional and I was sorry for it, since I had no intention of humiliating him, and he was humiliated. I had reproved him in the presence of company. A woman was coming out of the school office, gray-haired, but not matronly, with brown-paper cuffs pinned over the sleeves of her shirtwaist. She might have been Miss Fewkes, who used to be there. There was the same glint to her glasses, the same decisive lines from the pointed nose to the corner of the mouth, but she was not Miss Fewkes.

"Will you sit down please?" she said. "Doctor Harrison will see you in a few minutes."

I sat on one of the wooden chairs.

"You may look at the picture of the Roman Forum," I said to my son. "Maybe we'll go there someday. And don't snuffle. Blow your nose if you want to. Haven't you got a handkerchief?"

I had said the wrong thing again.

Thomas Wolfe

From "The Child By Tiger," September 1937

The years passed, and all of them were given unto time. They went their ways. But often they would turn and come again, these faces and these voices of the past, and burn there in George Webber's memory again, upon the muted and immortal geography of time. And all would come again—the shout of the young voices, the hard thud of the kicked ball, and Dick moving, moving steadily, Dick moving, moving silently, a storm-white world and silence, and something moving, moving in the night. Then he would hear the furious bell, the crowd a-clamor and the baying of dogs, and feel the shadow coming that would never disappear. Then he would see again the little room, the table and the book. And the pastoral holiness of that old psalm came back to him and his heart would wonder with perplexity and doubt.

Thomas Wolfe's elephantine vision of America was half Southern, half train window. He died of tuberculosis at age thirty-seven.

Paul Gallico's commercial successes in sportswriting almost kept him out of the heady realms of literature; he made it anyway.

Paul Gallico

From "The Snow Goose," November 1940

"Look, Philip," Frith said. Rhayader followed her eyes. The snow goose had taken flight, her giant wings spread, but she was flying low and once came quite close to them, so that for a moment the spreading black-tipped, white pinions seemed to caress them and they felt the rush of the bird's swift passage. Once, twice, she circled the lighthouse, then dropped to earth again. "She isn't going," said Frith, with marvel in her voice. "The princess be goin' t' stay." "Aye," said Rhayader, and his voice was shaken too. "She'll stay. She will never go away again. This is her home now—of her own free will."

William Faulkner

From "The Bear," May 1942

He heard no dogs at all. He never did hear them. He only heard the drumming of the woodpecker stop short and he knew the bear was looking at him. He never saw it. He did not know if it was in front of him or behind him. He did not move, holding the useless gun, which he had not even had warning to cock, and which even now he did not cock, tasting in his saliva that taint as of brass.

Then it was gone. As abruptly as it had ceased, the woodpecker's dry, monotonous clatter set up again, and after a while, he believed he could hear the dogs—a murmur, scarce a sound even, which he had probably been hearing for some time before he even remarked it, drifting into hearing and then out again, dying away.

Mississippian William Faulkner created mythical Yoknapatawpha county. To most Southerners it was terrifyingly unmythical.

Ernest Hemingway's terse style and adventurous life reminded the reader writing was a man's business and that the author had to be his own hero. Bullfighting, big game hunting and deep sea fishing only intensified the extreme delicacy of his ever-present fears about life.

Ernest Hemingway

From "The Great Blue River," July 1949

He may come behind the big, white wooded teaser that is zigzagging and diving between the two inside lines. He may show behind an outrigger bait that is bouncing and jumping over the water. Or he may come racing from the side, slicing a wake through the dark water.

When you see him from the flying bridge he will look first brown and then dark purple as he rises in the water, and his pectoral fins, spread wide as he comes to feed, will be lavender color and look like widespread wings as he dives just under the surface.

He will jump, and jump, and jump. Sometimes he will get the leader over his shoulder (the hump on his back behind his head) and go off greyhounding over the water, jumping continuously.

John O'Hara

From "That First Husband," November 1959

I have not made much of myself. I know that my judgeship came about through politics. My father had been on the bench and I had no doubt that some of the votes that came my way were given to me by innocent people who thought they were voting for my father. Obviously I had been in no scandal that would give me a separate identity, but even if I had been, I almost believe that the party and the people would have given me the benefit of the doubt. My family have lived in the same county for two hundred years, and the Otterbein name must be in the county records a million times. That may be a slight exaggeration, but only a slight one. When you think of it, a million times is only five thousand times a year, and in those two hundred years, the family has produced lawyers, doctors, ministers, schoolteachers, bankers, and even a couple of undertakers whose names would somehow get into the legal records of the county.

John O'Hara bragged his copy went straight from the typewriter to the printer. Although literary grandeur eluded him, he never became embittered, surviving his more glamorous contemporaries.

Kurt Vonnegut, Jr. built a fantasy out of the endlessly level reality of the American Middle West. He obliterated postwar pretentiousness with Cat's Cradle *and* Breakfast of Champions.

Kurt Vonnegut, Jr.

From "My Name Is Everyone," December 1961

For Harry's pleasure, and for our pleasure, too, we had him read from the scene where he beats up his wife. It was a play in itself, the way Harry did it. And Tennessee Williams hadn't written it all either. Tennessee Williams didn't write the part, for instance, where Harry, who weighs about 145, who's about five feet, eight inches tall, added fifty pounds to his weight and about four inches to his height by just picking up a playbook. He took off the coat and tie, opened his collar, then turned his back on Doris and me, getting up steam for the part. There was a great big rip in the back of his shirt too. He'd ripped it on purpose, so he could be that much more like Marlon Brando, right from the first.

"Is there a chance I'll get the part?" he said.

Arthur Miller

From "After the Fall," February 1964

I started to call you a couple times this year. Last year, too. Well, I lost the impulse. I wasn't sure what I wanted to say, and at my age, it's discouraging to still have to go wandering around in one's mind. Actually, I called you on the spur of the moment this morning; I have a bit of a decision to make. You know—you mull about something for months and all of a sudden there it is and you're at a loss for what to do. Were you able to give me two hours? It might not take that long, but I think it involves a great deal, and I'd rather not rush. Fine.

Arthur Miller's plays built a corona around essential American occupations. He wrote his masterpiece, Death of a Salesman, *while in his thirties, enjoyed both commercial and critical success.*

John Steinbeck brought the West into the mainstream of American literature. His heroes, like Tom Joad, symbolized the little man against the world, usually becoming victim rather than victor.

John Steinbeck

From "America and Americans," July 1966

One of the generalities most often noted about Americans is that we are a restless, dissatisfied, searching people. We spend our time searching for security and we hate it when we get it. For the most part, we are an intemperate people: We eat too much when we can, we drink too much, indulge our senses too much. We work too hard, and many die under the strain; and then to make up for that we play with a violence just as suicidal. The result is that we seem to be in a state of turmoil all the time, both physically and mentally.

Characters

In the early 1900's the *Post* began to run serials. It might be called pop art, fiction as recognizable as Andy Warhol's soup cans, and as saleable. The stories centered around comfortable characters, more real, perhaps, than the men who created them. Though most Americans would be hard pressed to match Tugboat Annie, Scattergood Baines, Alexander Botts, Little Orvie, Ephraim Tutt, Glencannon, and Jeeves with their makers, Norman Reilly Raine, Clarence Budington Kelland, William Hazlett Upson, Booth Tarkington, Arthur Train, Guy Gilpatric and P.G. Wodehouse, these authors were as rich and famous as movie stars, and their characters were as well known as the President. The *Post* even had a form letter for readers who demanded more. The letter said the authors were working as hard as they could and as soon as a new story was ready, the readers would be the first to know.

Few of these characters have any redeeming social value. They suit themselves, nobody else. With this concept readers identified. Who has not longed to be free of the responsibility of civil behavior.

William Hazlett Upson

From "Alexander Botts and the Young Inventor," Fall 1972

"The difference between the old methods and my new method is the same as between a gentle shove from a fat, lazy elephant, and a swift kick in the pants from a small but vigorous mule."

"It sounds good," I said. "Let's take this thing out and find a patch of soft, loose earth and see what it can do."

Pete's enthusiasm melted away. "I'm sorry," he said. "We can't."

"Why not?"

"So far, my pounder lacks one essential element. I have no air compressor. And I don't have enough money to buy one."

"What? You have conscientiously burrowed around in most of the best dumps and junkyards in this whole section of Vermont—you have gathered practically all needed parts, such as wheels, framework, and air hammers—but you have dismally failed to find an air compressor to actuate your remarkable mechanism?"

"Yes, I guess I have failed."

"Pete," I said, "I am disappointed in your attitude. Did Robert Fulton give up merely because he had no money to buy a boiler for his steamboat? Did the Wright Brothers quit because they had trouble finding a proper motor for their airplane?"

"Those guys had money. I don't."

"You soon will have. I am going to finance you. I don't have much in my checking account right now, but I am expecting a large payment very soon from the Earthworm Tractor Company. In the meantime my credit ought to be good enough. Kindly get in my car and we'll be on our way."

And we came back to Ripton with a very high-grade gasoline-powered air compressor.

Alexander Botts

Glencannon

Guy Gilpatric

From "The Hunting of the Haggis," January 1939

"Yes, yes, precisely! I've followed ye to a *T*, so noo ye can follow me to a whusky."

"Glodly!" said Mr. Glencannon. "However, Wully, I fear we dinna quite understond each other. I cudna use a billy goat's blodder, because I dinna want to mak' a futball, a bagpipe or a hot-water bottle. What I told ye I wanted to mak' was a haggis."

"A haggis?" Mr. Anstruther repeated again. "Ye mean a guid, auld, steaming, peppery, juicy, Heeland haggis? Weel, weel, weel, let's drink a drink to it! The only trooble is—er—er—— Trooble? Ho! If it's trooble ye're looking for, ye ugly brute, ye've only to——"

Norman Reilly Raine

From "Tugboat Annie," July 1931

Tugboat Annie stood at the wheel with a huge bean sandwich in one fist and a blue-granite mug of steaming coffee nearby, dividing her time between eating, steering and watching speculatively the head of Conroy, who stood on the forward deck, his hostile face turned toward the stormy waters of the strait ahead. She hailed him:

"Foul-weather Jack's abroad, so if ye like fresh air ye'll get plenty before the night's out."

But before he could deliver the spiteful comment that rose to his lips, one of the deck hands appeared in the pilot house.

He said, "Annie, Sam sent me to tell you that Shiftless is drunk as a fiddler's dog. He can't go on watch."

"What's that?" Tugboat Annie roared.

She lumbered hastily aft and disappeared down the engine-room housing. For a few minutes there was the sound of a minor hurricane below, dominated by her vigorous bellow. She reappeared, breathless and disheveled, followed by the oil-grimed figure of Sam, the engineer.

Conroy turned on her.

"Another sample of feminine muddleheadedness, eh, Mrs. Brennan?" he snapped sarcastically. "No extra fireman. Do you know what you're going to do now?"

"Yes," she wheezed, "I know. It's one problem you're going to answer for me."

Tugboat Annie

Mr. Tutt

Clarence Budington Kelland

From "Scattergood Baines—Invader," June 1917

"Tell you what I'll do," said Scattergood. "You men git back here inside of an hour with seven hundred and fifty cash, and lay it in my hand, and I'll agree not to sell groceries, dry goods, notions, millinery or men's or women's clothes in this town for a term of twenty years."

Within the hour they were back with seven hundred and fifty dollars in bills, a lawyer and an agreement, which Scattergood read with minute attention. It bound him not to sell, barter, trade, exchange, deal in or in any way to derive a profit from the handling of groceries, dry goods, notions, millinery, clothing and gents' furnishings.

He signed his name and thrust the roll of bills into his pocket. Then he picked up his mop and went to work as hard as ever.

"Say," Old Man Penny said, "what you goin' ahead for? You jest agreed not to."

"There wasn't nothin' said about moppin'," grinned Scattergood; "and there wasn't nothin' said about hardware and harness and farm implements either. If you don't believe me, jest read the agreement. What I'm doin', neighbors, is git this place cleaned out to put in the finest cash, cut-price, up-to-date hardware store in the state. And thank you, neighbors. You've done right kindly by a stranger."

Arthur Train

From "Tutt and Mr. Tutt—in Witness Whereof," May 1921

"Where did you get little Eva?" chirped Tutt, peering at his partner over his goggles through the door after the lady's departure.

Mr. Tutt's long wrinkled face wreathed itself in an expansive grin.

"Isn't she terrible!" he ejaculated.

"Some crocodile!" asserted the lesser Tutt. "I can see now what the fellow meant when he said that the female of the species is more deadly than the male! What kind friend passed her on to us?"

"Nobody—she came herself," replied the senior partner. "I think she must like my looks!"

"B-r-r-rh!" shivered Tutt, shielding his face with his hands. "I hope she won't take a fancy to me!"

"You're safe!" laughed his partner. "Mrs. Georgie Allison has rendered you immune to the attractions of the opposite sex for all time."

"Well, reverting to the subject we were discussing, what was the Lady Gorgon's name?"

"Mrs. Cabel Baldwin."

"Wife of the old fellow that married his trained nurse?"

Mr. Tutt gave a fervid start of surprise.

"What!" he ejaculated. "Really?"

"Don't you recall the case? 'Nurse Spearman'—and all that? It was in the papers," Tutt reminded him.

Scattergood
Baines

Jeeves

Booth Tarkington

From "The Terrible Shyness of Orvie Stone," June 1933

The upper surface of the rail of the balcony was flat and about three inches wide. Impelled by hatreds and by stinging and unbearable ambitions more powerful than himself, little Orvie climbed upon this rail and somewhat totteringly stood erect upon it. No one observed him immediately; even in the minds of his parents he had again become so inconsequent a factor in the pleasures of the day that his presence on the roof of the veranda had been forgotten.

Neither he nor anyone else understood this matter afterward; but, at the moment when he contrived to poise himself erect upon the rail, the punch bowl was to him the symbol or at least the suggestion of a tank of liquid far, far beneath a glittering figure upon a little platform high in the air.

"Look at me, Mamma!" little Orvie bawled star-

Little Orvie

P. G. Wodehouse

From "Jeeves and the Hard-Boiled Egg," March 1917

"It won't work. We can't get anybody to come."

"I fancy I can arrange that aspect of the matter, sir."

"Do you mean to say you've managed to get anybody?"

"Yes, sir. Eighty-seven gentlemen from Birdsburg, sir!"

I sat up in bed and spilt the tea.

"Birdsburg?"

"Birdsburg, Missouri, sir."

"How did you get them?"

"I happened last night, sir, as you had intimated that you would be absent from home, to attend a theatrical performance, and entered into conversation between the acts with the occupant of the adjoining seat. I had observed that he was wearing a somewhat ornate decoration in his buttonhole, sir—a large blue button with the words 'Boost for Birdsburg' upon it in red letters—scarcely a judicious addition to a gentleman's evening costume. To my surprise I noticed that the auditorium was full of persons similarly decorated. I ventured to inquire the explanation, and was informed that these gentlemen, forming a party of eighty-seven, are a convention from a town of the name of Birdsburg in the state of Missouri."

I was amazed. This chappie was a Napoleon.

"Eighty-seven, Jeeves! At how much a head?"

"I was obliged to agree to a reduction for quantity, sir. The terms finally arrived at were one hundred and fifty dollars for the party."

tlingly, standing upon the rail. "Look, Mamma! Look, Grandpa and Grandma! Look at me, everybody! Yi-i-i-i-i! Hurrah for me!"

The conclusion of his descent was complex. The impact was first, in a partially sitting position, upon the punch bowl. He caromed, upsetting the punch bowl, the table and his grandmother; but not the Governor, whose clothes, however, became mainly garnet. Little Orvie's grandmother sustained a bent rib, a thorough wetness, discolorations and an unsettling nervous shock. Little Orvie himself suffered no injury whatever, except the ruin of his clothes and being locked up in his grandfather's bathroom, unclad, for three hours before being taken home, put to bed and exhorted tragically and tediously. In fact, he became so bored with the passionate question, "What if you'd killed your dear Grandma dead?" that he finally went to sleep while it was being put to him.

Post Scripts

To a Lady

Lady, pretty lady, delicate and sweet,
   Timorous as April, frolicsome as May,
Many are the hearts that lie beneath your feet
   As they go a-dancing down the sunlit way.

Lady, pretty lady, blithe as trilling birds,
   Shy as early sunbeams plays your sudden smile.
How you quaintly prattle lilting baby words,
   Fluttering your helpless little hands the while!

Lady, pretty lady, bright your eyes and blue,
   Who could be a-counting all the hearts they broke?
Not a man you meet that doesn't fall for you;
   Lady, pretty lady, how I hope you choke!

—Dorothy Parker
October 1922

Of Fish and Men

The education of a true fisherman is a lesson of patience. In point of fact, there can be no such thing as an impatient fisherman. It cannot be denied, therefore, that insofar as fishing is the teacher of patience, it ought to be given credit in relation to the affairs of everyday life. If faith can move mountains, patience and faith ought to move the universe.

—Grover Cleveland
December 1903

Letter of a Self-Made Diplomat to Senator Borah

Tokyo, Japan

Dear Senator: Well, here I am, over in Nippon. I have to start right in, explaining the meaning of things to you, on account of you never having been anywhere: "Nippon" means "Sun." I have had very little trouble with the language. 'Course I don't know all the words, but I can carry on a pretty fair conversation with the words I have: "Nippon"—Sun—"Banzai"—meaning a word of exultation, as, say, if a Republican Senator would die from a Democratic stronghold, the yell among them would be, "Banzai! Banzai! Banzai!" It means a little more than joy. Then I can say, "Harry Carey." Now, "Harry Carey" in English means a darn good Western actor that can play any part; in fact he played Trader Horn. But the same word in Japanese means "to commit suicide." So I can say, "Hurrah, go commit suicide, in the Sun." Then they got a word, "Ohio," which means "hello," or "good morning." Over home, "Ohio" means the difference between being elected president and being just another ex-candidate.

—Will Rogers
March 1932

Epitaph on a Dull Parson

His congregation mourn his loss,
   To them a sad mishap;
May he be blessed—for he blessed them
   With many a pleasant nap.

—Anonymous
August 1849

Lines by a Clerk

Oh! I did love her dearly,
   And gave her toys and rings,
And I thought she meant sincerely
   When she took my pretty things;
But her heart has grown as icy
   As a fountain in the fall,
And her love, that was so spicy,
   It did not last at all.

I gave her once a locket,
   It was filled with my own hair,
And she put it in her pocket
   With very special care.
But a jeweller has got it—
   He offered it to me,
And another that is not it
   Around her neck I see.

For my cooings and my billings
   I do not now complain,
But my dollars and my shillings
   Will never come again.
They were earned with toil and sorrow,
   But I never told her that,
And now I have to borrow,
   And want another hat.

Think, think, thou cruel Emma,
   When thou shalt hear my woe,
And know my sad dilemma,
   That thou hast made it so.
See, see my beaver rusty,
   Look, look upon this hole,
This coat is dim and dusty;
   Oh, let it rend thy soul!

Before the gates of fashion
   I daily bent my knee,
But I sought the shrine of passion,
   And found my idol—thee;
Though never love intenser
   Had bowed a soul before it,
Thine eye was on the censer,
   And not the hand that bore it.

—Oliver Wendell Holmes
May 1842

Song

Gone, gone again is summer the lovely.
  She that knew not where to hide
Is gone again like a jeweled fish from the hand,
  Is lost on every side.

Mute, mute, I make my way to the garden,
  Thither where she last was seen;
The heavy foot of the frost is on the flags there,
  Where her light step has been.

Gone, gone again is summer the lovely,
  Gone again on every side,
Lost again like a shining fish from the hand
  Into the shadowy tide.
                    —*Edna St. Vincent Millay*
                    June 1928

A Rare Blake

A careless explorer named Blake
Fell into a tropical lake
Said a fat alligator
A few minutes later
Very nice, but I still prefer steak.

                    —*Ogden Nash*
                    July 1966

Moral Science

We may perhaps learn to deprive large Masses of their Gravity, and give them absolute Levity, for the sake of easy Transport. Agriculture may diminish its Labour and double in Produce; all Diseases may by sure means be prevented or cured, not excepting even that of Old Age, and our Lives lengthened at pleasure even beyond the antediluvian Standard. O that moral Science were in as fair a way of Improvement. . . .
                    —*Ben Franklin*
                    August 1780

To the Sundial

Thou silent herald of time's ceaseless light!
Say, could'st thou speak, what warning voice
  were thine?
Shade, who can'st only show how others shine!
In day's broad glare, and when the noontide bright
  Of laughing Fortune sheds the ray divine,
  The ready favors cheer us—but decline
  The clouds of morning and the gloom of night.
Yet are they counsels faithful, just, and wise.
  They bid us seize the moments as they pass—
  Snatch the retrieveless sunbeam as it flies,
  Nor lose one sand of life's revolving glass—
Aspiring still, with energy sublime,
By virtuous deeds to give ETERNITY TO TIME.
                    —*John Quincy Adams*
                    July 1842

Sonnet

The hope of truth grows stronger day by day;
I hear the soul of Man around me waking
Like some great sea its frozen fetters breaking,
And flinging up to Heav'n its sunlit spray,
Tossing huge continents in scornful play,
And crushing them with din of grinding thunder
That makes old emptinesses stare in wonder:
The memory of a glory past away
Lingers in every heart, as in the shell
Ripples the bygone freedom of the sea,
And every hour new signs of promise tell
That the great soul shall once again be free,
For high and yet more high the murmurs swell
Of inward strife for Truth and Liberty.
                    —*James Russell Lowell*
                    May 1843

BOOM AND BUST

WHAT GOES UP MUST COME DOWN

One day the Depression of 1929 will be as remote as those obscure financial panics that followed the Civil War and ruined hundreds of people, sending them flying out of the tallest buildings they could find. But not yet. It lingers in the American mind, an emotional encephalogram the end of whose plummeting line is always perilously close to the rainbow's pot of gold, the usual promise of this nation's prosperity. People who remember 1929 often confuse their youth with the low prices that prevailed and think of it as a good time. Prices were low but nobody had any money, and in a sense, like youth, the prices and the times were too good to waste on the Depression. Since then recession has come to be a more suitable term for less than ebullient economic conditions, a thorn by any other name. As always there are two sides to a depression: your side, and the side you read about. Graphs and unemployment indices make interesting conversation when you have a job; when you don't they become a dies irae, a dirge whose mournfulness is equaled only by the disastrously inward-turning spiral where people don't buy, manufacture decreases, and more jobs are lost. If the sky is darkest just before the dawn, the booms are brightest just before the busts.

"Working for the Yankee dollar," a slogan which made America think its power lay in its money rather than in its people, rose from the smoke of World War II, making the country conscious of the dangers of being a big spender instead of a big doer. Monetary isolationism is as impossible as human isolation; money without goods and services and people to back it up is merely paper; cash is simply the shorthand or symbolic expression of natural resources. The rich, contrary to popular belief, are no different from the poor, each depends on the other until he is fortunate or unfortunate enough to become his opposite. "Some goes up, and some goes down, and that's the way the world goes 'round," said Post writer Joel Chandler Harris's Br'er Rabbit.

(Right) One of artist J.C. Leyendecker's famous New Year's cherubs scans the ticker tape during the Great Depression, hoping for an upsurge. A lot of paper went into the basket before he saw it.

Taking Stock

The Neptune Pool, an azurean gem gleaming in the sunlight, was designed to provide a setting and reflections for the columns and arch of a graceful Greco-Roman temple that one of his agents picked up in Italy. When the marble-and-tile pool, holding 250,000 gallons of heated water, was finished, he was not satisfied with it. So it was torn apart and rebuilt to his satisfaction.

> —*Account of the building of William Randolph Hearst's pool at his San Simeon estate*

One of the outstanding features of this season is the way in which a majority of the American people are passing through a time of great discouragement without losing their sobriety. . . . There must be a depth and reality of patriotism, inarticulate though it be, in a people who have shown such patience, kindliness and friendliness in times so trying.

> —*1932 Saturday Evening Post editorial*

God gave me my money.

> —*John D. Rockefeller*

The machinery of existence had become more important than existence itself. The servants had outnumbered the family three to one. Moreover houses, horses, yachts, motor cars—all demanded constant attention; but unfortunately it was an attention that required no physical exertion. We had ceased absolutely to do anything for ourselves. Our wives grew fat from everlasting motoring. Even in our homes we went up and down stairs in elevators.

> —*Arthur Train, a Wall Street broker, on wealth, 1917*

It will be observed that all these causes of depression, with the exception of the early speculation, had their origin outside of the United States, where they were entirely beyond the control of our Government.

> —*Calvin Coolidge, 1932*

Mr. Getty has distinguished himself by reporting that he personally examines every single applicant; that he has been doing this, week in and week out, ever since the word got round in the late 30's that he was stupendously, redundantly rich, and that only twice has he yielded to a written entreaty.

> —*Wm. F. Buckley, Jr. on J. Paul Getty*

It must not be supposed that the trust-busting of a few years ago was a futile and misdirected effort. Big business has learned that some competition is desirable. It is more than reconciled to the abandonment of the old trust idea, such as the complete control of the oil industry by John D. Rockefeller and the railroad by E.H. Harriman. It is actually afraid of any attempt to restore these former imperial ambitions.

> —*Albert W. Atwood on big business, 1918*

When is it safe to invest? There are two answers. Both date from the beginning of the investment business: 1. Never! 2. Always! "Never" for the coward or the visionary. "Always" for the reasonable man; for it all depends upon what you call "safe," in a world peopled by fallible human beings.

> —*Edwin Lefevre, 1932 investment advice*

Recent bank failures in different parts of the country have been sporadic and of little general importance. The character of these failures has not shown a prevailingly weak condition, but has again disclosed defects of human character and institutions which only the millennium can remove.

> —*1929 Saturday Evening Post editorial*

. . . our American wage earner, employed or unemployed, has been giving an amazing demonstration of calmness, courage and confidence under the thoroughly distressing circumstances of the past few years—has, in fact, been staging an altogether remarkable social and civic phenomenon in the resourcefulness of his initiative, the steadfastness of his confidence in the future of America and American institutions, and especially in the coolness of his response to the red-hot preachments of the revolutionary soapboxer.

> —*from "The Hopeful American Worker" by Whiting Williams, 1933*

On October 24, 1929, $3 billion worth of paper profits had been wiped out in an hour, an average of about $50 million a minute. Grocers, seamstresses, housewives, and diplomats went from dream to debt. Efforts to make the crash appear temporary only made it worse.

July 28, 1932. Evicted by troops from the Capitol steps, a weary war veteran and his wife rest on a Washington, D.C. sidewalk. A few blankets and the flag are their only possessions. Economic conditions would get worse before twelve million unemployed found jobs.

Yoo-Hoo! Prosperity!

by Eddie Cantor

(August 1931)

Our President has done miracles for Europe. Maybe if we changed our name to Jugo-Bulgaria, he could do something for us. The future for Europe is simple. They're going to live on moratoriums. But what are we going to live on? I ask, what does the future hold for America? The bag.

Still, don't despair. Remember the proverb: when the wolf is at the door, don't look for the silver lining. While Hoover is busy with Europe, Cantor will take care of America. Since the depression began I've traveled all over the country—on foot—and after careful study of economic conditions wherever they've had any left, I've worked out a plan to bring prosperity right here.

The long gray line. Unemployment reached 12 percent, not including apple sellers. Bread was more important than social issues as these faces from New York's lower East Side show.

The entire Depression could be cured overnight. All you need to do is double up. Why should there only be nine men on a baseball team? And why only a football eleven? What is more wasteful than to have one jockey to a horse? Two chauffeurs in each car, two plumbers for each leak, two captains on each ship and two Presidents for each term. The Doubling System can work. It's so obvious I'm surprised nobody has thought of it before.

The apple sellers have been selling the wrong fruit. We could have brought prosperity back in six months if people would sell bananas instead of apples. The reason is simple. You eat an apple and you never hear from it again. But the minute you peel a banana, things start to happen. Somebody slips on the peel and soils his trousers. That makes business for the cleaner. The cleaner buys more benzine; the output of benzine increases. More people are engaged to extract benzine, to pack it, ship it and deliver it. Larger deliveries create a demand for more motor trucks and automobile companies start turning them out by the thousands.

Now figure out the millions of bananas that could have been sold by this time instead of apples, and picture the whole country busy cleaning pants, everybody busy, happy and prosperous. What the apple did for Newton, the banana could have done for President Hoover!

Reaping

by T. Cottrell Clarke

(September 1824)

Look around you and see if you cannot take some measures to improve your farm. Can you not drain the wet parts of it, and lead in streams upon the dry; remove stumps, stones, etc.; build walls; or prepare a place for compost. Can you not make a large stack of litter, in or near your barnyard, which you may cut down next winter; and with which you may litter your stables, hog-sties and etc. Gather the seeds that are first ripe, and preserve them carefully. Raise your own seeds, and you will know their quality. Do not cut corn stocks till the kernel is perfectly filled and somewhat hard. Break up greensward. Sow winter grain.

The American breadbasket is personified in this Illinois family, healthy and happily ready for a state fair in 1932.

The largest financial operation of its period—$50 million of United States bonds purchased by a group of leading bankers in New York.

Money Was Money

by an Old Fashioned Banker

(July 1932)

Now that George F. Baker has gone, only the merest handful of us are left whose banking life spans the sixty-odd years of money joys and money troubles from the booms and depressions following the Civil War to the booms and depressions that have been our part since the Great War.

"Sit down, sir, and let me look at your collateral notes."

Many things have come and gone. Many things have changed. But men have changed very little. In this the few of the old guard who are left would, I am certain, bear me out. By the old guard I mean John D. Rockefeller—as great a banker as a businessman—the Mellon brothers—the Ambassador to Great Britain, and R.B., the head of the Mellon National Bank—and E.T.

Stotesbury, the senior partner in Drexel and Co., of Philadelphia. They have seen, as I have seen, generation after generation riding the great merry-go-round trying to catch the brass ring. And I think that they would agree with me in saying that, although a few of us have learned a little, none of us has learned very much, and the public as a whole has learned nothing.

When I entered banking in the late 1860's, business was fitful and, they told me, rather bad. My job was to run errands and make myself useful at $200 a year. I was told that the bank I worked for ought to take down its sign and put up three balls, and that as bankers my employers were second-rate pawnbrokers.

As a banker, I should rise indignantly to deny that bankers are ever anything but the most stalwart supports of their communities. Since I am now writing anonymously, I can afford to be truthful. The truth is that nearly all the great financial disturbances which I know personally have been largely caused and certainly prolonged by bankers—not by the real bankers but by the men who, during booms, get into banks and banking firms.

At the first signs of trouble, the new bankers start heading backward more rapidly than they went forward and by crying "Wolf," they get depositors even more panicky than they are themselves. The inevitable crash finds the old-line banker holding the bag.

Nothing will substitute for experience in banking, and I would not qualify any man as capable of heading a financial institution and undertaking a proper responsibility to depositors, borrowers and stockholders unless he had been ripened by at least one panic and depression.

Helping Nature

by David Burpee

(June 1939)

My father used to travel upwards of thirty thousand miles each summer, visiting trial grounds and private gardens both in this country and abroad, looking mainly for vegetables. He scorned any specimen that was not perfect. His idea, like that of the country's first seed collector, Benjamin Franklin, was to hunt bigger, stronger, more abundant types and build purebreds by careful selectivity. To them, the great adventure was finding a good plant ready-made by Nature.

Today's vegetable originators do the opposite. They build plants to order. They wax enthusiastic over a specimen with unpalatable fruit because it has a single desirable characteristic. It resists the wilt, or it bears

two weeks early. Their whole scheme is to breed hybrids, and the big adventure is combining characteristics in one variety until it is just the answer to the housewife's or the chef's or the canner's current whim.

Breeding a better vegetable is a far more tricky undertaking than crossing strains to produce a new flower for your garden. In vegetables you have to change the very structure of the plant itself. Most of our old favorites in the vegetable garden were found ready-made by accident of Nature in some isolated garden. Most of the new favorites come to you as the result of the new magic of the plant geneticists. Today the average roasting ear wouldn't even recognize its own father and mother.

A seed company employee checks a new strain of zinnias on a California flower farm. W. Atlee Burpee, father of David and this firm's founder, was Luther Burbank's cousin. Together, all of these plant wizards helped feed American and make it beautiful.

Boyhood in Kansas

by Dwight D. Eisenhower

(April 1967)

Now that we had a large barn and acreage there were new items on the agenda each morning before school—milking the cows, feeding the chickens and horses, putting the stalls and chicken house shipshape. The legend which spread in later years was that I was always the last from bed. This may be true but I doubt it. Extra winks would not reduce the amount of work to be done. Mother and, above all, my brothers would not tolerate such escape from full employment.

Some mornings were worse than others. On washdays, all white clothes were boiled to kill germs. While one of us turned the washing machine, the others brought in water for heating in the reservoir, a five-gallon tank built as an integral part of a cookstove. No burden weighs

more on a boy's arm than a bucket of water. If he attempts to cut down the number of buckets by filling each to the brim, splashing and slopping mean mopping up floors. Nor does a bucket brigade, in the manner of colonial fire departments, help much when it is made up of boys in a hurry. We tried it.

All in all, we were a cheerful and a vital family. Our pleasures were simple, but we had plenty of fresh air, exercise and companionship. We would have been insulted had anyone offered us charity; instead, my mother was always ready to take some of her home remedies to anyone who was sick or suffering. The daily prayers of my parents did not fail to include a plea for the hungry, the weary and the unfortunates of the world.

(Below) Summer on the farm meant more than splashing in the swimming hole. There were also the long hours put into preparing 4-H projects for the fair. A young 4-H'er looks on with nervous anticipation as the county agricultural agent inspects her cow.

Debts and Taxes

by Calvin Coolidge

(March 1932)

Almost all units of government from the national treasury down are faced with a deficit. This comes at a time when many of them feel the necessity of enlarging relief expenditures. The result is a scramble for new means of raising revenue.

Some years ago it became apparent that tangible personal property and real estate were paying about all the taxes they could bear. To meet the cost of war, resort was had to very high income taxes, which were levied on the theory that those who had income could and must afford to make large contributions to public expenses. That seemed fair. With the increase in prosperity that the country enjoyed, large incomes increased rapidly, so that there was a great temptation to load more and more of the burden upon that source and release or disregard other and more stable sources of revenue. Now that large incomes have greatly diminished something must be done in a hurry to pay the expenses of government.

This situation raises questions of extraordinary difficulty. It is evident there are but three things to be done—increase taxes, increase debt, or reduce expenses. Not much thought has been given to curbing the cost of government. Increasing the debt means borrowing money to meet current expenses, which leaves the treasury in the precarious position of having an unbalanced budget.

That is always demoralizing. It can be done to meet a temporary emergency or for a specific purpose, but to borrow to pay ordinary running expenses of a government breaks down public confidence and very soon destroys credit. Some of our municipalities are already dangerously near this position. While no one questions the credit of the United States, a violent decline in government bonds recently gave warning that there is a limit to the borrowing power even of the strongest treasury in the world. When people saw that the national receipts last year were but $3,371,000,000, and that $236,000,000 of that came from foreign-debt payments, which are now suspended, while the expenses were $4,220,000,000, a cold shiver went down the financial spine of the public. Last year a deficit of more than 21 percent and this year a threatened deficit of about 40 percent were not pleasant to contemplate.

That was the immediate, pressing and even danger-ous situation that confronted the national treasury. Of course, we were a long way from being unable to meet our obligations, but we were in urgent need of more revenue to pay current expenses. Our situation is aggravated by a great shrinkage in all values, so that there remains little if any surplus out of which increased taxes can be paid.

We may wonder why this is the case when we know that in the past eleven years we have had four permanent reductions and one temporary reduction of Federal taxes and, by paying off about $8 billion of the nation debt, have made an annual saving of well over $300 million in interest. But all the money saved in one place has been expended, with some more with it, in some other place, so that the total cost of the Federal Government for the last fiscal year was considerably in excess of what it was eight or nine years ago. It is this expansion in the area of governmental activities, with the accompanying expansion of expense, that is a large factor in the present treasury difficulties.

Governments are necessarily continuing concerns. They have to keep going in good times and in bad. They therefore need a wide margin of safety. If taxes and debt are made all the people can bear when times are good, there will be certain disaster when times are bad.

Because our national wealth is more than $300 billion, some have thought our resources so nearly unlimited that we could pay any tax. But most of our wealth cannot be used to pay taxes. The collectors will not receive a farm, a home, a mill, a railroad or even an automobile. They want cash or bank credits, and cash or bank credits are strictly limited. Our property applicable to discharging a tax bill is a very different thing from the national wealth. To be safe and sound, taxes have to be earned. The only other source is capital, and taxes paid out of capital mean forced sales. When we arrive at that point we should like to close our eyes to what is sure to follow.

Of course, the national resources are still amply able to support the national credit. But it will mean balancing the budget, which must be done at a good deal of sacrifice and cannot fail to retard the revival of business. It is regrettable because it was mostly needless. If the same people who have lately been hastening down to Washington to protest that they cannot pay any more taxes had been half as diligent when the Congress was passing bills calling for billions of expense, they would not now be in such distress. They then sat supinely at home, leaving the public treasury and presidential vetoes to be overrun by a wave of extravagance. While the new taxes to balance the budget will be discouraging for business temporarily, it is the lesser evil, because an unbalanced budget would be disastrous. The national credit is our last resort; it must not be permitted to be impaired whatever the cost of maintaining it.

It may be wondered why the country did not realize sooner the dangerous position it was in or resist more energetically the imposition of such a burden of debt and taxes. The main answer is the indirect tax and the graduated income tax. The people at large do not see the indirect tax and have been deceived by the pretense that they paid no part of the high-rate income taxes. In both cases the result was the same; they thought someone else was paying the high cost of government. They listened to the claim that the few were being taxed for the benefit of many. When the time came, as it was sure to do, that the few found the high taxes could no longer be added to the cost of production, the many found themselves out of work. High taxes have not proved to be for their benefit, but are increasing their distress. While there were other causes for business depression, high taxes was an important one and is one of the main hindrances to a revival.

Another consequence of this method of taxation was the rapidly shrinking national revenue and consequently large deficit. The taxes were laid on uncertain and rapidly fluctuating sources. Big incomes were greatly reduced and small incomes were exempt. The result was loss of revenue at a time when it is a great burden to increase it.

More attention will have to be given in the future to broadening the base of the tax structure and seeking sources of revenue which do not shrink so rapidly as large incomes.

If we resort to borrowing, it must then be on the theory that, as we have no reserves, we will anticipate future prosperity and spend now what we think we may be able to save in the coming years. That may turn out well, but it is extremely hazardous. No one can be sure that public confidence will be restored and business thrive at the prospect of a large debt and future enlarged taxes. Living on past savings and borrowed money may be very delightful while it lasts, but it always results in a day of reckoning that is not pleasant. Spending money by private or public agencies before it is earned is not a conservation or accumulation, but a dissipation of capital, on which no sound or permanent business structure can be erected, but if long pursued leads in the end to universal bankruptcy.

Scarcely anyone questions the necessity of some increase of tax rates. But it seems apparent that such remedy ought only to be for the existing emergency that must be met to protect the public credit. The nation has the resources to provide for such action, and they must be used. But the only permanent remedy, the only relief for high taxes, is a reduction of public expenditures. Such a reduction must be made. Almost all our governmental units have been taxing, borrowing and spending beyond the means of the people to pay. Taxes remain unpaid. That causes forced sales of property and destroys values. The credit of many units is exhausted, so that no more money can be borrowed by them. The local governments have been the worst offenders and find themselves in the most serious difficulties. Nothing but drastic retrenchment will restore them to financial health.

The only remedy for the situation in which we find ourselves is an aroused public opinion. High expenses have created great debts and heavy taxes. The disaster these have brought is felt most keenly by the wage earners but the source of the evil is most apparent to our business interests. Many of these expenditures have been authorized by the appropriating power almost under duress. They did not want to do it. But the pressure was nearly all in one direction and there was little encouragement from the public in offering resistance.

The time has come for a combination, on a nonpartisan basis, of wage earners and businessmen for their mutual protection. They need to be organized, alert and vocal. Then the Congress and other bodies will listen because they will feel they have some support in resisting further expenditures and some encouragement in pursuing a policy of retrenchment.

Millionaires

by J. Paul Getty

(May 1965)

J. Paul Getty, probably the richest man in the world. He made his first million at the young age of 23, but in a still earlier business venture, at age 12, he recalls, "I used to collect copies of the Post *to sell every week in offices and homes."*

As soon as this is published, I know my mail will increase from an average low of 50 letters a day to 300, 400 or even 1,000. My two secretaries will be dealing with long letters from complete strangers, usually written in crabbed, almost indecipherable handwriting, and headed "Dear Paul." Some will be from cranks and religious maniacs, urging me to give away my riches for the good of my soul. A few, like one I received recently, will demand "one million dollars by return mail because you have so much of the stuff."

Perhaps it's the lack of consideration of the well-to-do solicitors for charities that irks me most. I'd never dare to do indiscriminate fund-raising among acquaintances of mine, let alone total strangers. As Groucho Marx once said, in an unforgettable hotel-lobby scene: "Boy, what are you shouting my name for? Do I go around shouting your name?"

When I was a boy, multimillionaires owned huge steam yachts, with large crews. I had one—until 1936. It gave me so much trouble I felt I was in the shipping business. If I ever buy a yacht again, it'll be a small one that I can handle.

The rich and the super-rich live in much the same way as the middle class, says Getty—they wear the same clothes, drive the same cars and live in more or less the same style.

Since multimillionaires have been stripped of so many status symbols and must live very much as other people do, they should be entitled to the same courtesies. If I go to a doctor, I should be charged the regular fee. If I go to a hotel, I should pay the standard charge for a room. And when I tip, I shouldn't be expected to tip more than the average man. It's rude and inconsiderate to overtip. It only makes things difficult—and embarrassing—for people who are not as rich as I am.

There was this business of the pay phone I had installed in my country house in England, to be used by my guests. When *I'm* staying with guests and have to make long-distance calls, I make a point of making them from a pay phone in the nearest town or village. I had the pay phone installed in my place because I knew my guests preferred it that way. And yet a spate of cartoons and letters resulted. You might have thought I was pathologically inclined.

With all these problems, why bother to become a millionaire in the first place? In my case, I inherited a certain amount of wealth and was determined to use that wealth constructively. I take a certain pride in running a corporation, if not more successfully than other people, at any rate just as successfully as most. I've never felt tempted to give my fortune away to buy my way to a better mood. There are people, of course, who have been destroyed, physically and morally, by their wealth. The same people, born poor, would have probably become alcoholics or thieves.

Though our rewards may be small, we are essential to the nation's prosperity. We provide others with incentives which would not exist if we were to disappear. If I were not using my fortune usefully, I would have little justification for having it in the first place. And if you then took it away, it wouldn't make all that much difference to me. At least I wouldn't be getting all those letters.

Love and Money

by John D. Rockefeller

(February 1898)

Who is the poorest man in the world today? The poorest man I know is the man who has nothing else in the world but money.

I believe it is a religious duty to get all the money you can, get it fairly, religiously, and honestly—and give away all you can.

I lived within my income in my early days. I paid my washerwoman and the lady with whom I boarded and I saved a little and put it away. I paid in the Sunday school every Sunday one cent. It was all I had to give. I had a large increase in revenue the next year. But when I got that increase I felt guilty—I felt like a capitalist. We had no trusts nor capitalists in those days. I remember the clothes I bought. I didn't patronize a fashionable tailor. The clothes were good, and such as I could pay for. Let me give you a word of advice: "Always live within your means."

What is success? Is it to get money? Well, is that success? If I had my choice today, I'd be a man with little or nothing but a purpose in life. It's not the money in itself that is so miserable. Money is good if you know how to use it. Let me give you a little word of counsel: know what you receive and how you spend it. Write down just what you do with it, and don't be ashamed to let your fathers and mothers see what you have written down.

My first business training was in keeping a ledger. It was the time when I began to spend my first earnings in my first struggle to get a footing. It was a very hard struggle. When I put my head on the pillow, the contents of my ledger kept running through my head until I awakened the next morning.

I came into sympathy with many undertakings, both religious and philanthropic. My opinion is that no man can trust himself to wait until he has accumulated a great fortune before he is charitable. He must give away money continually.

City men haven't had the struggles we had who came from the country.

John D. Rockefeller, Jr., with sons David, Nelson, Winthrop, Lawrence and John D. III, at the 1937 funeral of John D., Sr.

SPARE TIME

AMERICA AT PLAY

Our great-grandparents had eight children, chopped wood, ploughed fields, sewed the family's clothes, put up the family food, never missed church or tending a sick friend, and always helped build their neighbors' houses. In their spare time they made quilts, tended solariums, read and wrote three-volume novels and committed long passages of the Bible to memory. This was of course before the days of labor-saving devices. With the advent of washing machines, vacuum cleaners, electric stoves, and central heating, arts and crafts almost disappeared, suggesting a law in which creation varies inversely with the amount of time one has on hand.

America has produced no Shakespeare, no Michelangelo; its main masterpieces have been more of the earth than the mind, folk art rather than fine art, Huckleberry Finn and jazz instead of Hamlet and Mozart. Usefulness and sentiment have been strong elements in the pastimes and creations of the United States. Our monuments tend to have a Victorianism in them, almost as though they were elaborate and enduring stone valentines sent to fallen heroes and public figures in a heaven where senti-mentality is no longer pathetic but manly and brave. Young ladies of the nineteenth century plied their needles on mourning-pictures with an almost gleeful energy.

The effect of spare time—time created by laborsaving devices and mechanization—has been to to swell the work force and to put leisure on a commercial basis. Many companies demand that their employees take vacations, figuring resort hotel rooms are cheaper than hospital rooms, fishing less expensive than daily wool gathering.

"The purpose of an education," once observed the august dean of Barnard College, Virginia Gildersleeve, "is to teach you what to do with your leisure time." She felt the average American would always be able to get a job, always be able to make a living, but the difference between the forty-hour work week and the seven-day week needed real application of mind.

(Right) Croquet is a game that invites revenge. Turn-of-the-century America delighted in putting its foot down. Rockwell's player doubtless conceals serious muscle behind her Gibson girl sleeves.

After Hours

The public is aware that P.T. Barnum, proprietor of the famous American Museum in New York, is preparing to open a somewhat similar establishment in this city, at the corner of Seventh and Chestnut streets. We understand it is to be opened on the 28th. We warn Mr. Barnum that the Philadelphia public expects great things of him. Nothing short of a real live mermaid in the way of natural curiosities, and a terrific exhibition of some kind in the show line, will satisfy us.

—1849

This is the greatest people trap in the world ever built by a mouse!

—A weary visitor leaving
Disneyland

How much more inspiring life is when you have a dog, a tennis court, a pool, a sailboat, children, those amenities of life. You can do things based on them.

—A Marin County (California) housewife

Today, however, America has caught the germs of homesickness for elsewhere from the French and English. Florida has been reclaimed from the swamps and the Indians, the small automobile has been put within the means of stevedores, cooks, second-story workers and moderately successful story writers, and golf trousers may be worn in Western towns without causing the wearer to be shot. A road is cursed fluently by an automobilist if it is sufficiently bad to get his wheel spokes muddy. The businessman who can't knock off work for two or three months a year is regarded pityingly as being either a back number, a simp or a poor man.

—1922 account

Parents know their youngsters won't wind up in a beer hall. With a Happiness (ticket) Book a youth brings his girl to the Starlite, where we don't sell any alcoholic drinks. We even have attendants in the rest rooms to see that nobody spikes the soft drinks. The drive-in is the answer to the problems of wholesome amusement for teenagers.

—A drive-in movie theater
operator

SUMMER EXCURSION TICKETS—To all Northern and Eastern seaside, lakeside and mountain resorts, to Deer Park and Oakland, the Virginia Springs, Niagara Falls, Luray Caverns, Gettysburg, and to all other points where people gather in search of health and pleasure are now on sale at all Baltimore and Ohio ticket offices at greatly reduced rates. . . . Before selecting your route or resort consult B. & O. summer excursion book, in which shortest routes and lowest rates, via "Picturesque B. & O.," to all resorts are given from points on that road east of the Ohio River; profusely and artistically illustrated.

—1893 Baltimore and Ohio
advertisement

TWO LEARNED DOGS—TOBY AND MINETTO, from Europe, in consequence of the very general approbation manifested by those ladies and gentlemen who have seen this extraordinary novelty, will be continued every evening during the present week, at the Arcade, No. 73 second story, West Avenue.

The dog TOBY will answer questions in Geography, Arithmetic, and Astronomy, as well as almost any question asked. He will select from the Pack any Card that may have been drawn by the visitor; or when blindfolded, a card that may be only pointed at by either of the company, will be selected by him.

The dog MINETTO will leap through Hoops and Balloons, not much larger than his body; and will walk on his hind or front legs at command.

—1827 advertisement

The rush of Americans to Europe has not yet begun. It will be late in the season before those 400,000 Americans expected by the hotel and shopkeepers of Paris will apply for accommodations.

—1867

The great thing, in family recreation as in all pursuits, is to be yourself. If that means inventive leisure with the kids, fine, but if what you are good at is sitting and looking at the stones in the driveway, then teach your children how to do that.

—Harry Reasoner on how to spend
leisure time

An amateur chamber music quartet practices in the back of a Vermont barbershop before an audience consisting of an enraptured mouser.

My Boyhood

by Dean Acheson

(December 1962)

Only Christmas rivaled the Fourth of July on our calendar, a day by which preceding days were numbered ("only two more days before the Fourth," etc.), a fitting climax to weeks of purchases, comparisons and harassments of parents—"Why can't I have cannon crackers? I'm older'n Joe, and he can," etc. Dawn came early in July, and everyone took oath that first up would fire

salutes under the windows of sleeping friends. Broad Street was soon an embattled front, steady artillery fire interspersed with machine-gun fire—the word then was Gatling gun, out of Kipling—as one of us, with reckless extravagance, put off a whole package of firecrackers at once.

At noon brief peace and sanity returned as my father

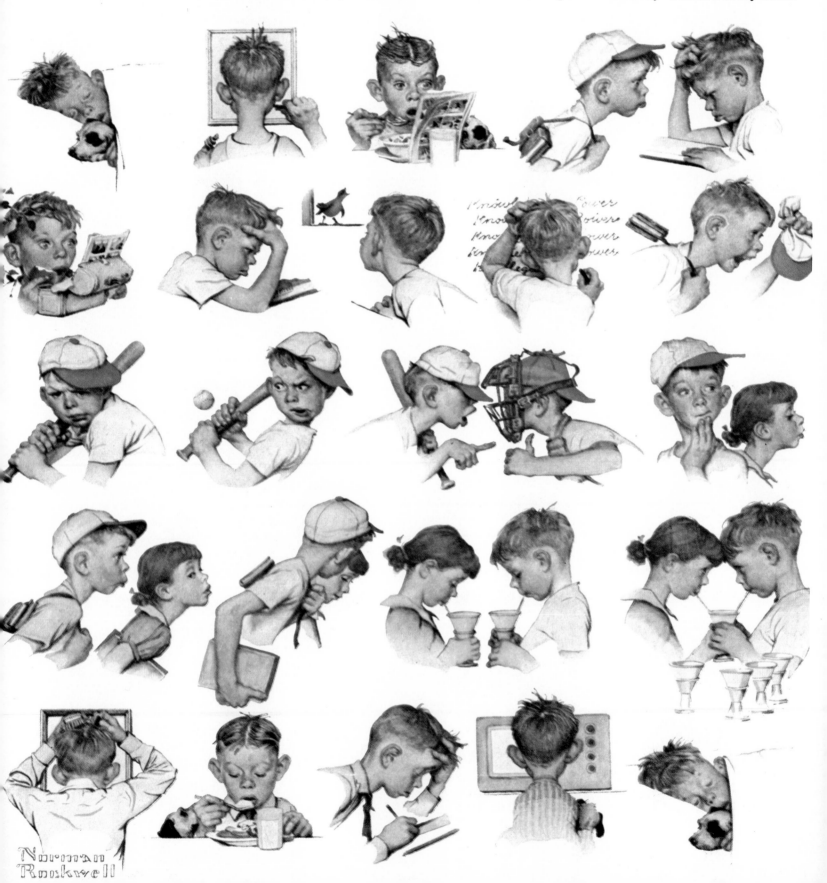

performed his one child-chore of the year, and a noble one it was. The eight children of our block on Broad Street climbed into an express wagon with the rest of their explosive equipment and a picnic lunch, to be carried off by him to a pond on the edge of town, too muddy and choked for bathing and appropriately called by us "Polliwog Pool." It lent itself, however, to such absorbing spectacles as blowing up the battleship *Maine*, an ancient toy boat wound up and started across the pond with a lethal cargo of a cannon cracker. At lunch my father aided digestion by telling Indian stories. At length, we jogged home ready to review the parade from the church steps and, after bath, bread, jam and milk, and the briefest pinwheels and Roman candles—bed.

The Tree

by Bob Considine

(December 1974)

My mother's Christmas trees always made talk. It wasn't because they were big—we never paid more than a quarter or fifty cents for a tree—or because they were ornately decorated. Our decorations were mostly homemade, like the plain tin star my father had fashioned from a bit of scrap metal, holy pictures won by our scholars at school, and a drawing of a grinning cat that my mother had had since she was a girl.

My mother's trees made talk because she always found it difficult to take them down.

People who didn't know her well and who dropped into the house for a cup of tea near the end of January would stop as if shot when they saw our Christmas tree still standing.

My mother always knew what they were thinking. She would say placidly, "It gives the room such a nice perfume, doesn't it?" They would nod uncertainly and glance nervously at the tree from time to time while they visited. They always went away a bit thoughtfully.

Louis Prang, a Boston card maker, adapted the English practice of sending cards at Christmas for the American market. The first card went out in 1843. By 1881, he was printing 5 million, including this cycling Santa and the parading dinner followed by bicarbonate of soda.

Dennis to His Valentine

by Joseph C. Lincoln

(February 1904)

I wint out to buy me a valentine, dear,
    That should spake me devotion to you,
And I saw a lot there and I saw a lot here,
    But 'twas sorrar the lot that would do;
For though ivery wan, from the best to the worst,
    Wid the fine dicoration was gay,
So flimsy they were, from the last to the first,
    That the first wouldn't last through the day.

They showed me wan fixed up wid lace here and there
    And a sweet, painted Cupid below,
But lace that is paper, me darlin', will tear
    And only is meant for a show.
And Cupids that's painted may flutter about
    So long as the sunshine is warm,
But what would you give for a love that washed out
    At the very first taste of a storm?

And so—though I hunted through street after street,
    It was niver a wan of thim there
That told half the love that I feel for you, sweet,
    And I came home agin in dispair.
But watch whin the clock says it's quarter past eight
    On the edge of the night of to-day,
And you'll see, slippin' in through the backyard front gate,
    A valentine comin' your way.

'Tis not very handsome, but shure it'll last
    Through the heat or the cowld or the rain,
And its love won't wash out, for the color is fast
    And is proof aginst sorrow or pain.
Its heart is as warm and true blue as a sky
    Wid the sunbeams of June all ashine,
And its name—Well, I hope you'll change yours by and by
    For the name of your own valentine.

"But I don't love him" became the romantic excuse for giving up millionaires, Adonises, and the boy next door. *Omnia vincit amor was a battle cry against the European custom of arranged marriages. But statistics show most Americans marry within their socioeconomic group.*

Poor Richard's Almanack

(March 1732)

The colonists responded to pamphlets the way later Americans respond to television. The wisdom was not always original—rehashes usually of Aesop or La Fontaine—but the approach was fresh, risqué and daring. No wonder they were usually printed

"Sunny, good for haying."
Almanack

One good Husband is worth two good Wives; for the scarcer things are, the more they'r valued.

There's more old Drunka than old D

Love your Neighbour; yet don't pull down your Hedge.

The Golden Age was never the present Age.

anonymously. Franklin's *Almanack* was a yearly event in the 1730's; he knew a great deal more about human nature than about agriculture, always preaching self-sufficiency. "I do not know a single article imported to the . . . colonies, but what they can either do without, or make themselves." His sayings have become part of the American vocabulary, applicable today as they were two hundred and fifty years ago. Were he alive today he might very well marvel at the constancy of our follies.

297

My First 80 Years

by Harry Truman

(June 1964)

I must have been asked a hundred times, "How does it feel to be eighty?" It's a foolish question in the first place because aging is a gradual process. I'm thankful that the pace has been gratifyingly slow in my case, so I can honestly say that I feel no different from the way I did at sixty.

I have been blessed with good health and a sound constitution, and I'm on record as saying I think I'll make ninety all right. My mother lived until she was ninety-four, by which time I had been President for more than two years. My Grandmother Young lived to be ninety-one, and I had an aunt who was ninety-seven. On the other hand, my father died comparatively young, at sixty-four, and my two grandfathers only reached their late seventies.

So, I have become the sixth oldest former President of the United States—both the Adamses, Jefferson, Madison and Hoover have lived longer than the age I have thus far attained (though I will pass John Quincy Adams in six months).

In achieving this distinction of a sort I have been honored beyond what any man could reasonably expect.

When I was about seventy, a reporter asked me about running again, and I told him I would when I became ninety. I was kidding him, of course. Some fool looked it up and found that it will be an off year when I reach ninety.

Recently I was asked about my own place in history. A reporter dug up a poll of seventy-five leading historians which was published in the *New York Times Sunday Magazine* a couple of years ago. This poll showed the greatest presidents to be, in this order, Lincoln, Washington, Franklin Roosevelt, Polk and, in ninth place, Harry Truman. I told the reporter I didn't think the poll meant a thing insofar as recent history is concerned; the historians didn't know any more than the pollsters did when they said I wouldn't win in 1948. Nobody will be able to assess my administration until about thirty years after I'm dead, and I'm going to live another ten, so they've got to wait a long time. It certainly is something I'm not going to worry about.

During my years as President I had to make many hard decisions, some of which I knew would offend a lot of people. But I never believed in hesitating, once I had all the facts in hand. And I never sought popularity with the press or with the polls. I have felt that a president who made decisions on what was popular, rather than what was right, was heading for disaster. If the President is right, he can get through to the people and persuade them, even if he has to risk terrible unpopularity at the beginning.

The hardest decision I had to make was the one to enter the Korean War. There has never been any doubt in my mind that I did the right thing, and in this case it seemed to be generally accepted as something we had to do. The Marshall Plan, the Berlin Airlift, the Point Four program, NATO and the atom bomb stirred up varying degrees of opposition, either before or after the event, but they all drew public approval, as I thought they would.

Last April General MacArthur was quoted in posthumous newspaper interviews as saying that he had been betrayed by fools in Washington. If he said such a thing, I guess he meant to call me the biggest fool of all. I have never made any remarks to reflect upon the character of General MacArthur, and I don't intend to make any now. But I have never had a moment's regret for the action I took. The only trouble was I waited so long.

I am a Democrat by inheritance and by conviction. All my ancestors were in sympathy with the Confederacy, and I grew up in an atmosphere where it would have been impossible for a Confederate to be a Republican. When I was a young National Guardsman, I visited my Grandmother Young, wearing my new blue uniform with red stripes down the pants legs. Grandma Young remembered when Union sympathizers came over from Kansas and butchered 400 of her hogs during the War Between the States, cut off the hams, slung them over their saddles and left. She said to me, "Do not wear that uniform in my house again."

My first memory of politics goes back to 1892, when Grover Cleveland was elected for the second time. I was eight years old at the time, and I remember how happy my father was at the Democratic victory. He rode a gray horse in the torchlight parade, and he decorated our weather vane with a flag, and red, white and blue bunting.

When I was sixteen, I was a page boy at the Democratic National Convention in Kansas City. I recall the bell-like voice of William Jennings Bryan, the like of which I have never heard since. At every election from the time I was twenty-two until I went off to the First World War I was Democratic clerk in Washington Township, and I had been postmaster at Grandview, Missouri. But I never really got into politics until 1922, when I was thirty-eight and was elected county judge—an administrative, not a judicial job—in Jackson County.

My own sympathy has always been with the little fellow, the man without advantages, and these have always been the people who responded to a politician named Harry Truman. I dislike seeing the growth of snobbery in this country. Nobody ought to feel that he is better than the other fellow simply because he's more prosperous or because he lives in a bigger house. We're all of the same breed. We all came over here from European countries and settled in various parts of the country. Some of us were successful and live in bigger houses. But no man should be ashamed of what he does, no matter what it is, so long as it is useful and honorable. Never, never scorn the man who works with his hands.

From the age of twenty-two to thirty-three I worked on the farm, and I worked hard. I plowed, I milked the cows, I fed the hogs, I pitched the hay. I got to know the farmhands who came out from the little towns and worked for us. Their usual wage was 10 cents an hour, $1.20 a day for a twelve-hour day. My father and brother and I always increased their wages when they worked for us—giving them $1.50 to $2.00 a day and their meals. These were hard-working, upright, good citizens. Most of them managed to get along, raise families and sometimes even send their sons to college. They were poor, but no man should look down on such people.

Since Lincoln's time there have been only four strong presidents: Cleveland, Theodore Roosevelt, Woodrow Wilson and Franklin Roosevelt. Without a strong president you get weak leadership, and such leadership sometimes results in chaos—which is what de Tocqueville predicted for the United States because he said the office of President was bound to be weak, at the mercy of Congress. The Constitution of the United States provides for a delicate balance among the three branches of the government, and each of the three must look after its own prerogatives. When I was a senator, I watched carefully to see that congressional preserves were not invaded; if I had ever been a judge, I'm sure I would have been just as anxious about the rights of the judiciary.

Last March President Johnson asked me to be his representative, along with Mrs. Johnson, at the funeral of King Paul of Greece. This was a kind gesture on the President's part because he knew that the Greeks remember me as the sponsor of the aid which saved them from Communism in their darkest postwar hour. (In fact, they have raised a statue to me in Athens; I only saw it out of the corner of my eye as I was driving by—I don't believe a living man ought to have a statue.)

When we returned to Washington, it was nighttime and the lights were squarely in my eyes as we left the plane. A voice said, "Welcome back, Mr. President." I couldn't see a thing, so I asked: "Who's that?" The voice replied, "The President of the United States." Oh, well, it might have happened to anybody.

Not long afterward President Johnson and I both made speeches at the opening of the New York World's Fair. His helicopter arrived late, just after I had finished speaking, and he walked down the front row of the platform toward the lectern. He shook hands with me, and he kissed Mrs. Truman on the cheek.

"There aren't many men I'd let kiss my wife," I said.

Recently, a television network offered me $50,000 to be a commentator at the 1964 convention, but I said no. A lot of people are willing to pay out money in such cases. When I left the White House, Mike Todd offered me a fabulous salary to head up a merger he was putting together. Several oil companies were after me; an insurance company wanted to pay me $100,000 a year to be chairman of its board. I said, "I put in ten of the best years of my life running a six-hundred acre farm. It was a bad time for farmers and I had to work hard to make a go of it. If you had come around then and offered me this job, I might have talked business with you." Of course, they didn't want me; they wanted the Presidency.

The Sagacity of the Dog

(December 1834)

A dog, which had been the favorite of an elderly gentlewoman, sometime after her death discovered the strongest emotions on the sight of her portrait when taken down from the wall and laid on the floor to be cleaned. He had never been observed to notice the picture previous to this incident.

Here was evidently a case of passive remembrance, or of the involuntary renewal of former impressions.

There were ten quaint lines in the corner of the picture, which conclude thus:

But in my dog,
Whereof I made no store,
I found more love
Than those I trusted more.

Years later, a brother paid a visit and was instantly recognized by the dog in consequence of a personal likeness.

There are over 26 million dogs in the United States. Registered. Americans spend $3 billion annually on their care—$5.5 million on food for them, $4.5 million on clothing (including leashes, collars, sweaters, ribbons, toys, cushions, doghouses, baskets, biscuits, and bones that are inedible, manicures, washes and sets), and $600 million on veterinarians' fees. In return, dogs never argue with their masters and never attempt to disguise their affection, especially for people who are not dog lovers. (Left) Butch, the all-time favorite Post cover character.

THE AMERICAN DREAM

SOMEWHERE OVER THE RAINBOW

The rocket that reached the moon in 1969 was launched in 1776. The founding fathers swore an oath on the outer limits of mankind; they believed in man's infinite capabilities, even those beyond their own vision. No one thought the rocket would get off the ground. Europe waited without much patience for the new country to fall apart so it could pick up the pieces. But the new country survived; it prospered, it triumphed, and even in times of its greatest prosperity it has listened to the voice of its conscience which is its young people. "Those who do not learn from the past are condemned to repeat it," said the American philosopher, George Santayana. To avoid the mistakes of its parents, youth must learn the victories of its grandparents which are often the same in the all-encompassing sweep of time. Our history books speak fondly of the courageous acts of a hundred years ago, but those same acts may have been regarded at the time as foolhardy and dangerous. Franklin and Lincoln believed in a Union but many of their constituents did not. Franklin believed inventiveness could not flourish without security and national pride, and Lincoln's motives were as economic as altruistic. America could only thrive, he felt, if it were at peace with itself, if its laws were stronger than its men.

As the nation enters its third century it senses a dream is never realized; old ideals can have value only as revelations of future goals. The architects of our nation were never afraid to make fools of themselves for a purpose, for a cause. They were never blindly patriotic, even when it might have stirred their followers to do the bidding of the young republic. Franklin's early experiments with electricity helped put men on the moon. His interest in science was sparked by some unknown teacher at the Boston Latin School more than 200 years ago. New Franklins are sitting at desks in classrooms all over the world. The space they stare out at will soon be peopled with their own image. They have great beginnings. The future belongs to them.

(Right) Sitting on top of the world, a young couple looks at the future and each other. Styles change, but dreams don't. Tomorrow frightens . . . and beckons.

Pursuit of Happiness

. . . to every man his chance—to every man, regardless of his birth, his shining, golden opportunity—to every man the right to live, to work, to be himself, and to become whatever things his manhood and his vision can combine to make him—this, seeker, is the promise of America.

—*Thomas Wolfe*

We are in a perplexing period of Change. We seem to be running in all directions at once—but we are running. And I believe that our history, our experience in America, has endowed us for the change that is coming. We have never sat still long; we have never been content with a place, a building, or with ourselves. Americans do not lack places to go and new things to find. We have cut ourselves off from the self-abuse of war by raising it from a sin to an extinction. Far larger experiences are open to our restlessness—the fascinative unknown is everywhere.

—*John Steinbeck*

One day a generation may possess this land, blessed beyond anything we now know, blessed with those things—material and spiritual—that make man's life abundant. If that is the fashion of your dreaming then I say: "Hold fast to your dream. America needs it."

—*Franklin Delano Roosevelt*

Old hopes have been reached and new horizons beckon us. This remains the land of the Great Experiment. The American story in the history of life on this planet is just beginning.

—*Lyndon Baines Johnson*

All my life I have tried to hold off the future by saying to myself that time is a fraud, that weeks, months, years which seem to stretch ahead forever are collapsible. Take your eyes off them for a moment and the future is only yesterday.

—*Dean Acheson*

The idea of novelty is indissolubly connected with that of improvement. No natural boundary seems to be set to the efforts of man.

—*Alexis de Tocqueville*

Preserve America therefore an asylum for the distressed of all nations, and a land of liberty for yourselves. Let the oppressions that forced them . . . to leave their native soil, teach you wisdom; let it teach you to value the envied blessings you enjoy, purchased by the perilous toil and stern virtue of your ancestors, therefore leave these blessings which they left you, unimpaired to your posterity.

—*Anonymous broadside, 1773*

We are a people still young and we know that we have not yet come to the fullest of our powers.

—*Pearl S. Buck on*
accepting the Nobel Prize

I see that you are impatient. I see that you are angry, and I say that you will have your chance to change the world. I say that you will succeed in your dreams. I pray that you will succeed as no other generation in history.

—*Billy Graham's message*
to the youth of America

I am still in touch with the youth of this country, and I see its idealism, its eager aspiration, its vigor. I do believe in our young people. They are good Americans, and we can count on them.

—*Herbert Hoover*

Ways must be found to motivate men and women to understand our predicament, to accept our responsibilities, and to accelerate our own mental revolution. A mental revolution in human values can and must be our salvation . . . Without an informed, sympathetic, and active public, all our programs, all our plans, all our competence and all our potential will not be worth one penny, one piastre, one sen, yen, or fen. This will be the flame we light. This will be the flame we tend.

—*Shirley Temple Black,*
closing statement on behalf of
the U.S. delegation, in the
Preparatory Committee for the
United Nations Conference on
the Human Environment, March 1972

Studying law by candlelight became a national pastime in the 1800's. Half of Congress passed the bar by the application of midnight oil.

The American Family

by Stewart Alsop

(July 1968)

Americans are less prone to ancestral worship than any other people—we have tended to follow the biblical injunction to "let the dead bury the dead." And yet ancestors can be interesting.

A couple of mother's collateral forebears made history—President Theodore Roosevelt, who was her uncle, and President James Monroe, who was her great-great-great-uncle. Father's family boasted no presidents, but it did include a poet or two, a rich man who refused to sign the Declaration of Independence on the grounds that it was a subversive document and a capitalist who advised Lincoln not to war with the South.

Father was very family-proud. He always resented it when the Alsops were referred to as "Roosevelt kin." Although they did not make history, father's family was very representative of American history.

Our eighteenth-century uncle, Richard Alsop, was one of the Hartford Wits. Although almost forgotten now, they made a bit of a splash in the colonies, and even in England, during the post-Revolutionary era.

Richard was, like many Alsops to come, a thoroughly conservative fellow. He had no more use for Thomas Jefferson than my father had for "that crazy jack," Franklin Roosevelt. His heroes were "the illustrious Adams," and first and foremost, "the great, immortal Washington," as Richard called the first President in a long panegyric written when Washington died.

The poem is dedicated to "Mrs. Martha Washington as a small tribute of esteem to her virtues and a testimony of individual sympathy in her affliction."

Mother's family was much more dashing, sophisticated and odd than the Alsop family. By the first half

Artist John Singleton Copley, born in Boston, painted many of our first patriots. In this self-portrait, he is surrounded by his family and the highfalutin silks of his life in England. Art critics consider his robust American paintings superior to the work he did abroad.

of the nineteenth century her maternal forebears, the Roosevelts, had become prosperous New York bankers and merchants.

In 1820, in New York, Betsy Mary Douglas met Captain James Monroe, nephew of the President of the United States, and they fell deeply in love. Most mothers would have been delighted. But Margaret Douglas was not pleased at all.

Young Monroe, she pointed out, was a most unsuitable suitor—he was virtually penniless, and besides, he was a career officer in the Army, and therefore could not lead a "stationary" life. But Betsy Mary was a determined young lady, and she accepted Monroe's proposal.

The American attitude toward ancestors is no doubt a healthy one. In this country a man is judged for what he is, not for what his ancestors were.

Ancestors seemed to me a boring subject. Now that I have found out more about them, my ancestors don't seem so boring anymore. I would like to have known John Alsop, that "soft, sweet man," and his nephew the Hartford Wit, and stern-faced Mary Wright Alsop. I would especially like to have known Betsy Mary—if she hadn't been so stubborn about marrying James Monroe, these lines wouldn't have been written.

Knowing something about his ancestors gives a man a sense of being part of a continuum, of a process of birth, death, and rebirth that started long before he was born, and will continue long after he is dead.

It is reassuring to know that all sorts of people have gone before. And in such times as these, it is also comforting to know that all sorts of people are still going to come after.

A frightening primness has replaced the sumptuous ease of Copley's Colonial family in this 19th-century portrait of the American family, replete with Bibles. On the wall is a picture of a tomb to remind the family of the loss of a loved one and mortality in general.

A 20th-century family poses with its 2.3 children in a moving van to symbolize the mobile society. Forty million Americans moved in 1972.

The American Dream

Generations

by Harry Reasoner

(July 1968)

Look back. When I was a boy, families knew what they did together. My father, restless, had begun the business of frequent moving a generation before it caught on, but we knew where the family *came* from—Humboldt, Iowa—and stayed at Grandpa's house and fought with our cousins.

People don't seem to have grandparents anymore, or if they do have them they live 1,000 miles away, or they live in an apartment and go to the theater and would be horrified at a dozen or so grandchildren coming for Christmas.

The fact is that we've moved away from our traditions, especially those of family leisure. So you've got to make your own traditions. It is important to do things together, and even more important to do the same things together at about the same time, year after year.

Times change though. By the time our oldest was thirteen—it was in 1960—he and his siblings had lived in Minneapolis, Manila and Connecticut, and they had got completely used to the idea that a postcard from traveling parents might come from Anchorage or San Juan or Seattle. But they had never driven across the country and cooked meals in roadside parks, or stopped in the heat of a Kansas afternoon to swim in a municipal pool.

So we loaded our then six children—and a girl from Scotland who was staying with us—into a station wagon. We strapped luggage on top. We tucked items of field cookery around our feet, and started off at five o'clock one afternoon. Only rigid common sense on the part of the lady of the house kept me from taking along the collie, because in 1927 we took the collie to California and "we always" is as important to fathers as it is to children.

We stopped in Humboldt and had a family picnic with what Reasoners are left there. On a hot afternoon we stopped to swim at a municipal pool in Kansas. My wife cooked spaghetti and meatballs in the sand of the Painted Desert, and we saw Disneyland and the Grand Canyon, and in the mornings at the motels people came out to really see if we could get all nine of us and the Thermos jugs into the car.

It has always seemed to me to be patently asinine to be a pal to your children. They don't need thirty-five- or forty-five-year-old pals; they need parents. They don't need friendly discussions with equals; they need responsible authority. I remember explaining to some of the older children, when there was a total of six youngsters in our family, that we would operate as a democracy: each of them would have one vote. And their mother would have seven votes, and their father would have fourteen. This is the authority youngsters lean on and which you cut down, step by step, as they grow older.

Togetherness doesn't necessarily mean sitting in someone's lap. It's a state of mind and an attitude.

by Phyllis McGinley

(July 1968)

There is nothing pundits love like a crisis. Give them something to deplore and they are as happy as a child with a Popsicle. Of all the topics of lamentation, the collapse of the American family is the most reliable.

"Ever and non," wrote a doomsayer in this very magazine at the beginning of the century, "rises a cry that the home is perishing from our midst and civilization must perish with it." Then he went on to explain what he believed was at the root of that doom. He had to reach farther than his hand-wringing brother today. There was no Dr. Spock to blame, no space program; the country was threatened by no unpopular wars, few divorces, fewer precooked dinners. The Bomb was not so much as a gleam in a scientist's eye, and the word "alienation" had not entered the mass vocabulary.

The message seems to be that the American family has *always* been in crisis, yet has always muddled through. And I, by nature an optimist, cannot entirely despair. From my suburban terrace I survey the betrayals, the accidents, the triumphs of middle-class American life and feel a kind of hope. Certainly this amiable village is as thorned with problems as any other community of its type. Generation misunderstands generation. Ideas and ideals of sex, politics, religion, the arts, have been radically altered in so brief a time that all heads swim. Here, too, we come across drugs circulating in schools and youth in flight from authority. But for one thing, these are the noisy singular, not the ordinary quiet, examples of family life in our region. And for another, parents here have never before worked so hard at understanding the forces of chaos that imperil their young.

At base, the American family, I rosily believe, is in pretty good condition, considering the brutal buffeting it has taken in the twentieth century. Scarred but intact it survives. It has not abandoned its aspiration; merely changed society's shape and its own. For there has been a revolution. It was apparent as long ago as the First World War, it quickened in the next few decades and has come, during the present years, to high climax. Yet it *is* a revolution rather than a mere rebellion. We are back where we began, on a frontier. Like the pioneer families, we face a wilderness where few new trails have been blazed. Though the wilderness is moral and psychological rather than geographic, the dangers are real.

New generations have tender consciences. They can afford them better than could we who were so engrossed in trying to ward off from our front porches the wolves of the Depression that we only paid lip service to good causes. Who among us in the Thirties or Forties would have clamored to join a Peace Corps, a Head Start, a neighborhood renewal project? We in youth wished to make our fortunes. Many now yearn to make a world.

I admire the new generation. And I believe the American family has never before had a better chance.

The average American is anything but average. In Norman Rockwell's "Family Tree," some of the ingredients that go into the final product are pictured clinging to the vine of an American dynasty. In Europe, such an end result would be called nobility.

Dynasty

by Cornelius Vanderbilt, Jr.

(January 1927)

What does the future hold for prominent American families, for those bearers of great names renowned in business, politics and society whose ambition it is to perpetuate and add luster to the dynasty? What are the chances, in these days of killing competition in every line of endeavor, for reproducing the strain of courage, intelligence and integrity which combined in the past to elevate the bearers of these names to positions of eminence? Frankly the outlook could be brighter.

Dynasties of the Old World were built upon the historical significance of names which stood for more than the materialistic things of the New World. Great deeds of courage and daring, romantic achievements of honor and integrity, laid the keel for long lines of genealogy which were to follow. Ancestral domains wherein bold knights and fair ladies courted, wedded and lived happily ever after became part and parcel of the social system. Modernity changed somewhat the manner in which things were done. Glistening armor, Elizabethan hoops, curtsies and toppers passed with the chivalrous era of Queen Victoria. Through each period of history we find suffering and intolerable conditions among the less well-to-do, brought about by the social hierarchies. And then overnight we have the days of terror, the guillotine and the bloody revolutions which did away with the dynasties and completely reorganized the face of society.

The late Theodore Roosevelt it was who with one hand laid bare the folly of an American nation in its attempt to emulate the courts of an empire. In a speech made just after he had met with rebuff from a portion of the financial hierarchy of the land, he said, "Quack remedies for the achievement of a social sphere are generally as noxious to the body politic as to the body corporal."

Roosevelt, though to the manner born, never attempted to foist his social or financial connections upon anyone. The colonel rather ridiculed the attempts of certain interests to form small coteries for the edification of a chosen few. Like all great Americans born to rule and to be ruled, he could not see the use of exclusiveness. The future of this land, he held, lay within the grasp of every man and woman who would put shoulder to the wheel of progress, of education, of achievement.

As an example to the nation, he sent his children to public school; they were trained all their lives not to emulate those who lived in gilded halls and wore silks and satins, but to follow those who came from the good, decent, honest stock of working men and women.

By this act perhaps more than by any other single one, Roosevelt made it known that financial dynasties in this country could not hope to succeed if they attempted to make of their descendants individualists, who, when joined together in their little groups, would become merely collective groups of individualists again.

Frankly, because I have had the experience, I rather favor the Rooseveltian theory. At its base it is the American theory, and young Theodore and his brothers, Archie and Kermit, will go further toward the perpetuation of a name than many other well-known families who rebuffed the late President in those active days.

Fifteen years ago, or thereabouts, while I was attending one of the numerous private schools to which I have been sent, the headmaster said to me, "No use your trying to do something in life, young man."

"Why?" I asked him.

"Oh, simply because no clever man ever has a son who amounts to anything. A family rebuilds itself every other time. One man makes a fortune, his son dissipates it; his grandson by necessity is forced to work, and if he has inherited anything worthwhile, as he surely must have, he duplicates the achievement of his grandparent in some other line of endeavor. Thus American finance repeats itself."

A rich man's son finds the stiffest kind of competition in every line of endeavor, from the sons not only of the moderately well-to-do but of the very poor as well. And many a rich young man has gone down before this kind of competition, with which he has never learned to cope.

The man who is coming to the top in every profession today is the man who bends every agency at his command to help him perform the task he is trying to achieve. Thus the really clever young man tirelessly climbs step by step to the position he most desires, while his financially more opulent adversary looks on in wonder and amazement.

America was born of freedom. It has continued great because through the ages men of mettle have risen here and there and stood firm upon the convictions of the masses. We have had our Washingtons, our Jeffersons, our Lincolns, our Roosevelts. Liberality of thought, liberality of speech, liberality of action, each in its place, to urge us further forward. Socialism, communism, while they exist, will never gain headway in this land of ours as long as the temperate qualities of great men make themselves felt when there is need of it.

Our destiny—the destiny of our people and of our land—is certain to be more and more glowing. The sun will never sink upon the horizon of the proper proportion of people, events or situations with us. That is why our form of government is so much more flexible than the governments of other nations, and so much more sought after.

The Dream

by Isaac Asimov

(February 1974)

"I'm dreaming," I said. It seemed to me that I had said it aloud. I knew that I was in bed. I was aware of the bedclothes. I was aware of the scattered city lights peeping through the slats of the Venetian blinds.

Yet *he* was there. As alive, as living, as real—I could reach out and touch him, but I dared not move.

I recognized him. I've seen enough pictures of him. He did not look quite like his pictures, for he was old, very old. White hair fringed his head. I recognized him. I simply knew who he was.

We stared at each other and all the world faded away—the bed and the bedclothes and the room. I said, "You're Benjamin Franklin."

He smiled slowly and said, "Of what year are you, my good sir?"

I was silent. He waited patiently and then shook his head.

"Then I will speak first," he said. "I am old enough to have naught to fear. It is New Year's Eve of the Year of our Lord, 1790, in the fourteenth year of the Independence of the United States, and in the first year of the presidency of George Washington. And in the last year of poor Benjamin Franklin, too. I will not last the new year. I know that.

"I do not die prematurely. In a fortnight and a few days I will mark my eighty-fourth birthday. A good old age, for it has made my life long enough to see my native land become a new nation among the nations of the Earth, and I have had something to do with that. We have a Constitution that was hammered out, not without pain, and will perhaps serve. And General Washington is spared to lead us.

"Yet will our nation last? The great monarchies of Europe remain hostile and there are dissensions among ourselves. British forces still hold our frontier posts; Spain threatens in the south; our trade languishes; the party spirit grows. Will our nation last?"

I managed to nod my head.

He chuckled almost noiselessly. "Is that all you can say? A nod? I asked for two hundred years. With this new year coming in, my last year, I asked what the United States might be like on its two-hundredth birthday."

He paused and then his voice seemed stronger, as though he were preparing to face whatever might be.

"The United States, then, still exists in your time?"

"Yes!"

"In what condition? Still independent? Still with the princely domain we won from Great Britain?"

"Still independent," I said, and I felt myself grow warm with the pleasure at bringing great news. "And far larger. It is a land as large as all of Europe, with a population of more than two hundred million drawn from every nation. Fifty states stretch from the Atlantic to the Pacific, with the fiftieth leaping the sea to the Hawaiian Islands of the mid-Pacific."

"Does the nation prosper?"

"The richest on Earth. The strongest."

Now Franklin paused. He said, "You say that because you think to please me, perhaps. Richer than Great Britain? Stronger than France?"

"If you asked to have the future revealed to you, would it be lies you would hear? The time has not been all bliss. If we are a mighty Union of states now, under our thirty-seventh President in unbroken succession from George Washington, it is because we have survived a long and bloody War Between the States. In this present century, we have fought war after war overseas. We have had periods of economic disaster and periods of political corruption. It has not been the best of all possible worlds, but we have survived and we are the richest and strongest nation on Earth."

Franklin said, with infinite satisfaction, "Yours is an age in which natural philosophy, then, is highly advanced, I see."

"We call it science now," I said, "and you are right. We fly through the air and can circle the globe in less time than it took you to go from Boston to Philadelphia. Our words streak at the speed of light and reach any corner of the globe in a fraction of a second. Our carriages move without horses and our buildings tower a quarter of a mile into the air."

He was silent and for a time seemed to be attempting to absorb what might have seemed like wild fantasy.

I said, "Much of it stems from you. You were the first to penetrate the nature of electricity and it is electricity that now powers our society. You invented the lightning rod, the first device, based on the findings of pure science, that defeated a natural calamity. It was with the lightning rod that men first turned to science for help against the universe."

"And now," he said, "you live in a great world that has grown curiously small; a world far smaller than my thirteen colonies of 1754. Around the world in a day, you say? Words at the speed of light? The astronomer royal, Mr. Bradley, had worked that out to be some 180,000 miles per second."

"That is right; 186,282 miles per second."

"Even to the exact mile? And yet your world is as divided as our American states once were."

"More divided, I fear."

"I catch a dim view of devices that make war deadly," he said.

"We have bombs that can destroy——"

But old Franklin waved his hand. "Do not tell me. I see enough. And yet with the chance of universal destruction, there remains no certainty of peace?"

"The nations are armed and hostile."

"The United States arms also?"

"Certainly. It is the strongest nuclear power."

"Then man does not advance in wisdom as he does in power?"

I shrugged. What could I say?

Franklin said, "Are there no enemies against which the nations can unite? We tried to unite against France, but relied too greatly on Great Britain to feel the absolute need. We did unite against Great Britain, at last, when we stood alone."

I said, "There is no power against whom the nations of the world feel the need to unite. There is no enemy from beyond the Earth to threaten us with universal defeat and slavery."

"Are there no enemies other than those who are living beings?" asked Franklin, angrily. "Is there not ignorance? Is there not misery? Is there not hunger and disease, and hatred and bigotry; and disorder and crime? Has your world changed so much that these things do not exist?"

"No. We have them. Not all of man's material advance has ended the threat of those things you mention."

"And mankind will not combine against this immaterial foe?"

I said, "No more than the colonies combined against

France; or even against Great Britain until bloodshed in New England brought them a clear and present danger."

Franklin said, "Can you wait for a clear and present danger? What you call a nuclear war would make it too late at once. If matters advanced to the point where your complex society broke down, then even in the absence of war, you could not prevent catastrophe."

"You are correct, sir."

"Is there no way, then, to dramatize the——" His head bent in thought. He said, "You spoke of a War between the States. Are the states still at enmity?"

"No, the wounds are healed. In the years after that war, the nation was engaged in building the West. In this great colonizing venture, all the states, north and south, combined. In that common task, and in the further common task of strengthening the nation, smaller enmities were forgotten."

Franklin thought about that for a while and I was afraid he would say nothing. Then, his voice growing stronger, he said, "I am a practical man, my friend, and if brotherhood were merely a matter of lofty ideals, I doubt it would be adopted. But it is a necessity, is it not? Can the world afford to remain a collection of separate, mutually hostile nations? Can it afford to endure the kind of wars that can now be fought, with weapons men can now wield, with the kind of death that can now be delivered?"

"That is very true, sir, but how can we possibly convince people who are filled with hatred and distrust of each other?"

"The devil take hatred and distrust," said Franklin. "Of what use are they in the face of facts? Did we not have the same things in the case of our thirteen colonies? But we had a flag that stated the truth baldly—a serpent divided into thirteen parts, and under it the slogan, 'United or Die.' What else is it for your world of two centuries hence, but unite or die?"

"Yes, but sir, the ingrained prejudices and distrust——"

"There must then be . . . compromise . . ." came the whisper. Franklin was fading fast.

"What kind of compromise? How?" I asked.

"Compromise," came a last breath of sound, and he was gone.

This historic photo of planet earth is proof of her limited resources and frail and vulnerable atmosphere. Africa appears at left
on the globe. (Right) The space shuttle will be operating routinely
by 1980, to learn more of man's psychological limits in space.

Space

by James C. Fletcher

(May 1973)

The splashdown of Apollo 17 in the Pacific in December 1972 marked the completion of one of America's greatest adventures—and proudest achievements. For, in a very real sense, on the way to the moon we rediscovered Earth.

The unforgettable view from the moon showed all mankind that our own planet Earth is unique in the solar system, and that its resources are not as they had seemed for so long—unlimited.

Thus, in many respects, Apollo is far from over. The value of its achievements will not be fully known and understood for years to come—which is one of the reasons astronaut Eugene Cernan has called it "not an end, but a beginning."

Now, with the launch of our first experimental manned orbiting laboratory in 1973, called Skylab, we are augmenting the instrumented approach with the physical presence of man's mind and senses. When on board Skylab, the astronauts monitor surface and atmospheric phenomena, make specific checks on the health of crops and forests, contribute detailed photo-mapping of land masses, inland waterways and rivers, oceans and their currents, and gather a host of other environmental data.

The real key to America's future in space, however, is the revolutionary new multipurpose "Space Shuttle." Work is now underway on this reusable space vehicle which will be launched like a rocket, fly in orbit like a spacecraft and land like an airplane. It will give us economical and routine access to space, and will be useful for both manned and unmanned missions.

The Space Shuttle is much more than just a new vehicle. It is a whole new approach to space. It builds on present technology, but it also is a breakthrough that must be made to reduce operating costs to a fraction of those expended for present "throwaway" launch vehicles.

The Shuttle will open the laboratory of the space environment not just to specially trained astronauts, but to engineers, scientists, technicians and others who will be able to accompany their experiments into orbit.

Scientifically and technologically, we are laying the foundations for America's greatest epoch. Touching upon virtually every area of human endeavor, the space program offers one of our best hopes of making Spaceship Earth a safe and desirable place to live for future generations.

A Great Society

by Lyndon B. Johnson

(October 1964)

Forty years ago I left my high school diploma at home and headed west to seek the fame and fortune that I knew America offered. Almost two years later I came back to Johnson City, with empty hands and empty pockets. I came back because I realized that the place to begin was the place that I had been all the time.

Here, at this time, is the starting point of the path that leads to the future. Our society can be a place where we will raise our families, free from the dark shadow of war and suspicion among nations. It can be a place where our children will grow up knowing that success in life depends only on their ability and not on the color of their skin, or their religion, or the region of their birth. It can be a place where America is growing not only richer and stronger but happier and wiser. For whatever the strength of our arms, or whatever the size of our economy, we will not be a great nation unless we pursue excellence.

The great society rests on abundance and liberty for all. It demands an end to poverty and racial injustice. But that is just the beginning. The great society is a place where every child can find knowledge to enrich his mind and to enlarge his talents. It is a place where leisure is a welcome chance to build and reflect, not a feared cause of boredom and restlessness. It is a place where the city of man serves not only the needs of the body and the demands of commerce, but the desire for beauty and the hunger for community.

It is a place where man can renew contact with nature. It is a place where man honors creation for its own sake and for what it adds to the understanding of the race. It is a place where men are more concerned with the quality of their goals than the quantity of their goods. But most of all, the great society is not a safe harbor, a resting place, a final objective, a finished work. It is a challenge constantly renewed, beckoning us toward a destiny where the meaning of our lives matches the marvelous products of our labor.

Aristotle said, "Men come together in cities in order to live, but they remain together in order to live the good life."

It is harder and harder to live the good life in American cities today. The catalogue of ills is long. There is the decay of the centers and the despoiling of the suburbs. There is not enough housing for our people or transportation for our traffic. Open land is vanishing and old landmarks are violated. Worst of all, expansion is eroding the precious and time-honored values of community with neighbors and communion with nature. The loss of these values breeds loneliness and boredom and indifference.

Our society will never be great until our cities are great. It will be our task to make the American city a place where future generations will come, not only to live, but to live the good life.

We have always prided ourselves on being not only America the strong and America the free but America the beautiful. Today that beauty is in danger. The water we drink, the food we eat, the very air that we breathe, are threatened with pollution. Our parks are overcrowded, our seashores overburdened. Green fields and dense forests are disappearing.

Once the battle is lost, once our natural splendor is destroyed, it can never be recaptured. And once man can no longer walk with beauty or wonder at nature, his spirit will wither and his sustenance be wasted.

A third place to begin building the great society is in the classrooms of America. There our children's lives will be shaped. Our society will not be great until every young mind is set free to scan the farthest reaches of thought and imagination.

In many places, classrooms are overcrowded and curricula are outdated. Most of our qualified teachers are underpaid, and many of our paid teachers are unqualified. We must give every child a place to sit and a teacher to learn from. Poverty must not be a bar to learning, and learning must offer an escape from poverty.

But more classrooms and more teachers are not enough. We must seek an educational system which grows in quality as well as in size. This means better training for our teachers. It means preparing youth to enjoy their hours of labor. It means exploring new techniques of teaching, to find new ways to stimulate the love of learning and capacity for creation.

We hear it said from time to time that the day of the individual is passing. We are told that this is the age of the oversized organization—of big business, of big unions, of big government. We hear that the individual is being smothered by giant concentrations of power.

Earlier generations also prophesied that the individual had reached his final frontier. Our ancestors complained bitterly when the West was won, leaving no new avenues of adventure or escape. At the turn of the century, prophets were predicting that men would be devoured by the monster corporation. During the dreary Depression years, some concluded that the future, if there was a future, belonged to the totalitarian society.

History has a habit of upsetting dire calculations. I believe that the pessimistic prophecies about our future are mistaken. We can shape a destiny in which the individual finds rich rewards.

In all areas of public and private enterprise, we must understand that important ideas cannot be fashioned on an assembly line. The wit who told us that a camel was a horse designed by a committee deserves a medal.

We can and we must set priorities for individual accomplishment, and avoid mediocrity as the standard of success.

I believe that thirty years from now Americans will look back upon these years as the time of the great American Breakthrough—toward the victory of peace over war; toward the victory of prosperity over poverty; toward the victory of human rights over human wrongs; toward the victory of enlightened minds over darkness.

DO UNTO OTHERS
AS YOU WOULD HAVE THEM
DO UNTO YOU

Ship of State

by George Washington

(May 1789)

Among the vicissitudes incident to life no event could have filled me with greater anxieties than that of which the notification was transmitted and received on the fourteenth day of the present month. On the one hand, I was summoned by my country, whose voice I can never hear but with veneration and love, from a retreat which I had chosen with the fondest predilection, and, in my flattering hopes, with an immutable decision, as the asylum of my declining years—a retreat which was rendered every day more necessary as well as more dear to me by the addition of habit to inclination, and of frequent interruptions in my health to the gradual waste committed on it by time. On the other hand, the magnitude and difficulty of the trust to which the voice of my country called me, being sufficient to awaken in the wisest and most experienced of her citizens a distrustful scrutiny into his qualifications, could not but overwhelm with despondence one who (inheriting inferior endowments from nature and unpracticed in the duties of civil administration) ought to be peculiarly conscious of his own deficiencies. In this conflict of emotions all I dare aver is that it has been my faithful study to collect my duty from a just appreciation of every circumstance by which it might be affected. All I dare hope is that if, in executing this task, I have been too much swayed by a grateful remembrance of former instances, or by an affectionate sensibility to this transcendent proof of the confidence of my fellow citizens, and have thence too little consulted my incapacity as well as disinclination for the weighty and untried cares before me, my error will be palliated by the motives which mislead me, and its consequences be judged by my country with some share of the partiality in which they originated.

I dwell on the pure and immutable principle of private morality with every satisfaction which an ardent love for my country can inspire, since there is no truth more thoroughly established than that there exits, in the course of nature, an undissoluble union between virtue and happiness; between duty and advantage; between the genuine maxims of an honest and magnanimous policy and the solid rewards of public prosperity and felicity; since we ought to be no less persuaded that the propitious smiles of Heaven can never be expected on a nation that disregards the eternal rules of order and right which Heaven itself has ordained; and since the preservation of the sacred fire of liberty and the destiny of the republican model of government are justly considered, perhaps, as deeply, as finally, staked on the experiment entrusted to the hands of the American people.

Besides the ordinary objects submitted to your care, it will remain with your judgment to decide how far an exercise of the occasional power delegated by the fifth article of the Constitution is rendered expedient at the present juncture by the nature of objections which have been urged against the system, or by the degree of inquietude which has given birth to them. Instead of undertaking particular recommendations on this subject, in which I could be guided by no lights derived from official opportunities, I shall again give way to my entire confidence in your discernment and pursuit of the public good; for I assure myself that whilst you carefully avoid every alteration which might endanger the benefits of a united and effective government, or which ought to await the future lessons of experience, a reverence for the characteristic rights of freemen and a regard for the public harmony will sufficiently influence your deliberations on the question how far the former can be impregnably fortified or the latter be safely and advantageously promoted.

To the foregoing observations I have one to add, which will be most properly addressed to the House of Representatives. It concerns myself, and will therefore be as brief as possible. When I was first honored with a call into the service of my country, then on the eve of an arduous struggle for its liberties, the light in which I contemplated my duty required that I should renounce every pecuniary compensation. From this resolution I have in no instance departed; and being still under the impressions which produced it, I must decline as inapplicable to myself any share in the personal emoluments which may be indispensably included in a permanent provision for the executive department, and must accordingly pray that the pecuniary estimates for the station in which I am placed may during my continuance in it be limited to such actual expenditures as the public good may be thought to require.

Having thus imparted to you my sentiments as they have been awakened by the occasion which brings us together, I shall take my present leave; but not without resorting once more to the benign Parent of the Human Race in humble supplication that, since He has been pleased to favor the American people with opportunities for deliberating in perfect tranquillity, and dispositions for deciding with unparalleled unanimity on a form of government for the security of their union and the advancement of their happiness, so His divine blessing may be equally conspicuous in the enlarged views, the temperate consultations, and the wise measures on which the success of this Government must depend.

Washington's first inaugural address, from which this is excerpted, appeared in the May 1789 issue of Franklin's *Gazette*.

The U.S. frigate Constitution *rolls out into Boston harbor on her annual turnaround, a ceremony intended to promote even wear. She was christened "Old Ironsides" by American sailors in the War of 1812 who saw British shot falling off her oaken sides; Paul Revere manufactured the copper sheathing on her bottom, and Oliver Wendell Holmes's poem aroused public sentiment to preserve her in 1828. After a 1927 restoration, the ship visited 90 U.S. ports on both coasts and was seen by 4,500,000 people.*

Acknowledgments

Special acknowledgment: Stanley Schindler and Steven Elliott of Sachem Publishing Associates, Guilford, Connecticut. Washington researcher, Andrew J. May. The Danenberg Galleries, New York.

Pages 22 and 23, 27, 296 and 297: Painted by Norman Rockwell for the editions of POOR RICHARD'S ALMANACKS issued by The Limited Editions Club and The Heritage Club, copyright © 1964; reproduced by arrangement with The Cardavon Press, Inc., Avon, Connecticut.

"Freedom from Fear" by Stephen Vincent Benet. Copyright © 1943 The Curtis Pub. Co. Copyright renewed © 1971 Thomas C. Benet, Stephanie B. Mahin and Rachel Benet Lewis. Reprinted by permission of Brandt & Brandt.

From BREAKTHROUGH by Richard Carter. Copyright © 1965 by Richard Carter. Reprinted by permission of Simon & Schuster, Trident Press Division.

From P.T. 109 by Robert J. Donovan. Copyright © 1961 by Robert J. Donovan. Reprinted by permission of McGraw-Hill Book Co.

"Blowin' in the Wind," words and music by Bob Dylan. Copyright © 1962 M. Witmark & Sons. All rights reserved. Used by permission of Warner Bros. Music.

From AT EASE by Dwight D. Eisenhower. Copyright © 1967 by Dwight D. Eisenhower. Reprinted by permission of Doubleday & Co., Inc.

From "The Bear" by William Faulkner. Copyright © 1942 The Curtis Pub. Co., renewed 1970 by Estelle F. Faulkner and Jill Faulkner Summers. Reprinted by permission of Random House, Inc.

From "Babylon Revisited" (Copyright © 1931 The Curtis Pub. Co.), reprinted by permission of Charles Scribner's Sons from TAPS AT REVEILLE by F. Scott Fitzgerald.

From THE SNOW GOOSE by Paul Gallico. Copyright © 1940 The Curtis Pub. Co., renewed 1968 by Paul Gallico. Reprinted by permission of Alfred A. Knopf, Inc.

"This Land is Your Land," words and music by Woody Guthrie. TRO—Copyright © 1956, 1958 and 1970 Ludlow Music, Inc. Used by permission.

From MY HOPE FOR AMERICA by Lyndon B. Johnson. Copyright © 1964 Random House, Inc. Reprinted by permission of the publisher.

From "The World through Three Senses" by Helen Keller, Ladies' Home Journal Copyright © 1941 Downe Publishing, Inc. Reprinted with the permission of Ladies' Home Journal.

From "Alibi Ike" by Ring Lardner. Copyright © 1915 The Curtis Pub. Co. Reprinted by permission of Ring Lardner, Jr.

From THE SPIRIT OF ST. LOUIS by Charles Lindbergh. Copyright © 1953 Charles Scribner's Sons. Reprinted by permission of Charles Scribner's Sons.

From "Woman: A Technological Castaway" by Clare Boothe Luce. Reprinted with permission from the 1973 BRITANNICA BOOK OF THE YEAR. Copyright © 1973 Encyclopaedia Britannica, Inc.

"Fashion: A Bore War?" by Marshall McLuhan is from WAR AND PEACE IN THE GLOBAL VILLAGE. Copyright © 1968 by Marshall McLuhan, Quentin Fiore and Jerome Agel, published by Bantam Books, Inc. Reprinted by permission of the publisher.

"Song" by Edna St. Vincent Millay. Copyright © 1928 The Curtis Pub. Co. Reprinted by permission of Mrs. Norma Millay Ellis.

From "The Real John Paul Jones" by Samuel Eliot Morison. Copyright © 1959 The Curtis Pub. Co. Reprinted by permission of the author.

"A Rare Blake" by Ogden Nash. Copyright © 1966 The Curtis Pub. Co. Reprinted by permission of Curtis Brown, Ltd.

From "That First Husband" by John O'Hara. Reprinted by permission of Random House, Inc., from THE TIME ELEMENT AND OTHER STORIES by John O'Hara. Copyright © 1972 by Random House, Inc.

From "Tugboat Annie" by Norman Reilly Raine. Copyright © 1931 The Curtis Pub. Co. Reprinted by permission of Brandt & Brandt.

From "My Life with Babe Ruth" by Mrs. Babe Ruth. Copyright © 1959 by Mrs. Babe Ruth. Reprinted by permission.

From "The Decline of Greatness" by Arthur Schlesinger, Jr. Copyright © 1958 The Curtis Publishing Company, Inc. Co. Reprinted by permission of the author.

From "Alexander Botts and the Young Inventor" by William Hazlett Upson. Copyright © 1972 The Curtis Pub. Co. Reprinted by permission of Brandt & Brandt.

From "Why Do We Read Fiction?" by Robert Penn Warren. Copyright © 1962 by Robert Penn Warren. Reprinted by permission of the William Morris Agency, Inc. on behalf of the author.

From THE WEB AND THE ROCK by Thomas Wolfe. Copyright © 1939 Harper & Row. Reprinted with permission of the publisher.

(On pages with two or more photographs from different sources, letters (a), (b), etc., indicate position, top to bottom or left to right.)
American Museum of Natural History, 56(b); Ray Atkeson, 8-9; Ollie Atkins, 14-15, 16-17, 33(a), 146, 147, 149(a); The Bettmann Archive, 61, 92, 93(b), 98, 112, 113, 155, 157(a), 162, 163, 169, 170, 187(c), 199(a), 234(a), 236(a), 237, 254, 256, 258(b), 261; "Blackberry Winter," "My Earlier Years," William Morrow & Co., 1972, 117(a); Black Star Photos by John Lanois, 10-11, 167, by Charles Moore, 308; William Boozer, 260(b); Boston Public Library, 217(b); Brown Brothers, 63(b), 217(a), 222(b); W. Atlee Burpee Co., 278-279; Chautauqua Association, 199(a); Ruth Chin Photography, 38, 39(a); Chrysler Corporation, 206; Columbia Pictures, 178(b); Corcoran Gallery of Art, 194(a); Culver Pictures, 93(a), 175(b), 176, 178(a), 179(b) (c), 186-187, 187(b), 188(e), 189(b) (c), 226(a), 227(b); Dell Publishing Co., 262(b); Eastman Kodak Co., 205(a); James Faust, 184, 185, 245; Ford Motor Company, 203, 204(b); Franklin Institute, 27(b), 204(a); Ray Manley, 12-13; General Mills, Inc., 221(a); General Motors Corporation, 205(c); Thomas Gilcrease Institute of American History and Art, Tulsa, 94-95; Globe Photo, by John R. Hammond, 174(a); Senator Barry Goldwater, 121; Arthur Griffin, 42-43; Hallmark Cards, Inc., 292, 293, 294; Harper, Row, 259(b); Illinois State Historical Library, 151(c) (d), 153(c); Indiana State Library, 132(a), 133, 157(b), 276; International Museum of Photography, 100; Thomas Jefferson Memorial Foundation, 31; Helen Keller Birthplace, Tuscumbia, Ala., 116(b); Stanley Kramer Productions, 175(a); Alfred A. Knopf, 260(a); Library of Congress, 58, 60, 101, 116(a), 137(b), 148(a), 149(b), 194(b), 195(a), 248, 249, 250(a), 251, 252, 253, 255; Lincoln National Life Foundation, Fort Wayne, 153(b) (d); Little, Brown & Co., 259(a); Lucian Lupinski, 265, 266, 267; Michael Philip Manheim © 1974, 21, 319; Ray Manley, 12-13, Pat Marble, 211(b); Metro-Goldwyn-Mayer, Inc., 178(c), From the MGM release GONE WITH THE WIND © 1939 Selznick International Pictures, Inc. Copyright renewed 1967 by Metro-Goldwyn-Mayer, Inc., 181; Metropolitan Museum of Art, Gift of I.N. Phelps Stokes, Edward S. Hawes, Alice Mary Hawes, Marion Augusta Hawes, 1937, 250(b); Museum of Fine Arts, Boston, 30, 126,127, 307; Museum of Modern Art/Film Still Archives, 172(a), 173, 179(a), 180, 198(b), 257(b); National Aeronautics and Space Administration, 189(f), 193, 314; National Archives, 150-151, 151(b); National Foundation (March of Dimes), 207; National Gallery of Art, 56(a), 57, 306; Notre Dame Sports Information Service, 229(a); Oakland Museum Andrew J. Russel Collection, 148(b); Oklahoma Historical Society, 99; Lloyd Ostendorf, Dayton, 152; Paramount Pictures, 183; Polaroid Corporation, 204(c); Lewis Portnoy, 233; Random House, Inc., 262(a); RCA, 205(b); Dave Repp, 236(b); RKO General, 182(b) (c); Rockwell International, 315; Franklin D. Roosevelt Library, 119; Theodore Roosevelt Association, 154(b); Theodore Schwartz, 117(b); Charles Scribner's Sons, 257(a); Sears, Roebuck and Co., 84-85; Bill Shrout, 53; Ron Smith, 234(b); The Taft Museum, Cincinnati, 104-105; United Press International, 62, 63(a), 64, 65, 200, 201, 202, 220, 221(b), 222(a), 223, 224, 226-227, 232, 258(a), 285; United States Department of the Interior, 33(b), 132(b), 153(a); Universal Pictures, 186(b); Valley Forge Historical Society, 144, 145; Viking Press, 263; White House Collection, 136, 137(a); Wide World Photos, 39(b), 186(c), 188(d), 189(d) (e), 228, 229(b), 230, 235, 274, 275, 284(a). All paintings and drawings not otherwise credited are the copyrighted property of The Curtis Publishing Company or The Saturday Evening Post Company.

An effort has been made to trace the ownership of all text and photographs included. Any errors or omissions will be corrected in subsequent editions, provided the publisher is notified.